American Baby

American Baby

Baby

A MOTHER, A CHILD, AND THE SHADOW HISTORY OF ADOPTION

GABRIELLE GLASER

VIKING

VIKING

An imprint of Penguin Random House LLC
penguinrandomhouse.com

Photos on pages 24 ,50, 86, 93, 146, 153, 162, 268 courtesy of Margaret Katz
Photos on pages 176, 217, and 225 courtesy of Kim Rosenberg

Library of Congress Cataloging-in-Publication Data

Names: Glaser, Gabrielle, author.
Title: American baby : a mother, a child, and the shadow history of adoption / Gabrielle Glaser.
Description: New York : Viking, 2020. | Includes bibliographical references and index.
Identifiers: LCCN 2020005338 (print) | LCCN 2020005339 (ebook) |
ISBN 9780735224681 (hardcover) | ISBN 9780735224698 (ebook)
Subjects: LCSH: Rosenberg, David, 1961–2014. | Katz, Margaret Erle. |
Adopted children—United States. | Adoption—United States—History—20th century. |
Adoption agencies—Corrupt practices—United States—History—20th century. |
Teenage mothers—United States—Social conditions—20th century. |
Birthparents—Identification.
Classification: LCC HV875.55 .G59 2020 (print) | LCC HV875.55 (ebook) |
DDC 362.734092 [B]—dc23
LC record available at https://lccn.loc.gov/2020005338
LC ebook record available at https://lccn.loc.gov/2020005339

Printed in the United States of America
1   3   5   7   9   10   8   6   4   2

Set in Fairfield LT Std
Designed by Cassandra Garruzzo

*To Margaret, to David,
and to all families separated
by a culture of secrecy*

Contents

Prologue

I met David Rosenberg for the first time on a rainy spring afternoon in 2007, at a dialysis center just outside Portland, Oregon. He was sitting in a beige vinyl chair, tethered to the machine cleaning his blood. I was working on an article for the local paper about the kidney transplant David was soon to undergo, thanks to the organ donation from a friend. We had spoken on the phone to arrange the interview, and I was surprised that David suggested we meet for the first time in what felt like such an intimate setting. He immediately disarmed me with his sense of humor: "Are you kidding? I'm stuck there for four hours three times a week," he said. "It's not like I could be out doing errands." When asked how I would find him, he laughed out loud. "I'm the olive-skinned bald Jewish guy with glasses," he said. "Can't miss me."

David's description was accurate, and in the crowd of mostly quite-pale descendants of Scandinavians, he was easy to spot. Within a moment of my sitting down, we started playing Jewish Geography, the game in which Jews who meet each other for the first time try to identify people they have in common. Even before I took out my notebook, it was clear he wanted to be forthcoming. Maybe it was that dialysis centers, sitting so squarely at the intersection between life and death, aren't conducive to small talk.

The kidney donation tale was uplifting, and I planned to follow

David, his friend and donor, Marshal Spector, and their families for an article about the Jewish concept of *tikkun olam*—healing the world—that would run just before the Jewish New Year, four months away. But as David began to talk, I realized that the story was deeper. Many living organ donors are family members, but David had been adopted as an infant and had no known relatives who could give him a kidney. A cantor in a large Portland synagogue, he was beloved, and many people in his tight-knit community had stepped up to offer theirs. Doctors had decided the best match was Marshal. Early in their relationship, they'd discovered an uncanny connection: Marshal's great-grandfather had been a rabbinical teacher of David's adoptive father in a Romanian city before World War II.

As a clergyman, David presided over deeply personal events, participating in his congregation's greatest joys and deepest sorrows. "Especially private ones," he said, tapping his broad chest proudly. I wondered where our chat was headed. I was there as a reporter, not a confidante, and my job was to take down everything he said in the notebook on my lap. Dialysis centers are loud—the machines whizz and whir incessantly, and it's hard to hear above the noise. He moved toward me as if to convey something intimate.

David told me he had another motive for wanting to publicize his circumstances. These were still early days for social media, but homemade videos and links to newspaper articles had started to go viral, and David hoped the story about two guys on the Western frontier whose ties stretched back to the old country would circulate among Jews nationwide. He knew only one detail about his own past, he said: in 1961, the year he was born, his mother had been a Jewish girl "in trouble" in New York City. He paused for a moment, and looked away.

His wish was that somewhere on the vast Internet, she would see his black eyes, his thick, strong hands, cleft chin, and broad smile, and recognize him as her son.

David wasn't looking for new parents; the couple who adopted him after surviving the Holocaust loved him deeply—and he them—and gave him every advantage. Both had died long ago, and David didn't feel he was betraying their love by trying to discover more about his identity, medical history, and the woman who, as he put it, gave him up. "I want to know more," he told me that day. He pointed to the blood-filled tubes that crisscrossed his body. "You know, for my kids."

OVER THE NEXT YEAR, I grew close to David, his wife, Kim Danish Rosenberg, and Marshal. I got to know their children. After I moved from Portland to New Jersey in 2008, we stayed in touch and visited occasionally when I returned to Oregon to see my family. Things with David weren't good: Despite the new kidney, his health was failing. Just months after the transplant, he had been diagnosed with a lethal form of thyroid cancer. One time when I met him at a hipster coffee shop in Portland—where he walked in carrying his own Diet Coke—he told me he was still hoping to find some relatives. He just didn't know how.

As the years passed, David's interest in finding his biological mother, even as he was running out of time—especially as he was running out of time—never really left my mind. I understood how difficult it would be for him to find her, given that the laws in New York, like in many other states, kept the original birth certificates of adoptees closed, meaning that only state officials and adoption agency social workers were allowed to see them. Years before, David had inquired briefly about his adoption, but learned that searching would require the written permission of his adoptive parents, who had already died. That brief interaction was enough to confirm David's suspicions that he was unwanted. So, perhaps fearing more rejection, he let it go. We didn't really talk about it, and it seemed too painful for me to ask. I wasn't a journalist covering him any longer; I'd become his friend. Yet whenever I was in Manhattan, I'd find myself absentmindedly looking at Jewish grandmothers on the bus, in supermarkets: Could that be her?

〜

ISSUES OF FAMILY IDENTITY have long fascinated me. My own ancestors were Jewish tailors from a shtetl in Poland who reinvented themselves as gentile farmers in Oregon. From 2003 to 2008, I covered adoption, surrogacy, and reproductive technologies as a beat at the *Oregonian*. I was drawn to stories about the increasingly complex, scientifically enabled ways of creating families. But it was only when I saw *Philomena*—the 2013 biopic about a mother's search for the son she was coerced into relinquishing for adoption in postwar Ireland—that I started thinking more broadly about how adoption in the same period might have affected Americans.

The movie focuses on Philomena Lee, a young Irishwoman who became pregnant after a brief romance. Shamed by her family and small community for having premarital sex, she was forced to live in a convent where she worked as a laundress along with other young, unmarried pregnant women. When she almost died in labor, the Mother Superior told Philomena it was fitting punishment for her sins. She stayed there, paying off the purported debts incurred for her room, board, and delivery until her son was three years old, and then watched in horror as a wealthy American couple drove away with him after offering a sizeable "donation" to the Mother Superior. The nuns told Philomena to forget about her boy, as he would most certainly have forgotten about her. This proved untrue.

I read the book that spawned the movie and my thoughts returned to David and the woman who gave birth to him. I began asking myself some questions that even I, as a mother of three daughters and as someone familiar with this topic, hadn't fully considered. How could a woman ever be expected to forget a baby she had carried for nine months? What would it take to "move on" from the experience, especially if one knew nothing about where the child had ended up being raised and by whom? From my coverage of open adoption, in which the birth mother chooses, and often remains in contact with, the adoptive family, I knew that *that* process was often wrenching for birth mothers, despite their continued presence in their children's lives. Many of the women I'd interviewed described a deep, longing sadness that never quite went away.

Philomena, of course, always remembered her baby, and never gave up hope of finding him. I found myself wondering whether David's mother might have had a parallel experience, then dismissed the thought. Adoption in the United States in the postwar years was surely different from the punitive, moralistic, and secretive approach of the Irish Catholic Church. It had to be. Didn't it?

In early May of 2014, David's name popped up on my caller ID. I was late to catch a train, but I picked it up. Cancer had reduced his sonorous tenor to a whisper that was hard to hear. He asked me if I was sitting down. "I am now," I said, and took a seat on my bed. Kim had given him a kit from 23andMe, the DNA-testing company, for his birthday. Five months later, he had big news.

"I found my birth mother," he said, his excitement uncontainable. "Her name is Margaret Erle Katz, and she lives forty-five minutes from you." He had already plotted the distance between our addresses on Google Maps. "You have to meet her," he said.

It turned out that his birth parents had married, and he had three full siblings. He'd spoken with the youngest, Cheri, a woman he embraced as his "baby sister." Like him, she was also a professional vocalist: she was an opera singer in Berlin. He'd watched her performances on YouTube, and she was his female clone.

If only, he said, he'd known sooner.

"Margaret didn't want to give me up," he told me. I heard David's voice catch. "She's loved me my whole life."

I began to realize that the story of how David and Margaret lost and then found each other—and of the political, scientific, cultural, and economic forces that caused and then enforced their separation—was part of a far larger story. Their story wasn't an aberration; it was representative of a much larger reproductive- and human-rights story that encompassed generations of American women and their sons and daughters, many of whom were exploited for profit and for science. It was an important chapter of American social and cultural history hiding in plain sight, undergirded by a soothing narrative that had repackaged the reality of what it meant to adopt, what it meant to be adopted, and what it meant to surrender a baby you gave birth to. Margaret Erle, I would be stunned to learn, was one of more than 3 million mostly unmarried young women who conceived during the decades after World War II and found themselves funneled into an often-coercive system they could neither understand nor resist. They endured their pregnancies in secret, sometimes with distant relatives, or as servants to strangers. Many were shipped far from their families to the hundreds of maternity homes that dotted cities and towns in nearly every state. They gave birth alone, and were then pressured or forced to surrender their newborns to strangers who hadn't explained that in doing so, many of these young mothers would never see or hear about their children again. This unheralded surge in births out of wedlock came just as battles over contraception and abortion were beginning to dominate the public conversation, and continued until 1973, the year *Roe v. Wade* made abortion legal nationwide.

The silence surrounding this massive experiment in social engineering is hardly surprising. In the 1950s and '60s, America embarked on a frenzy of homemaking and family-building unlike in any previous period of history. Images from the baby boom portrayed an ideal (white) breadwinning father and a beautiful mother who stayed home with several children, all living happily in a pretty new suburb. But in fact, there were lots of families living outside that tidy picture. Millions of couples were unable to conceive and did not yet have the benefit of advanced reproductive medicine. The need to adopt was viewed as shameful as becoming inconveniently pregnant. A woman who had engaged in out-of-wedlock sex and one who was embarrassingly infertile in an era of relentless fecundity had both failed some new test of social acceptability, and the solutions to the problems they represented were found in silence and secrecy.

Many of the same demographic and social forces that had launched the baby boom propelled the explosion in unwanted pregnancies and adoptions. Birth rates had dropped during the Depression and war, but now the prosperous postwar economy, fueled by generous government loans for college and new suburban homes, catapulted millions of white Americans into the growing middle class. In previous generations, young, unwed couples who found themselves with unexpected pregnancies married quickly and kept their babies. But the shifting cultural landscape had made shotgun weddings for teenagers much less appealing, at least to rules-following parents who had withstood the deprivations of the Depression and World War II and now had aspirations to achievement. These surprise pregnancies were an obstacle to a better life that needed to "go away." For the millions of couples who could not conceive and were longing to join the baby boom, the plight of those women was an opportunity, the ideal solution to a painful problem. The babies were desirable; the mothers were not.

The adoption business comprised an array of individuals and institutions, from researchers whose pseudoscience justified the advantages of unproven practices in child assessment, to the social workers addressing family crises, and adoption agencies that frequently benefited economically and professionally from each woman they persuaded to relinquish a child. When it was publicly discussed at all, the accepted narrative was that adoption was in the best interests of everyone involved: it gave birth mothers the chance to escape the stigma of unwed motherhood, spared their children the shame of illegitimacy, and offered infertile married couples the chance to become parents.

The one thing that few, it seemed, thought to consider was the lifelong emotional impact on women who were hidden away in shame during pregnancy, expected to lie about it ever after, and then told to put their babies out of their minds. Few invested much thought in the feelings of the adoptees who were brought up to think their birth parents hadn't wanted them, and that—regardless of how cherished they were—they were their adoptive parents' "second choice" to biological offspring. Family members, social workers, obstetricians, agency officials, clergy, and lawyers all promised that adoption worked out for everyone "for the better." Adoptees would blend seamlessly into their new families, the theory went, and if they wanted to know about their biological origins one day, they could "look" when they were adults. (Although with families who had wanted and loved them so much, why would they bother?)

But as David and millions of other adopted people would come to learn when they turned eighteen, the promise of finding birth parents was largely an illusion. Nearly every state had laws that sealed the records that would allow children to find their original identities. The adoption agencies involved in many of these arrangements claimed they had a duty to protect the privacy of the birth mothers, despite having little, if any, evidence that they had either been promised confidentiality or were continuing to insist upon it.

As I dug into archives and interviewed scores of birth mothers and adoptees, I came to understand the dynamics behind these decades of entrenched secrecy. I realized that the way the United States dealt with unplanned babies in the decades after World War II—when abortion was illegal, contraception was forbidden even for married couples, and discussion of sex and reproduction was taboo—revealed a great deal about this country. Again and again, the nation's powerful religious and political institutions collaborated to control women's lives and the destinies of babies born out of wedlock. Today it is socially acceptable for women (and men) to raise children on their own. But for many adoptees and their birth mothers, the shame lingers, the skewed principles of the past remain in place—and the conflict about whose rights deserve protection rages on.

For David and Margaret, and for countless others, the miracle of modern genetics smashed open the secrecy created by the politicians of the twentieth century. DNA testing kits made it possible for David and so many others to spit into a vial and locate distant, or not-so-distant, family members, facilitating reunions that seemed unimaginable just a decade before. Through the advocacy of adoption reformers, who argue that access to one's own original birth certificate is a human and civil right, several states have finally opened their records, turning the random chance of a DNA search into a certainty for people who happened to be born there. This transparency has exposed incalculable emotional costs paid by birth mothers and adoptees alike. Even the joyful reunions are bittersweet, shadowed by the fundamental, unanswerable question: Why did you give me away?

Every family, every adoptee, every birth mother has their story. This is David and Margaret's.

Their tale—whose basic contours they share with millions of Americans—is one of loss, love, and parallel searches for identity: one a mother who lost her firstborn; the other a son grafted onto a family of loving strangers, wondering where he had come from.

1.

Family Matters

When Margaret Erle was six years old, her favorite toys were dolls. She combed their hair and bathed them, kissed their hard plastic foreheads, and rocked them to sleep. Margaret liked to imagine what her own grown-up life would be like one day, away from her New York City apartment. She imagined a spacious house with lots of rooms and even more trees, a big, strong husband, plenty of children, and a menagerie of animals. Whenever she had time to herself, she retreated to her soft pink room and sang lullabies to her dolls. She swaddled them, talked to them, washed and pressed their dresses.

Soon enough, her desire for make-believe had faded: by the time she was eight, she had real babies to tend to. The outgoing Margaret was so trustworthy, parents in her neighborhood asked her to watch their children. Her mother, Gertrude, fretted that she was too young, but Margaret pointed out that she'd had plenty of experience taking care of her little brother, Allen, who was two years younger. And by the time she was finishing fourth grade, Margaret had a busy after-school and weekend schedule, wrangling strollers up and down stairwells and wheeling babies around her block. She boiled bottles and knew instinctively how to hold infants' heads and change their diapers. The giant pins made her a little nervous at first—what if she poked a leg?—but she got the hang of it quickly. She got a dime each time she babysat.

After school she helped Gertrude in the kitchen, peeling carrots and potatoes as soon as her hands were deft enough. She wasn't allowed to touch knives—she could hurt herself, hurt someone else, be reckless. Margaret was helpful and eager, but also careful. Gertrude, who showed little approval and even less affection, had rules, and one was expected to obey.

Like most of her friends in Manhattan's Washington Heights in the 1950s, Margaret was the child of Jewish refugees from Nazi Europe. Her German-born parents never spoke of their past comfortable lives, of the tragedy they'd evaded. Now they waited for disaster in America, even as their kids plunged into its promise. Nobody was warier than Gertrude, who had wounds she both felt and wore. Deserted by her first husband, Gertrude was dealt an even crueler blow when she was diagnosed with breast cancer at fifty. She felt that the surgeons who removed her breast also stripped her of her identity as a woman, leaving her with scars that stretched from her collarbone to the bottom of her rib cage, red ropes beneath her porcelain skin. A few months after the operation, Margaret came home unexpectedly and caught a glimpse of Gertrude as she dressed behind the bathroom door, opened to let steam escape. Gertrude, suddenly aware of her daughter's gaze, slammed the door shut with one hand as she tucked her bulky foam prosthesis into her bra with the other one.

Silence was how the family coped with their pain: Nobody talked about the breast cancer that had also maimed Margaret's aunt and grandmother. And nobody ever mentioned the relatives the Nazis murdered, or for that matter, the war itself. In fact, any longing for the bourgeois world of music, food, art, and culture Gertrude and Josef had left behind in Europe was also unspoken. While Margaret felt loved by her extended family—cousins, a grandmother, and aunts and uncles who had miraculously reassembled nearby—what the family had lost hung over her childhood like an invisible veil. Her parents spoke German to relatives, and to each other when they were angry, but Margaret knew better than to ever ask questions about what they were discussing.

She also didn't ask questions about the pretty blonde that Josef met when he took her and Allen to a nearby park on weekends. Josef always greeted the young woman, Irene, warmly. A few minutes later, Irene's mother would show up to push the children on the swings while Josef and Irene disappeared, they said, to go chat at a diner for an hour. Margaret somehow understood that coffee was a euphemism. When the two returned, they always seemed in high spirits.

Silence extended to puberty and sex as well. When she got her period at twelve, Margaret had no idea what was happening, so she asked a girlfriend what to do. The friend instructed her how to use sanitary napkins, and Margaret, embarrassed by her own lack of knowledge, pretended to know more than she did. Older girls called menstruation "the curse," and that's certainly what it felt like, another secret not to be broached. Although no one explained its meaning to her, Margaret sensed that it was some kind of milestone in her own femininity. The timing couldn't have been worse: it seemed to have arrived just as her mother's had vanished. She borrowed pads from her aunt, and wadded up the used ones at the bottom of the garbage can.

The Erles were modern Orthodox, abiding by kosher dietary laws and strictly observing the Sabbath as a day of prayer and rest. Margaret was an active member in her synagogue, Congregation Beth Israel, where she attended Hebrew school and joined her peers for Torah study groups over bagels on Sunday mornings. She learned to read Hebrew, and drew strength from the ancient prayers she chanted in the separate women's section. While other girls gossiped, Margaret would concentrate on studying. But the synagogue offered another outlet: it was a sanctioned escape from home.

Gertrude had grown up comfortably in Fulda, a small German city with a medieval monastery, a town square with brick Gothic arches, and timbered buildings with fairy-tale spires. Gertrude's father, a shoemaker, had a shop on the ground floor, while the family lived in an airy apartment on the floor above. After high school, the striking brunette took a job as a bookkeeper, and yearned for horizons beyond Fulda. Alone, she set out for the United States, landing in New York in 1927, where she became a governess. One day, a photographer who admired her high cheekbones, ruby lips, and patrician carriage approached her to offer her work as a hat model. Before long, her elegance attracted the notice of a debonair young printer, and they married after a brief courtship. But when the stock market collapsed in 1929, his business did, too, and a year later he disappeared without a word. Gertrude came home from work one day to find herself locked out of her apartment. Her husband had failed to pay the rent for months.

Humiliated, she had to rely on friends for help, and later learned that her spouse had taken up with a wealthy woman. Eventually they dissolved their marriage. Divorce was shameful, and rare. For a religious Jew, it was more stigmatizing still, and Gertrude fell into deep despair. After a few years, she rallied, forcing herself to socialize at a club for German émigrés. There she met a baker named Josef Erle.

The son of a cattle dealer, Josef was the oldest son of thirteen children. He had held a respected job as a yeshiva teacher in the small town of Baisingen and had grown increasingly concerned after the Nazis came to power in 1933. When his father died in 1935, Josef became adamant that the family flee. Two of his married sisters already lived in the United States, and signed the required affidavits promising they would financially support their immigrant relatives. Josef drained the family resources, selling cattle, the house, silver, and china to secure visas for eleven family members before finally leaving Germany himself in 1938. Exhausted and penniless, he arrived in New York at age thirty-five. He shortened his name from Erlebacher to Erle on Ellis Island, still harboring hopes for a new start. It didn't take long for his dreams to dwindle: New York was saturated with Jewish refugee-scholars, and without fluency in English, a teaching position—or any office job—was impossible to obtain. So Josef took the work he could find, landing a job in a relative's bakery. The focus of his life shifted from intellectual inquiry—starting out the day dressed in a tailored jacket and tie—to grueling manual labor. Every morning he rose before sunrise and walked to the bakery, where he put on a white apron and cap and learned to make yeasty challahs and sandwich bread. Josef never complained about his new vocation, but after work, he spent a good half hour coughing before he'd light the first of his many evening cigarettes. Inhaling flour and powdered sugar all day further strained his lungs.

As the war raged in Europe, Gertrude and Josef, by then in their late thirties, put their faith in the future, marrying in 1940. Gertrude was thirty-nine when she had Margaret in 1944, and forty-one when she gave birth to Allen two years later. On the outside, they seemed like the ideal American family. But photographs show more than just new-parent fatigue: although they proudly held their hopeful new Americans—the symbol of their family's unlikely survival—their faces looked worn and solemn, as if the future itself was not to be trusted. Little, it seemed, was going their way.

Shortly after the war ended, Josef bought a pastry shop of his own, where he crafted jam-filled rugelach, rich chocolate babkas, and elaborate wedding cakes. His creations were as delicious as they were beautiful, but his timing could not have been worse. By the late 1940s, New York supermarkets had begun overtaking smaller specialty stores, and the one near Josef's shop offered cheap, mass-produced cookies and cakes. The new bakery lost money from the start, and went under two years later. Colleagues and friends urged him to declare bankruptcy and walk away, but Josef refused. He insisted on paying back all the relatives from whom he'd borrowed.

Josef's economic misfortune was at odds with the boom times that defined postwar America. By the mid-1950s, the easy lives of the lucky were on national display on television, in newspapers, and in women's magazines designed to advise women how to navigate their newfound affluence. Slim mothers in high heels smiled as they loaded dishwashers in their spacious suburban homes, and handsome fathers in fedoras sailed their shiny new cars along ribbons of new highways. This dazzling universe eluded Gertrude and Josef, who lived in a noisy railroad flat three floors up from belching buses at the foot of the George Washington Bridge. But Josef told his children they should aspire to a more comfortable, secure life.

Gertrude, who woke daily to her scars, fears, and indignities, did not share his optimism. Once slender and glamorous, she was now a plus-size housewife, flying into rages at a moment's provocation. She may have lacked power over her larger world, but within her apartment, her will reigned. Mild-mannered Josef, who often worked double shifts, was no match for her. Money was tight in the Erle home, and Josef, bowed by his failure as a provider, kept track of finances to the nickel. Often the couple bickered over bills, but even at her young age, Margaret understood that the disputes were about something larger.

Many adults who knew them sensed the tension and showed Margaret extra affection. A doting aunt and uncle, tailors, made her beautiful woolen coat-and-hat sets. A friend of her mother's, a divorcée without children, took her to the ballet, to movies, and to watch kids dive for coins in Sheepshead Bay. Sometimes Margaret took the bus to visit Josef's sister at her sprawling suburban house in New Jersey. In the summer, she went to Jewish summer camps in upstate New York. Margaret loved the outdoors, and looked forward to a month of fresh air and sunshine. But she welcomed an even greater freedom: being far from her mother.

One emotion Gertrude did not withhold was her contempt for men. Even on hot days, she insisted that Margaret wear cardigans, never showing her bare shoulders. She grudgingly permitted Margaret to go out on a few dates, but when it came to physical contact, she had strict rules. "Don't let them touch you," she warned. "Don't give them the wrong idea."

MARGARET—NO SURPRISE—spent as much time out of the apartment as she could. She took on even more babysitting jobs so she could have her own spending money, and after school went home with classmates to do homework and try on new makeup and hairstyles like teenage girls across the country. In the evenings at home, she focused her attention on the larger world. She watched the nightly news with Josef, horrified at reports from the growing unrest in the Jim Crow South. She read articles on South Africa's apartheid and wrote a school paper arguing for its abolition. She often talked to Josef about the news, and he reminded her that injustice existed everywhere. He led by example with kindness. He knew all the families—Puerto Rican, Italian, and Greek—in their nineteenth-century brick building, and always asked after everyone's health.

Josef reserved a special understanding for Old Lady Rosen, a Holocaust survivor who wagged her crooked finger at all children who crossed her path. At some point, Mrs. Rosen learned that Allen charged kids in the building a dime to watch the woman in the building opposite as she took off her clothes, and then paraded naked, in front of the window each night. "HaShem will punish you all!" she warned them. Yet Josef instructed his children to treat everyone with respect—especially Mrs. Rosen.

"God loves everybody," he told his daughter. "You never know what someone else has gone through," he added. "Have compassion. Don't ever think you're better than someone else."

When Margaret entered junior high school in 1956, she got good grades and threw herself into the arts. She sang in the school choir, helped sew costumes, painted elaborate set backdrops, and relished the camaraderie of her fellow theater lovers. Teachers rewarded her with roles in musicals and a prized spot on the dance team, where she stood out enough that recruiters from disc jockey Alan Freed's *The Big Beat*, the television precursor to *American Bandstand*, invited her to be a regular background dancer. Gertrude objected at first, but when neighbors commented that they'd seen Margaret on TV, her doubts gave way to tight-lipped pride.

Margaret had always been pretty, with wavy thick brown hair and dark almond-shaped eyes, but in seventh grade her tomboy's frame bloomed into an hourglass figure, and she started sensing a shift in the way people reacted to her. She felt as if she'd gone from a sweet little girl to an object—whose, she wasn't sure. At home, Gertrude hectored her to cover up, cover up, cover up. Her uncles started giving her quick pecks on the cheek, not their customary hugs. Margaret was baffled when suddenly bus drivers waited for her. Strangers whistled, men she'd known her whole life held open doors, and high school athletes asked her out on dates.

Nobody, though, was more attentive than George Katz, the tall sixteen-year-old pitcher on the high school baseball team. He had espresso-colored eyes, thick black hair he slicked back with Brylcreem, a deep dimple in his chin, and an athlete's cool. George first spotted Margaret at her friend's party, dancing the Lindy Hop with her pals in a pair of green plaid capris and a matching top. Every time fifteen-year-old Margaret looked up, she noticed George staring as he stood near the sandwich table. By then, she had grown accustomed to appreciative male glances, and occasionally she looked up and smiled. After an hour of watching her, George leaned over to his best friend, Hank Edelman. "See that girl?" he said. "I'm going to marry her."

2

Teenagers in Love

S oon enough, Margaret and George began meeting after school for tuna melts at a diner, or for egg creams at a soda fountain on weekends. They'd go to the movies, but didn't really watch: the back row was a great place to kiss. She wasn't a sports fan, but when she came to George's games, the team always won. Baseball players are superstitious, and even the coach was persuaded that Margaret brought good luck. He convinced his friend, her last-period Spanish teacher, to excuse her for away games. He always agreed to let her go.

George was smitten—and persistent. He wanted to see Margaret as often as possible, calling from a nearby pay phone to ask her to meet him in her building's lobby. Gertrude fumed, and forbade Margaret to go out. She wasn't the only disapproving parent. George's father, Frederick, the co-owner of an army-surplus business, was equally discouraging. In New York City's émigré Jewish community, the Erles simply were of a lower class.

Born to a wealthy, educated Viennese family, Fritz, as his friends called Frederick, was a law student when the Gestapo arrived at the Katzes' elegant neobaroque home in June of 1938, shortly after Hitler annexed Austria. Fritz and his father, Isidor, were among the first of thousands of Austrian Jews to be deported to Dachau, an abandoned munitions factory where Jews, gay people, Roma, and suspected political enemies were taken for what the Nazis called "protective custody."

At Dachau, the Nazis forced the men to construct new cells, build roads, and drain marshes. Jews were assigned the most physically demanding tasks, yet denied morning bread rations even as they stood in line alongside other prisoners who received them. They were often the target of spontaneous beatings, and whenever they began, Fritz, a tall man with thinning blond hair, would stretch his arms out to try to protect his father. "Beat me instead," he'd cry. His pleas had no effect. They were both lashed with rubber truncheons and horsewhips.

During the many months they were detained, Fritz's mother, Karoline, sold art and jewels in Vienna to negotiate her husband's and son's release from Buchenwald, the second camp to which they'd been transferred. Fritz got a visa to England on the proviso that he would leave the Reich immediately, without any family members. A few months later, the young man who'd grown up in a home with Persian rugs, opera, and servants found himself living in damp former army barracks in Sandwich, Kent, eating meager wartime rations of bread, margarine, pickled eggs, and cheese. The camp had been converted to a holding place for mostly single Jewish men from Germany and Austria.

Fritz had no word from his parents, and worried constantly about their safety. Fritz spoke little about his year as a laborer, a shattering detour from his plan to become an attorney. A lone photograph from 1939 shows him sitting in the crowded barracks, the arms of a fellow refugee draped around his bony shoulders. He smiles uncertainly.

George's mother, Lizzie Lederer, also suffered wrenching losses. Early in the evening of November 9, 1938, Lizzie went out with some friends to a dance at her local public school in Vienna. It was just four days past her eighteenth birthday, and as a secular Jew, she had many gentile friends and classmates. That night, she danced a waltz with a blond Austrian boy who seemed exceedingly nervous.

She returned home shortly before ten. Just as she was getting into her nightgown, she heard a knock at the door. Her mother answered. In the hallway stood the boy from the dance. Lizzie, hearing his voice, emerged from her bedroom as he motioned her toward him. His face looked stricken.

"What is it?" she asked. "What's wrong?"

He leaned close to Lizzie and whispered that people were coming that night to "hurt the Jews" and destroy their property. "What?" Lizzie asked.

"There's nothing I can do and you can't say I told you," he said. "They'll kill me and my family if they find out. But I wanted to warn you."

"What should we do?" she asked.

"Hide," the boy told her. "Quickly."

The family fled down the stairs of the apartment above their china store and hid in the cellar beneath it, clutching one another for warmth in the dank, airless space for hours during the night. Above, they could hear shouting and breaking glass. In the morning, Lizzie rose to find the family's store demolished. Every plate, every teacup, every bowl was smashed, and the air was filled with smoke. As she glanced down the block, Lizzie could see why: in the synagogue at the end of it, the round stained-glass window embedded with an iron Star of David was glowing orange as flames consumed the roof above.

Vienna's orderly streets had been transformed into an apocalyptic scene. The sidewalks were littered with debris from Jewish apartments and stores. Smoke filled the autumn sky, and storm troopers and Hitler Youth units goose-stepped along the boulevards. There were rumors of rapes and suicides.

German officials claimed that what came to be known as Kristallnacht, a series of attacks on synagogues and Jewish-owned businesses across Germany and Austria, was a spontaneous eruption of popular rage in response to a Jewish teenager's murder of Ernst vom Rath, a German diplomat serving in Paris. (In fact, it was encouraged by Nazi propaganda minister Joseph Goebbels.)

Lizzie's parents, Olga and Walter, instantly understood that nothing in their prosperous lives would ever be the same. And since they shared the same olive skin and black hair as their daughter, they realized there was no possibility of ever passing in Vienna—or anywhere else within the Reich—as gentiles. The family calmly discussed its options. While her parents had money to escape, they couldn't bear to leave Lizzie's sick grandmother. Instead, they arranged for their daughter's passage to Britain on the Kindertransport, the rescue effort in the nine months before the war's start in 1939. During that time, British citizens took in an estimated ten thousand mostly Jewish children from throughout Central Europe. Lizzie was days beyond the cutoff age of seventeen, but the officials accepted her. For the next year, Lizzie lived with an English family in Kent, helping with housework and taking care of their children.

At some point in 1939, she met Fritz at a small gathering for Austrian Jewish refugees. Their parents had been friends in Vienna, and the pair began dating. Not knowing the fates of their families, the two clung to each other, and married on December 24, 1939. They immigrated to the United States, and had George in 1943.

Like the Erles, the Katzes never discussed their grief. It was too raw, too painful. In time, Lizzie would learn that her parents had died in the camps, and that the Nazis had shot her grandmother in her bed soon after she left for England. Fritz, meanwhile, never stopped trying to find his lost family. He scoured the personal-notice section of the *Aufbau*, the German-language newspaper for refugees worldwide, for word from them, and repeatedly placed ads for them himself. Five years after his arrival in America, he received a letter from his father, postmarked Alexandria: they had escaped Vienna and survived the war in Egypt. Fritz sent for them, settling them in a nearby apartment. His family was intact, but he never stopped lamenting the aristocratic life he had left behind.

And the baker's daughter Margaret Erle, he declared, was beneath his son. Like Gertrude, he was rigid, disciplined, and concerned about appearances. And Fritz, who wore sharkskin suits and silk ties, made himself abundantly clear: the Katzes had standards. They lived in an elegant apartment in Inwood, a quiet, tree-lined neighborhood at the northern tip of Manhattan. Every aspect of their lives marked them as superior to the Erles. Even their building, Fritz noted, set them apart. It had an elevator.

THE MORE FRITZ AND GERTRUDE tried to separate the young pair, the more they wanted to be together. They used pay phones to make dates, and met in the neighborhood, away from view. When George invited Margaret to his prom at the Copacabana in early June of 1960, Gertrude shouted, "Over my dead body!" and padlocked the door of their third-floor apartment. Margaret crept out the fire escape, her baby-blue pumps and borrowed fur stole in hand as George waited in the luncheonette around the corner. A week later, Margaret sneaked out to meet him again at a party in a nearby synagogue. Gertrude was so enraged when she noticed Margaret missing that she marched up the street in her housedress to find her daughter. She stomped into the reception hall, screaming that her daughter didn't have permission to be there. Margaret, mortified, hid in the bathroom and then darted out the back door. Once home, she locked herself in her bedroom before Gertrude could get there.

But on one occasion, Gertrude actually behaved. As much as the Erles observed traditional Jewish practices, they embraced some secular American customs, including a big party for Margaret's sixteenth birthday. For Jewish girls in New York, the parties were sometimes as formal as weddings—compensation for the fact that boys were feted at age thirteen with lavish bar mitzvahs. (Wide acceptance of bat mitzvahs for girls, championed by feminists, was still years away.) For days before Margaret's party, Gertrude and Margaret's aunt Rosel prepared a feast: huge platters of pastrami, roast beef, and turkey; big bowls of different salads. Josef baked a giant sheet cake and decorated it with white icing, blue trim, and blue roses that said "Happy Sweet 16 Margaret." It matched her white-and-blue dress. George came, and the two danced to Bobby Darin. He hardly left her side all night. But that didn't stop Gertrude from resorting to subterfuge: she claimed she'd spotted George kissing one of Margaret's friends in the hallway.

Margaret Erle and George Katz on their prom night
at the Copacabana nightclub, June 1960

Occasionally George braved Gertrude's intimidation, and the two would sit in the living room, watching TV shows Gertrude had to personally approve, or on Margaret's bed with the door ajar. Gertrude would march down the flat's hallway past her daughter's room, fiddling with the empty glass bottles in the metal milkman's box that sat outside Margaret's door, just so she could peek. Sometimes she paid Margaret's little brother, Allen, a nickel to snoop too.

A few weeks after Margaret turned sixteen, George handed her a velvet box with a silver ID bracelet he'd engraved with her name and "Love, George" on the inside. Margaret tossed it back at him. She had dreams of college—not settling down. Her parents had made clear they could only afford to pay for Allen's higher education, so Margaret knew she'd have to fund her own. She salted away money from babysitting jobs and doubled up on classes in order to graduate early, so she could start college part-time. She wanted to become a social worker: she wanted to help people.

As autumn fell into winter, kissing in the bitter gusts of nearby parks didn't feel quite so romantic. So the young couple found a backup plan. Margaret's friend Paula lived around the corner from Margaret, and her divorced mother worked. Paula had a boyfriend, too, and on cold afternoons, her apartment became a trysting place for the two couples.

By February, the kissing had advanced to petting. Everybody, it seemed, was doing it, despite the high school newsreels and dating manuals that warned girls they'd come to regret it, and blamed them if they didn't discourage it. But it was exciting, and it felt too good for either of them to stop. And one cold afternoon in early March of 1961, the young couple had intercourse for the first time on Paula's rug. They had never discussed the direction their relationship was taking, or even sex itself. It wasn't planned, of course—they hadn't even taken all their clothes off—and George didn't have a condom (not that birth control had ever been a topic of open discussion). Margaret knew from her friends, and a few embarrassed glances at confession magazines, how babies were conceived—sort of. Startled and scared, she rushed to the bathroom to stanch her bleeding with toilet paper. She came out, shaken, several minutes later, smoothing her pleated skirt, and announced to George it would never happen again. "What if God punishes us?" she asked him.

Margaret had never had a bite of pepperoni pizza, touched a shrimp, or even set foot in a Chinese restaurant. She didn't smoke. She didn't drink. She lit Shabbat candles, dropped portions of her meager earnings in her family's tzedakah boxes so that war orphans in Israel might find families to adopt them, and said the Shema, the cornerstone of Jewish prayers, every morning and night. But she had crossed a line, and she was terrified. She knew from her mother's—and the synagogue's—dictates that sex before marriage was off-limits, something only "bad" girls did.

Now she was one too.

3.

"We're Going to Have to Take Care of This"

For weeks, Margaret's thoughts raced. She loved George, and he loved her, and she knew they would make a life together. Sometimes the word "sin" crossed her mind, but whenever it did, she dismissed it. How could what she had done with George actually be *bad*? How could she be bad? Her father, the gentlest person in Margaret's universe, always reminded her that treating people with loving-kindness was among Judaism's most sacred tenets. She was always good to people, even to her mother. Didn't that matter more than anything else?

But as the days grew longer, so did Margaret's fears. She tried to focus instead on the coming holiday of Passover, the Jewish celebration of the escape from slavery in Egypt. She helped her mother scrub, rid the house of leavened products, and ready the apartment for the relatives who'd come for the Seder. As her father read the Haggadah, the text describing the book of Exodus, Margaret reflected on the images of oppression she saw in her own life. She thought about the disturbing pictures from the South she'd seen on television: the lynchings, the "Colored Only" signs on train cars and drinking fountains, and then the hopeful, dignified lunch-counter sit-ins that ended with mob beatings.

At the end of Passover, she and George celebrated by having a slice of cheese pizza, and a few nights later they went to a Rangers game—George was a huge fan, and went to as many games in nosebleed seats as he possibly could. In the bathroom during intermission, she discovered that she had spotted a bit, and breathed a huge sigh of relief: she'd gotten her period after all. But in May, it didn't come, and by this time her breasts had swollen so much she had to fasten her bra on the last set of hooks. Still, she pushed away the fear that she might be pregnant. Come on: the first and only time she'd had sex? (Had she even *had* sex? She wasn't entirely sure.) And besides, nobody could be that unlucky.

She bought a girdle with her babysitting money, and exchanged her formfitting pants for peasant tops, a beige tent dress, and skirts she could fasten with a giant safety pin across her thickening waist. But one warm morning as Margaret stood in her thin cotton nightgown ironing a dress in her tiny bedroom, she noticed her mother eyeing her body.

"You're pregnant, aren't you, you *Hure*," Gertrude hissed, using the German word for "whore." Margaret looked down, intent on her pressing. "Of course not," she replied.

"You're a liar," Gertrude cried. She lunged for the steaming iron, grabbed its plastic handle, and hurled it at her daughter, shrieking, "What kind of person are you?!"

Reality eventually overcame Margaret's bright optimism. What's going to happen to our lives? she wondered. George, eighteen, had just been offered an athletic scholarship to Ohio State University, while Margaret, barely a month past her seventeenth birthday, had doubled up on coursework in order to graduate that summer, nine months ahead of schedule. She had wanted to get a head start on college so she and George could finish at the same time. She had it all planned: they'd get married once they had both earned degrees, and start their lives together properly.

Late that afternoon, she mustered the courage to tell George, who was at work nearby in a craft store. She rang the shop bell, then waited near the entrance while he asked his boss for a short coffee break.

George ushered her outside, his heavy arm around her shoulders. "I might be pregnant," she blurted, tearing up. "What are we going to do?"

"We'll get married," he told her. "Don't worry. We'll figure out what to do."

"But how?" she insisted.

"We will," he promised her.

THE NEXT DAY, she met George on the subway platform near her house. He handed Margaret a pearl ring with two tiny diamonds. "It'll all be OK," he assured her. She hoped he was right, but they had both heard what could happen to girls like her: the classmates who'd been sent away, the cousins of friends, the "loose girls" who had to leave town to help a purportedly sick aunt, only to return to whispers. The catastrophes she anticipated multiplied. What would happen when Fritz found out? He and Gertrude could see to it that the couple never saw each other again.

Trying to buy time until they could figure out a plan, George told their friend Mark Imberman that Margaret was fighting with Gertrude, and asked if she could come stay with him and his widowed mother for a few weeks until the storm blew over. After dinner a few nights later, Margaret waited until eight o'clock, when Gertrude, Josef, and Allen sat down in front of the TV. It looked like an ordinary family tableau: Allen and Gertrude sat on the couch watching *The Donna Reed Show* while Josef relaxed in an easy chair, the tip of his cigarette glowing orange in the dim, smoky room.

Her father laughed at one of Reed's innocent capers, and Margaret took a deep breath. "I have a job as a mother's helper in Queens," she blurted.

Margaret studied her mother's face in the eerie light of the tiny black-and-white images, but Gertrude acted as if she hadn't heard. Josef looked up for a moment and said simply, "OK." Margaret gathered her suitcase, the blue hatbox that carried her makeup and her curlers, and crept out of her building to the sidewalk where George was waiting below. Gertrude said not another word.

Mrs. Imberman welcomed Margaret as if nothing at all was amiss, and showed her to the upstairs room of her grown daughter. It was a bright white, with a homey rag rug on the floor and a soft chenille bedspread. Ruffled curtains decorated a large screened window overlooking the backyard. Margaret could see fireflies shimmering in the darkness.

George came to visit on weekends, and in the evenings the boys played sock hockey in the basement as they listened to pop records. Margaret's high school coursework was finished, and she knew her diploma would arrive in the mail over the summer. George had graduated too. Soon they would both start college.

Some sunny Sundays, Margaret, George, Mark, and a group of other friends took the subway to Rockaway Beach. While the rest of the kids sunbathed and dove into the waves, George and Margaret visited the arcade. George, with his pitcher's arm, threw balls at weighted targets, winning every time. Carnival workers would unwind long strips of colored tickets he could redeem for prizes. Opposite the cheap stuffed animals and knickknacks were shelves of home goods. After his first victory, George looked at Margaret and asked, "A toaster or Pyrex?" He carted the new appliance back to his apartment and hid it under his bed.

For a few weeks that summer, Margaret felt calm. She took magazines outside to read in the backyard, stretching her legs out in the sun. Away from Gertrude's steely gaze, she wasn't constantly on guard. Margaret busied herself by helping Mrs. Imberman with the housework. One afternoon, they chatted nonchalantly as they pinned wet laundry on the clothesline. For the first time, Margaret lived in a house utterly lacking in tension. Mrs. Imberman never raised her voice in anger. Sometimes noisy blue jays would dart into the yard for bugs, their metallic cries as loud as seagulls'. She found herself dreaming that she and George might live in a house this nice one day, away from the city noise. She couldn't help but notice that her clothes were getting tighter. She kept hoping it was Mrs. Imberman's cake.

A few weeks later, Margaret stood at the kitchen sink after dinner, her hands plunged into dishwater. The dusk sky was the dark blue of late summer, and she could hear crickets chirping outside. Mark went into the living room to watch television, and in the reflection of the window she could see Mrs. Imberman approach her. She gently touched her shoulder. Margaret turned around, fearful of what she would say.

"My dear," Mrs. Imberman told her, "you need to see a doctor."

Margaret felt her stomach lurch to her knees. She didn't look up, didn't say a word. Deep down, she'd known she'd been running away— from her mother, from her future, from the truth. She felt her body go cold with the reality of her situation. She was a pregnant teenager with no skills to speak of, and she was going to shame her family. She dried her hands and called George.

"You have to come get me," she said, trying not to cry. "I need to come home."

When George arrived the next afternoon, he had dark circles under his eyes. They were both quiet on the walk to the subway. On the train back to Manhattan, Margaret slipped her left hand, the tiny pearl ring on her ring finger, into George's right palm. "We're getting married," he whispered. "It's going to be all right. Everything is fine." But since they were both minors in the state of New York—at the time, the legal age for marriage was eighteen for women, and twenty-one for men—they would need their parents' approval. The chances of that were vanishingly slim.

George carried Margaret's bags up the stairs to Margaret's apartment. They were silent as they approached her door, hoping Gertrude would be out. But they heard the hectoring voice of Gertrude's beloved health guru from the kitchen radio. She met them in the hallway in her housedress, radiating disgust. George spoke before Gertrude had a chance to.

"We want to get married," he told her.

"We're going to look for a place to live," Margaret added.

Gertrude waved her hands in the air. "Married?" she screamed. "Married?! You're not getting married—you're teenagers!"

She came toward Margaret angrily, then shot a look at George. "What about your scholarship?"

"We'll figure it out," he said, standing between his scared girlfriend and her mother.

She waved the wooden spoon in her hand toward George's face. "Leave!" she commanded.

He looked at Margaret. "Go," she told him, shaking with dread. "Go."

He squeezed her shoulder, and turned to look at her as he opened the door. She waved him on, and the door clicked shut.

No sooner had George reached the landing than Gertrude began screaming, her cheeks red with rage. "You seduced him," she shouted, her mouth so close to Margaret's face, she could feel her mother's spittle. "You're an embarrassment to this whole family. Good girls don't do this." She hurled more insults in Yiddish and German; they landed like grenades.

"We're going to have to take care of this," she finally announced and went to the telephone in the living room, stabbing her index finger into each number hole on the rotary dial. "I need to make an appointment for my daughter," Margaret heard her say. "It's urgent."

She hung up, then narrowed her dark eyes. "Can you imagine what this looks like?" she demanded. "You think you can keep a man that way, by being that kind of girl? He'll be gone in no time. You know why? You're used goods."

Margaret rushed to her room, pushed her dresser against the door so Gertrude couldn't harangue her, and sobbed into her pillow.

In the subway car to Gertrude's doctor's midtown office two days later, mother and daughter sat in frozen silence—Margaret panicked, Gertrude livid. At the doctor's office, they sat on opposite sides of the waiting room as Gertrude angrily thumbed through a *Reader's Digest*. Margaret was too petrified to move.

A nurse in a white dress, crisp white cap, and thick white stockings summoned them into the examination room. Margaret looked at the steel exam table, covered with fine white tissue paper, and shuddered. Then the gynecologist, a kindly older man named Dr. Grunstein, entered. "My daughter's pregnant," Gertrude announced.

"All right, then," he said gently. "Let's just see."

He instructed Margaret to remove all her clothes, and the nurse handed her a cotton gown. Margaret stepped out of her tent dress, and Gertrude, observing from a chair, gasped when she saw her daughter's naked swelling body.

Margaret climbed onto the examining table, shivering even though the room was warm. The nurse placed her bare feet into cold metal stirrups, and as Margaret lay with her legs splayed, she realized she was more exposed to Dr. Grunstein than she'd been with George. The gray-haired older man inserted a cold speculum, probed her cervix, and palpated her belly. Margaret stared at the ceiling, with no idea what he was doing, or why; she'd never been to a gynecologist before. Gertrude issued loud, pained sighs from her chair across the room.

"When was your last menstrual period?" the doctor asked.

"Early March, I think," Margaret responded. Nobody needed a lab test to confirm the obvious: she was almost six months' pregnant.

"Get dressed, dear, and come into my office," he told her. He patted her foot. "We'll take care of this." Margaret wondered what that meant. Perhaps Dr. Grunstein could help her in a way Gertrude could not.

When Margaret was dressed, she and Gertrude entered Dr. Grunstein's office. Books lined the shelves, and an image of female reproductive organs was affixed to the back of the door. Margaret stared at them, trying to understand her own.

The doctor began to tell Margaret and Gertrude about a maternity home where Margaret could spend the rest of her pregnancy, and about a Jewish adoption agency that would place the baby in a good home. "No need for anyone to ever know," he said matter-of-factly, writing down the information on a slip he handed to Gertrude. No one had asked Margaret a single question about what she wanted.

As she was leaving, Dr. Grunstein gave her a weary smile: "Come back when you're married and pregnant," he said. "I'll make sure no one ever finds out."

It was all so confusing. He made her pregnancy—her *baby*—sound like nothing important, an everyday experience her mind would soon erase.

"You can forget this ever happened," he assured mother and daughter, before picking up the phone and arranging for them to visit the Louise Wise agency on the Upper East Side that same day.

As they left to go, Dr. Grunstein approached them both to shake hands. He said goodbye, and then added in a lowered voice: "The building has a discreet back entrance for families in your . . . situation."

From the back corridor of the Wise agency office, Margaret caught a glimpse of the gleaming front entryway for Wise's very different clients: adoptive parents. The giant white wooden door facing the street had intricate glass panels on either side, and a Palladian arch overhead. It led to a vestibule and a vast foyer with chic Danish-modern furniture, a polished black-and-white-marble floor, plaster pillars, and a dark green rubber plant. Margaret had never seen anyplace so elegant in her life.

A receptionist whisked them to a modest upstairs waiting room, and motioned for mother and daughter to sit in a small private room with a single chair and a vinyl love seat. Margaret smoothed her dress, damp from perspiration. Moments later, a social worker with a clipboard summoned Gertrude. At first, Margaret stared down and tried to study the floor tiles. Then she flipped through a worn pile of *Saturday Evening Posts*, but none of the words registered. Instead, she thought about the tiny apartment she and George might be able to afford in some cheap part of the city—a studio downtown, perhaps, away from their parents.

She waited for what seemed like forever. Finally, the same woman summoned Margaret into a back room with a broad desk. Shades covered the high windows. She asked questions about Margaret and Gertrude's family history—their looks, their features, their height, their health. Gertrude said that she and Josef were born in Germany to middle-class merchant families, and had emigrated before the war. She was forthright about her breast cancer, and that of her mother and sister. Margaret told of her interest in dance, music, and theater.

Finally, the social worker asked Margaret questions about the "purported father" and his background too. "Purported father?" Margaret asked. "I know who my baby's father is. His name is George Katz."

The woman smiled with her mouth closed. "I see," she said. "Well, tell us about *him*." Margaret began to describe him: six feet one, with olive skin and eyes, a talented baseball player with a father who co-owned a military surplus store and a mother who was a secretary, both from Vienna. All of their parents, she added, spoke German, and both families were observant. The woman nodded.

"What does this all mean?" Margaret asked. "Why are you asking all this?" Even at the adoption agency, she clung to the idea that she could keep her baby.

Then the social worker presented a stack of papers before her. "These are the relinquishment papers you'll need to sign to get the adoption underway," she explained. Margaret looked on in disbelief. She wasn't even sure what "adoption" meant. The woman pushed a pen in her direction, but Margaret refused to pick it up. "I'm not signing anything," she said.

"You will too," Gertrude said.

"I'm not signing anything," Margaret repeated, her voice rising. She slipped her purse over her forearm and stood up. "I'm leaving."

"We'll be back," Gertrude told the woman.

Margaret didn't realize it, but while Margaret was alone in Louise Wise's waiting room, Gertrude had signed a permission form that would place Margaret at Lakeview, a maternity home owned by the Louise Wise agency. It was located on Staten Island, a borough of New York City reachable, at the time, only by ferry. At seventeen, Margaret was still under Gertrude's legal thumb.

On the subway home, Gertrude again harangued her. She sat close, spitting rage into Margaret's ear. "I did my very best with you," she told her. "I did my very best." She cast her eyes on Margaret's belly. "Do you know how your father has worked to support you? Do you know what we've sacrificed for you? Now look what you've done—you've ruined your life and your reputation. And ours! You're getting what you deserved."

Margaret tried to summon sympathy for her mother, in addition to her guilt and fear: Gertrude had lost a husband and a breast, and now her teenage daughter was pregnant. Maybe she even had an inkling about Josef's relationship with Irene. Margaret just kept repeating that she loved George, that he loved her, that they were getting married. Gertrude sneered. "Marry—a girl like you? Men fool around with your kind. Then they marry good ones."

She paused for a moment, narrowed her eyes, and looked again at her daughter's belly. "You," she said, "are not one of them."

When they arrived back home, Margaret lumbered up the stairwell behind her mother, focusing on the worn grooves of the marble steps, praying none of her neighbors would see her. She caught a strong whiff of Pine-Sol on the stairs—the super mopped with it twice a week—and felt overcome with nausea. The familiar and homelike odor now smelled like rotting garbage.

Once inside the apartment, she barricaded the door once again, flung herself on her pink duvet cover, and sobbed.

A while later, she heard her father coughing in the hallway before his key turned in the lock. Gertrude wasted no time in telling him the news, screaming in German that their daughter had ruined everything the family had worked so hard to build. Margaret turned up the volume on her transistor radio as high as it would go, but despite the tiny earpiece lodged in her ear, she heard the word "*Hure*" again and again. She gazed down at her body. Her curves had given way to mounds she hardly recognized.

While her mother carried on, Margaret grabbed her purse, and stole out the apartment door. She raced down the staircase and to the corner to the pay phone. George answered. She could hear the television in the background.

Her words rushed out: "My mother took me to the doctor," she blurted. "It's official: I'm pregnant. They're sending me to Staten Island, to a home for unwed mothers."

She spoke so quickly, George scarcely had time to answer.

"Goodbye," she said. "I love you."

George, speaking within earshot of his parents, could only say, "Me too."

Margaret hung up and ran back upstairs. Gertrude was still shouting in one endless loop.

Even Josef, who had always doted on Margaret, could do nothing in the face of his wife's rage. Then Gertrude picked up the phone and called the Katzes. Fritz answered, and Margaret could hear the two screaming at each other. She crept off her bed to eavesdrop from the hallway. The shouts were so loud Margaret could hear Fritz's booming voice from even a room away. There seemed to be one thing upon which they both agreed: Margaret was a tramp.

Margaret stayed in her room during dinner.

Before bedtime, Josef went into the bathroom, and a few moments later, he knocked softly on her door. Margaret opened, almost too anxious to face him. He looked at her sadly. "I'm sorry this happened to you, Margaret," he said gently. "There's nothing I can do." He turned to go, coughing down the hallway as he walked away.

⌇

THE NEXT EVENING, Fritz called the Erles. "Your daughter must get an abortion!" he screamed at Gertrude, who responded by threatening to sue George, eighteen, for statutory rape (the age of consent in New York was seventeen; Margaret was sixteen when she'd had sex).

Fritz had his own reasons to be angry. Not only did he see the pregnancy as jeopardizing George's educational future, it also upset Fritz's plans for his son. Fritz had always dreamed that George would marry the daughter of his business partner. Their army-surplus store was thriving, and a marriage could consolidate resources for an ideal American future.

Fritz and Gertrude hadn't even met yet, but they already hated each other—and each other's children. Margaret tried to envision a meeting in which they all sat down to discuss the situation rationally and arrange a small, quick wedding. Yet the more she heard the two parents screaming, the more she realized it could never happen. Most excruciatingly, there was no discretion in this conversation. The telephones in both apartments were in the living room. Nothing was secret now.

4.

Girls in Trouble

People had always had sex before marriage, but after the war, something in the social calculus shifted. Young men who went off to war as virgins returned from their years in Europe and Asia sexually experienced—and unwilling to resume chaste relationships with their stateside sweethearts. Teenagers also had newfound chances to explore their sexuality. In the increasingly affluent United States, they had unsupervised time and space in the expanding new suburbs: bedrooms they didn't have to share; basement rec rooms; the back seat of the family Buick. The opportunities to have sex were everywhere. But in a conservative nation, there was neither birth control nor sex education and that combined with teen privacy to make unwed pregnancy a biological inevitability. The number of babies born to unmarried mothers more than tripled between the years 1940 and 1966, rising from 7 per 1,000 births to 23 births per 1,000.

None of these statistics helped Margaret, who felt—was made to feel—isolated in her status as a "girl in trouble." She had good reason to think she was alone. Almost without exception, the images she saw all around her conveyed the American ideal: a calm, orderly universe in which white couples were creating calm, orderly families. Strong, commanding men were fathers, wed happily to morally upright mothers who had a carefully cultivated persona of rectitude. This new norm was a stark contrast to that of the 1940s, in which female sexuality seemed so volatile that good-looking women were described as "bombshells" and "dynamite." And no wonder: Wartime women in the United States didn't just have sexual power. They signed up by the hundreds of thousands for the armed services, and hundreds of thousands more stepped into traditionally male jobs, building ships and aircraft, manufacturing munitions and driving trucks. But once the war was over, so was their independence. Women, so recently valued for their skills and forbearance, were sent back home to the growing new and remarkably chaste suburban hearth. In the midst of the biggest demographic growth in history, the baby boom, their most important job was to be mothers. Between 1946 and 1964, American women—of every marital status— gave birth to an estimated 78 million infants.

Somehow, though, the specifics of how all these babies came to be was almost entirely airbrushed out of popular culture and polite conversation. By the early 1950s, female sexuality, once hailed as explosive, now seemed almost as frightening as communism. Censors tried to banish any hint of sex in novels and films. And yet at the same time women were prized for their fertility. Those who lacked the voluptuousness of Marilyn Monroe or Lana Turner could get help from the fashions of the day. With fabric rationing over, billowing skirts with petticoats emphasized curves, and an arsenal of undergarments bound and padded flesh into hourglass shapes whether they were natural or not. Even high school girls strapped themselves into tight bullet bras, and wore thick elastic girdles for cinched waistlines.

It was an era of contradiction and hypocrisy. Promote your sexuality, but don't have sex until you're married, then promptly become a mother. To make matters worse, sex education was almost nonexistent, and advice to young women was at once vague and conflicting. One constant: unmarried girls had to bear the responsibility for whatever took place between them and their boyfriends. Consider this 1957 newsreel, which aired in high school health classes across North America. It begins with a girl named Mary rushing out of her boyfriend Jeffrey's car one evening. He runs to follow her up her front steps, apologizing. Mary ignores him and bounds up the stairs to her bedroom, her face stricken as she furiously brushes her hair at her vanity table. Her mother looks on, concerned. Finally Mary confesses that she and Jeffrey had stopped and parked. "And then things seemed to happen, until we nearly . . ." The older woman's expression shifts from one of concern to dark disapproval. She recoils from her teenage daughter, crossing her arms. "It was so close," Mary cries, on the verge of tears. "Suddenly I realized what we were about to do. I asked Jeff to take me home. I guess he felt ashamed too—he said he was sorry, that it was his fault."

"Do you think it *was* his fault?" the bathrobed mother asks, her mouth pursed in a tight line.

As Mary's mother's comment suggests, it was up to girls to protect their honor. In the 1950s, abstinence was the only socially acceptable option for young people with surging hormones. In one popular guide to how girls should conduct themselves, the author offered the following admonition: "Girls!" she implores. "There's a limit! . . . When you sense that your emotions and the boy's are becoming too much aroused, suggest going to the corner for a Coke, or going for a walk." Taking any other path could have disastrous consequences: "sex feelings" might make you want to go further, and could lead to "unwed intercourse," lifelong guilt, and pregnancy. Better to get to know a fellow through a wholesome activity like bowling.

It was reasonable for parents and other adults to worry that "unwed intercourse" among teens could lead to pregnancy, since there was almost no way for them to obtain birth control. Condoms were all but off-limits to young people—they were kept largely behind the counter, and pharmacists, acting in loco parentis, often demanded proof of age. Access to the birth control pill, approved by the FDA in 1960, was prohibited even for married couples in some states until 1965, when the Supreme

Court issued its historic ruling in *Griswold v. Connecticut*. And abortion, of course, was illegal—and risky—in most states until the landmark *Roe v. Wade* decision in 1973.

The rules were utterly perplexing. You were sold glamorous formfitting dresses for proms and Sweet Sixteen parties. Yet you were supposed to be a virgin as you recited your vows, then magically morph into a sex kitten on your wedding night, wearing a frilly see-through full-length nylon nightgown—or more weirdly, a set of short sheer pajamas called baby dolls.

Sensing some intriguing data, Alfred Kinsey, a studious professor of zoology in Indiana who collected bugs and edible plants, had set out in the mid-1930s to make sense of human sexuality—an unexplored realm of science. What he found exposed the gap between how Americans pretended they behaved sexually, and what they actually did.

In 1948 Kinsey presented copious (and controversial) research he'd collected from thousands of subjects across the United States for more than a decade in a three-pound book called *Sexual Behavior in the Human Male*. In 1953 he presented his findings on women in *Sexual Behavior in the Human Female*. Both rocketed to the top of the *New York Times* best-seller list, selling hundreds of thousands of copies, despite the fact that the paper rejected advertising about the books and declined to review them.

At the time, most Americans professed to believe that those who didn't hew to an established set of sexual rules were degenerate. The laws reflected this: adultery, homosexuality, and premarital sex were criminal in most states. Children were taught that masturbation caused a variety of maladies, from hairy palms to insanity and blindness. Yet Kinsey's books revealed that almost all men, and a majority of women, masturbated; that most men and half of women had had premarital sex; that half of men and a third of women had cheated on their spouses; and that more than a third of men, and 13 percent of women, had had homosexual experiences.

Americans may have found the male studies shocking, but they simply refused to accept that their grandmothers, mothers, and daughters had active (and varied) sexual lives. Many insisted that Kinsey drew his six thousand female subjects from prostitutes. Indeed, not only young people were expected to act with decorum and self-restraint; married couples were too. On one side of popular culture, romance was presented in such a desexualized way that a television show featuring two of the country's most beloved TV stars—Lucille Ball and Desi Arnaz—showed the real-life husband and wife sleeping in twin beds. Almost everybody loved Lucy, but when she became pregnant during filming in 1952, CBS executives and the show's advertisers agonized about how to conceal her growing girth. (Until that moment, visibly pregnant women had never appeared on film or television.) Ball and Arnaz, though, insisted that Lucy's pregnancy would resonate with her 10 million viewers, and that it be written into the show. CBS was so nervous, it hired what sounds like the beginning of a bad joke—a rabbi, a priest, and a minister—to review the script for "taste." Ball, as audacious off-screen as she was on, evaded censors by using French in the episode when she tells Ricky she's expecting: it was titled "Lucy Is Enceinte." In the end, the joke was on CBS: an astounding 44 million people tuned in to watch the 1953 episode about the birth of Lucy's baby.

Meanwhile, a new upstart named Hugh Hefner was raising the banner of sexual freedom in Chicago. Kinsey had challenged American prudery with science. Hefner confronted it directly, with a new magazine he debuted in 1953 called *Playboy*. While there had been previous skin magazines, Hefner aimed for a mainstream audience. He intended *Playboy* as a new lifestyle guide for middle-class men (and not incidentally, teenage boys) who lacked role models for the country's newfound consumerism, and he commissioned articles on cocktail mixing, travel, dining, advice on how to buy the right cars and stereo equipment. Of course, what really propelled the popularity of his magazine was the publication of topless centerfolds every month. His first was Marilyn

Monroe—remarkably, she didn't receive a dime of the $500 he paid for the images—but soon thereafter his models took on a more attainable air. Although Hefner himself had grown up in a strictly religious home and had married the first woman he slept with (the couple later divorced), he offered Americans an entirely new concept: wholesome sexuality. Not only bad girls liked sex, Hefner was fond of saying—good girls enjoyed it, too, and they didn't have to be married to do it. Photos of his centerfolds—Playmates of the Month—accompanied lists of their alleged hobbies, turn-ons, and sports. His first message to readers was this: "We don't expect to solve any world problems or prove any great moral truths."

Hefner's subscription rates often topped those of *Life* and *Time*, and in 1960 he began expanding his company to include Playboy Clubs, in which "bunnies" dressed in impossibly tight strapless satin costumes with balls of cotton attached to their derrières, served men cocktails and meals with deep backward dips they had to master in order to get hired. Critics, most famously Gloria Steinem—who had written about her experiences as an undercover bunny—slammed Hefner for his blatant objectification of women. It became easy to dismiss what Hefner, padding around the Playboy Mansion in his silk robe and captain's hat, arms draped around women many decades his junior, would come to represent. But the magazine, and the man, were far more complicated than the frivolous bunny imagery he defended as "playful." Under his direction, the magazine criticized the Vietnam War and championed a host of progressive causes: abortion rights, civil rights, the decriminalization of marijuana, and especially the repeal of nineteenth-century sex laws. He integrated his staff and his club memberships and provided female employees with tuition reimbursement.

Playboy's complexities reflected the rapidly shifting cultural landscape—and morals—of a new generation of Americans. The chasm between the prim and the playboy became even more evident in 1956, when Grace Metalious, a young mother of three, shocked the United States with her blockbuster novel *Peyton Place*. It depicted premarital sex, extramarital sex, unwed motherhood, and incest in a small New Hampshire town. It sold millions of copies, spawning a sequel, a movie, and a prime-time TV series—and unlike *Playboy's* consumers its readers were overwhelmingly female. The book was a phenomenon, offering readers a form of socially acceptable voyeurism.

Americans had competing narratives for other, more sanctioned relationships. Newspaper society pages gave breathless reports of weddings, from descriptions of the bride's gown to the name of each of her attendants. The media lavished coverage on Elizabeth Taylor's serial unions, beginning in 1950 with Conrad Hilton Jr. when she was eighteen; paparazzi besieged Marilyn Monroe's civil ceremony with Joe DiMaggio in 1954; and millions watched Grace Kelly's televised marriage to Prince Rainier in 1956. The marriage rate spiked, and in 1950, the marriage age dropped to its lowest point since the 1890s, to just over twenty years for women, and just under twenty-three for men.

One guide to marriage—with the straightforward title *How Every Girl Can Choose, Win, Hold and Enjoy a Man*—offered women explicit advice for landing their dreamboat. In chapter after chapter, the author advises young women how to dress, speak, eat, and act. Among the tips: always be admiring of men; let your escort order for you in a restaurant; avoid halitosis at all costs; and if you are bottom-heavy, for heaven's sake, stay away from horizontally striped skirts. Not only appearance was to be curated—so were personalities. If a girl recognized herself as a "Timid Sue," a "Frozen Fran," or a "Temperamental Tess," she'd be out of luck—unless she picked up and moved to places where men outnumbered women. In Alaska, Nevada, or Idaho, even hapless women would have better prospects.

As a teenager in the Manhattan of the late 1950s and early '60s, Margaret was reading high school textbooks, not Kinsey, marriage guides, or

Peyton Place. But she had nonetheless grasped the essential contradiction of the era. Good Girls Didn't—and yet, like so many others, she had.

Margaret was part of another major trend. Unlike previous generations, adolescents who'd come of age after the war were developing social and financial autonomy. Like most kids, she and George had chores. But new appliances, from dryers to power lawn mowers, gave parents and children far more time on their own, and they had more money to spend during it. By Margaret's sixteenth birthday in 1960, the 18 million teenage Americans represented a new force of their own: consumers who contributed an estimated $10 billion a year to the economy. Many kids had after-school jobs, and like Margaret, millions of girls had regular babysitting gigs. (Parents now had time—and money—to go out on regular "date nights," and the demand for sitters was sometimes so great that families in some growing new towns started wage-bidding wars.) As a demographic wave, they were beginning to create their own teen subculture that defined its own media, music, and institutions. They created their own social bonds, cliques, and clubs.

Advertising officials were quick to recognize the new market—and that the young buyer was more valuable, long-term, than an older one. Musically, teenagers were their own new country, one with a racier approach to male-female relations. Youngsters in the 1940s had to listen to Dad's Bing Crosby records on the living room Victrola. But by the 1950s, they could buy portable record players they listened to on their own. George had a turquoise one, and he and his friends listened to music of which their parents disapproved: Elvis Presley, Chubby Checker, Little Anthony and the Imperials—music that Alan Freed, the DJ on whose show Margaret was a backup dancer, had introduced as "rock 'n' roll"— African American slang for sex—on mainstream radio.

Elvis represented a kind of young freedom all his own. He grew his hair long and combed it back in a bad-boy pompadour. He stood onstage with his legs spread apart, gyrating and twitching. He sang the African American music of the Mississippi Delta whether or not polite society found it acceptable. And yet this giant group of hormonal adolescents had little knowledge of sex (how would they, when even a pregnant Lucy looked like she lived in a dorm room?), and certainly no access to birth control. The social messages were mind-bogglingly conflicted: Do it, don't do it. Everybody does it, but nobody is supposed to. As Margaret often heard: Just keep your skirt down, and your panties up. That's all there is to it.

Margaret was coming of age with a generation that was asserting its independence in an era of social rigidity. But its strides only went so far. She was also part of a growing demographic of young women who for decades would feel shame, and stay silent.

5.

"Children of Your Own One Day"

In mid-September of 1961, Margaret prepared to leave for Lakeview, the maternity home on Staten Island. As was common at the time, there was a wait for one of the home's thirty-six beds. A few evenings after their visit to Louise Wise, the agency called Gertrude to say that a spot had opened up, and that Margaret could check in the next afternoon. Margaret called George from the corner pay phone to tell him, and they arranged to meet in the morning at the craft store where George worked, to say goodbye. It was a warm day, but she covered up with her thick wool winter coat. She felt her throat constrict as she eyed the big corner building with board games and toys in the window. She hardly understood what was happening.

George looked up as she entered, and rushed to greet her. They stepped outside. She looked up at him and said, "What's going to happen to us?" They didn't have a piece of paper, but they were already a family. "We can still build a life together, can't we?" she asked.

He nodded. "Margaret," he told her, taking her hand to his heart, "happily ever after."

Margaret and George looked like any other teenage sweethearts, meeting for a quick kiss. "Hey," a colleague called out to George. "You guys look so cute!" George, who had gotten a Polaroid camera for his eighteenth birthday, took it with him almost everywhere—including, that day, to work. The colleague suggested, "Why don't I take a picture of you two lovebirds?" Before they could object, he snapped the shot.

Margaret and George on the warm September day in 1961 when she left for the Lakeview home for unwed Jewish mothers. She was more than six months' pregnant, and tried to hide her belly underneath her winter coat.

IT DIDN'T TAKE MARGARET long to discover that there was, in fact, no lake, and no view. Lakeview was a stately three-story Italianate building on a quiet, secluded street. It had giant picture windows overlooking a yard so thick with tulip trees and oaks, she felt like she was in the middle of a forest. Margaret could hardly believe the island borough south of Manhattan was still part of New York City. She felt so far from her bustling, gritty neighborhood of Jews, Greeks, Italians, and Puerto Ricans; kosher butchers and pizzerias; liquor stores and candy shops; her nosy downstairs neighbor, Old Lady Rosen. She was so far from everything familiar. When Margaret and Gertrude pulled up to the front entrance, the taxi driver who had picked them up at the ferry lurched to a stop. He pulled Margaret's suitcase out of the trunk, set it down on the sidewalk without looking up, and hurried back to his running cab before Gertrude had time to ask him to wait. "How am I going to get out of here now?" she muttered to her daughter.

Gertrude signed Margaret in at a small admissions desk in the foyer, and asked the receptionist to call her a cab. "Goodbye," she said, and without another word she turned and walked through the giant wooden door.

The housemother came to greet Margaret in a large salon in the back of the house.

Like the taxi driver, the middle-aged woman with glasses and a gray belted dress kept her distance, and motioned for Margaret to sit opposite her on one of two matching navy-blue couches. She delivered some sobering advice: First, don't reveal anything about yourself, your family, or even your neighborhood. Second, come up with a fake name before you meet the other girls. Third, don't get close to anyone. Fourth, and most important: "Forget this ever happened," she said, batting her hand backward, as if swatting away a mosquito.

She showed Margaret to a third-floor room with three beds under a deep cornice and a small window overlooking the changing autumn treetops. It was so lush, it reminded Margaret of Mrs. Imberman's. The housemother motioned to the empty bed against the far wall and left. Margaret began to put her things away in the small bureau and shared closet. She had brought her tent dress and some giant blouses, a pair of stretch pants, white cloth sneakers, a nightgown, slippers, and a quilted blue bathrobe. One teenager and a young woman in her twenties sat on their beds. The girl in the middle bed stood up to shake her hand. "I'm Pam," she said. But was that even her real name?

Despite her fear and exhaustion, Margaret knew two things for sure: she had no intention of creating a pseudonym; and while she might be staying here, she was keeping her baby.

The older roommate said her name was Linda, and that she had come from Chicago. She spoke very little. But Pam was friendly, barely showing, and came from a wealthy town on Long Island. She gave her last name, and squeezed Margaret's hand. "They tell us not to make friends," she said, "but who are they kidding?"

Before the war, Lakeview authorities confiscated the girls' clothing when they arrived, issuing uniforms in their stead—blue dresses with big white collars covered by starched white aprons the director believed offered a "redeeming touch." The matching outfits also served as a deterrent to runaways—in those days, Lakeview officials insisted that mothers stay in the home for six months in order to breastfeed their infants, and many young women had taken off with their babies.

A decade later, the introduction of antibiotics, infant formula, and vaccines had made it safer to separate mothers from their children soon after birth.

By the early 1950s, girls were allowed to bring their own clothing, then left behind their old maternity garments for others. Pam showed Margaret the closet where faded pink dresses, oversize stained white blouses, and black pants with stretched-out pregnancy panels all hung like so many sad ghosts. There was also a stack of cotton underpants so large they looked like they would fit a giantess. Margaret looked down at her rapidly disappearing waistline and wondered: Would she, too, be that big?

At six o'clock, the three dozen girls filed down the stairs to a large, windowless dining room abutting a huge white kitchen with gleaming stainless-steel countertops and the biggest refrigerator Margaret had ever seen. The long table was loaded with pitchers of orange Tang and loaves of sliced white bread with margarine.

She watched as all the girls sat down, some holding their bellies from below, others resting their hands atop them as they chatted quietly. The girl next to Margaret tucked her long rayon napkin into her collar, and stretched it over her stomach. "When you get further along, you lose your lap." She shrugged. "Your spills land all over yourself, and you don't want to look like a schlump." Margaret watched as the heavyset, curly-haired cook put the food on the table. The first night, she set down giant trays of meat loaf, mashed potatoes, and canned peas. After dinner, some of the girls got up and cleared plates, and Margaret rose to help too. The girl with the big stomach told her that first-week girls never had table chores, and to check her week's assignment on a large chart in the dining room. A few minutes later, the cook brought out yellow and green squares of Jell-O. Margaret was astonished. Sugary drinks and desserts? No fresh vegetables or fruit? For pregnant women? Gertrude, she knew, would be shocked.

After dinner, she learned that she was on sweeping duty, one of several rotating tasks that also included setting and clearing the table, scrubbing countertops, washing dishes, and peeling potatoes. As soon as she put the broom in the closet, Margaret retreated to her room, took a shower, and went to bed. She woke up early the next day so disoriented she had to think for a moment about where she was. She'd always had her own room, but now she heard the other girls' breathing, and their beds creak as they shifted. The sun peeking through the aluminum blinds shone on Pam and Linda as they slept, and she felt her throat close with panic. How had she ended up trapped there?

Over the next week, Margaret learned sketchy details about the others. The women ranged in ages from a thirty-two-year-old secretary to a girl who had just turned fourteen. Margaret couldn't tell whose name was real and whose wasn't, but she realized they were all in the same bucolic prison. The artifice was disorienting. On one hand, the cook made sure the women spurned by their own community followed the dietary laws of their faith, never serving pork, shellfish, or dairy and meat together at the same meal. And then there was a basket of thin

gold wedding bands by the door, for the girls to slip over their ring fingers whenever they went out. Some kept them on all the time.

Pam didn't divulge the circumstances of her pregnancy—few girls
did. Many, it turned out, were as ignorant about sex as Margaret had
been. One girl said her mother had only ever told her she and her brothers had been "brought by the doctor." Another said her mother had told
her babies were simply plucked by their parents from cabbage patches,
and a third girl said that when her nephew had asked her much-older
sister about his arrival, her sister answered, "I planted a seed in my
body, and it grew, and that's how you were born."

Lights were supposed to be out at ten, but of course roommates
whispered, and within a few evenings even the taciturn Linda opened
up. "That's what you think," she would say when Margaret talked about
George's intentions to marry her, and the family they were planning.
Margaret felt her heart stop. What if Linda was right?

Over the next week, Margaret came to understand that the kind and
gentle cook was the only person at Lakeview who talked to the girls as if
nothing about them was wrong. Elsewhere in the house, Margaret felt she
was being constantly watched—and judged. That was deliberate: Lakeview's aim was to reform the wayward girls during their stays there. Not
only did they keep them under near-constant observation, supervisors
read both incoming and outgoing mail, as well as some journal entries.
(One young woman who complained about the intrusiveness was dismissed as "disturbed.") Administrators made sure to limit chatter among
the girls, keeping them occupied with typing classes and craft sessions, or
teaching them skills that might help them learn how to "keep house"—if
they were lucky enough to keep their shameful secret and marry one day.

THE SCENE AT LAKEVIEW was replicated in maternity homes across the
country as the number of unwed mothers rose from 125,200 in 1946 to
403,200 in 1972. Various institutions addressed the "problem," and mater-

nity homes sprang up to house, and seclude, young pregnant women. By 1965, there were more than two hundred such homes in forty-four states. The majority were run by national religious groups: Catholic Charities, the Salvation Army, and the Florence Crittenton Mission. Lakeview, of course, was run by Louise Wise Services. The agency, at first called the Free Synagogue Child Adoption Committee, was founded in 1916 by Louise Wise, wife of the famous Reform rabbi Stephen Wise. At her agency's inception, Wise's main focus was to find middle-class Jewish homes for thousands of Jewish immigrant children who'd been abandoned or orphaned in New York. Large numbers of Jews fleeing pogroms and poverty in Central and Eastern Europe had arrived in New York in the late nineteenth and early twentieth centuries. Many found work in the city's crowded, disease-ridden sweatshops, creating strains that often fractured families.

After World War II, as unwed pregnancies spiked and the middle class grew, so did the Wise agency's mandate. It began to deal almost exclusively in arranging the adoption, by Jewish couples, of the babies of unwed Jewish mothers. The couples paid a fee based on their incomes. At the time, New York law stipulated that the religion of birth mothers match that of the adopting parents or institutions "when practicable," and the Wise agency was the preeminent organization on the East Coast for Jewish families, both for couples seeking to adopt and for girls who had found themselves "in trouble." But there was also something else afoot: after the horrors of the Holocaust, there was an added compulsion, largely unspoken, to rebuild the Jewish family.

By the late 1950s, the number of infertile couples clamoring to adopt babies was skyrocketing, and the demand for adoptable (that is, healthy and white) babies outstripped supply. One couple adopting in the 1940s was told that there were thirty couples for every child available. By the early 1950s, the gap had narrowed, but there were still ten couples competing for every baby surrendered for adoption. It was a situation that even a federal employee described as a "seller's market."

The reasons for this demand were demographic and cultural. Birth rates had dropped dramatically during the Depression as married couples postponed starting families, and the war years lowered them further as millions of men were deployed overseas. After the war ended, ads beamed into American living rooms sent the message that domestic happiness and security were built on the rock of the modern, nuclear family, anchored by a pretty, conventional mother. (This family image, after all, was part of what made Americans superior to Communists: behind the Iron Curtain, children went to gloomy day care centers while their mothers slogged in factories in ugly uniforms, their hair mashed into hairnets.)

As unwed motherhood increased nationwide, by the 1960s, Wise and other large agencies could not accommodate the growing number of girls who needed to be sequestered during the final months of their pregnancies. In 1955, Louise Wise acquired control of Lakeview from the Jewish agency that had founded the home in 1905, and around that time also bought two additional properties in Manhattan: one on West Eighty-Second and one on East Ninety-Fourth. The nationwide homes housed only a small fraction of the unwed pregnant girls and women in the final trimesters of their pregnancies. One estimate found that only about 25,000, or 16 percent, of pregnant white women took up residence there each year. Among black women, that number was far lower. While some homes offered integrated housing, many of them categorically excluded black women. (Debate on whether to do so was often a topic at Louise Wise, where some were eventually accepted.)

Louise Wise homes were funded in part by Jewish philanthropies and sliding-scale adoption fees they charged adoptive parents, but like other homes, they charged the girls' families themselves. The price to hide one's daughter was not insignificant, costing as much as several hundreds of dollars for a four- or five-month stay. Some homes extracted labor in exchange for a bed and care. At a Salvation Army home in Portland,

Oregon, in 1968, "indigent" girls like Delores Swigert were housed on the third floor. They were assigned the tasks of cleaning and doing laundry for all fifty-nine girls who resided there, while girls whose parents contributed money for their stay only had to set the table. In 1970, at the Florence Crittenton home in Phoenix, where she lived with a hundred pregnant women, Marilyn Mendenhall shared kitchen chores with another girl. They were on their feet for hours, scrubbing dishes and spooning out meals to the other girls. In 1965, at Seton House in Richmond, Virginia, Carol Schaefer's job was to scrub and buff the long linoleum hallway between the foyer and the home's Catholic chapel. Girls there had to knit sweaters for other people's babies, attend daily Mass, and stuff envelopes for the church.

Many homes were like Lakeview—repurposed old mansions whose once-spacious bedrooms got chopped up to bunk the new volume of pregnant women. At a Salvation Army home in Jersey City, and at St. Anne's in Columbus, Ohio, as many as twenty girls slept crowded in the same dormitory room. In some homes, conditions were so cramped, some girls slept on sofas and examining tables.

Many homes functioned as minimum—or even not-so-minimum—security prisons. Unchaperoned excursions were often prohibited, and some homes looked, and felt, like jails. When women dared step outside Phoenix's Crittenton home for fresh (hot) air, they were reminded just where they were: the low-slung structure was surrounded by a twelve-foot chain-link fence that was topped with barbed wire. They were told that it was for their "protection."

Not surprisingly, girls often formed cliques and ranks just like teens in any high school. Letters were a great driver of status. At Portland's Salvation Army home, girls who received phone calls, visitors, and letters when the postman came at 4:00 p.m. were the most admired. Swigert, who was sixteen during her confinement, only received mail from her brother Don, who was in Vietnam. He wrote her almost daily, but letters from siblings were low on the scale of desirability. Ones from boyfriends were the most important, followed by those from parents.

While Jewish New Yorkers shipped their daughters on a ferry to the Staten Island woods—few Jews lived on Staten Island, so it would be unlikely that the girls would run into anyone familiar—thousands of wealthy parents from around the country sent their daughters to an even more remote location: Kansas City, Missouri. From the early twentieth century until the *Roe v. Wade* decision, Kansas City was the national epicenter for young unwed pregnant women. As it was the central hub for each of the country's main rail lines, parents could deposit their daughters on a train from nearly anywhere in the United States and have them arrive, alone and bewildered, at the city's Union Station. The women would descend from the train with their suitcases, stroll through the grand marble concourse, and meet a prearranged driver underneath the station's giant pedestal clock. The driver would usher them to the back seat of a car, and travel throughout the sprawling, prosperous city to one of many maternity homes.

Most prestigious and well known was The Willows Maternity Sanitarium, an ornate brick structure just a mile from the station. The Willows offered seclusion, and advertised it as artfully as one might for a swank rehab facility.

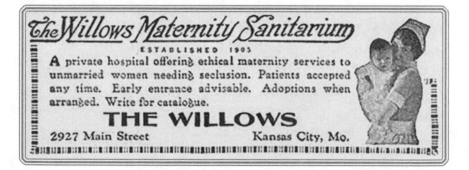

An ad for The Willows Maternity Sanitarium. It printed elegant
pamphlets and sent them to thousands of obstetricians nationwide.

Perched at the top of a limestone hill, The Willows' immense rose-and-vine-covered pergola also shielded patients from view. The home advertised to doctors nationwide, and catered mostly to what it called "higher-grade unfortunates" from every state in the union. One of its pamphlets also described its bargain services for lesser "quality" women, "just like those in department stores handling the choicest trade has its basement with less expensive goods."

The Willows banked on its allure as a tony refuge—the Ritz or the Waldorf for unwed mothers, as one woman described it. Indeed, it cost more to pay for a daughter's stay there than it did to send her to finishing school. Its fee for a four-month stay in 1962 was $1,600, including medical care, massages, and delivery, which amounts to $13,300 in today's dollars.

While religious homes sought to reform the girls and set them back on the "correct path," The Willows offered complete pampering throughout their confinement. It had a library of classics and a piano in the parlor, so that the girls might share some "gaiety." Most important, patients could avail themselves of specific services designed to conceal any hint of pregnancy: "A special system of abdominal and perineal massage has been originated for preventing striae gravidarum [stretch marks] and as an aid to labor. The abdominal markings of a single girl, caused by carrying a child, are telltale signs that might be discovered at any time and cause her misfortune to become known. This combination of massages, including the skin, perineal, and vaginal massage, has been successful in sending numbers of girls, who have taken them, away from The Willows without marks or signs to show of their experience." The services did not mention tactics for coping with private grief or shame.

Kansas City's central location—along with Missouri law—was convenient for childless couples too. When it came to adoptions, Missouri state regulations lacked—to put it mildly—red tape, and the state had earned a national reputation as a "baby mill." For decades, tens of thousands of couples arrived there to pick up babies, armed with only a financial statement and three letters from character witnesses. Couples could arrive in Kansas City in the morning, come to places such as The Willows with their documents, and leave by nightfall with a child, no questions asked. Home studies were performed after the fact, not before. Kansas City's geography was marketed as a benefit too. Its distance was thought to somehow magically "ease . . . isolating mothers and their babies from each other."

AT LAKEVIEW, administrators focused less on moral reform than on practicalities. The bored, worried girls were instructed to sew clothing they could wear once their bodies returned to their normal size, knit adult-sized sweaters and hats, and crochet couch covers. Not everyone was interested in this busywork, and sometimes the sessions were torturous—one sewing teacher was such a bully, she drove some girls to tears. But the tasks helped Margaret keep her mind focused, and she made a plaid skirt and vest for her aunt Rosel's young daughter. In knitting class, Margaret worked diligently on scarves she was making for George and her father.

Because Margaret had finished high school, she wasn't required to attend the daytime lessons in math and English led by local substitute teachers. So she pored over newspapers, newsmagazines, and books from the house library, which were filled with chaste classics by Alcott and Austen. Margaret was more interested in another girl's contraband copy of Leon Uris's *Exodus*, with a warning to keep the steamy novel under her pillow. Confined to Lakeview, she fantasized about the characters' fearlessness and determination as they fought to build the Jewish state. She and George would show the same spirit in forming their family.

As the fall progressed, Margaret felt her anxiety growing. Alone in bed at night, she worried. She *was* damaged goods. What if Linda (and

Gertrude) were right, and George met someone else he liked better   a virgin? What if her parents never spoke to her again? She comforted herself with the wild idea that as a last resort, she could convert to Catholicism and become a nun. She could hide from her shame, and still serve God. But then she'd yank herself back to reality, breathing deeply and praying. She sang lullabies to her baby in German, a language she was certain the administrators didn't understand, and daydreamed about being married to George and feeding their baby in a new high chair. She tried to push away her fears of being abandoned—George, after all, called several times a week on the house pay phone and, amazingly, was allowed to visit. Almost nobody ever phoned the other girls, and visitors were rare.

When he stopped in on Sunday afternoons, he and Margaret would sit in the common room on the couch, under the watchful eye of the housemistress. Once, when no one was looking, he put his muscular palm on Margaret's belly while the baby was kicking. "What's going to happen to us?" she asked him.

"It's all going to work out, Margaret." As proof, he produced Polaroids of his haul at a Manhattan arcade that week: one set of Pyrex cookware, another of CorningWare pots. "See?" he said, smiling. He bent down to kiss her.

"Young man," the housemother said, "that conduct is not allowed here." She asked him to leave.

Occasionally Margaret and the other girls took the bus to some nearby shops. A chaperone would accompany them to the five-and-dime for sanctioned purchases: gum, candy, tissues, lipstick, sewing patterns, knitting manuals, and wool. One chilly day in late October, Margaret asked a heavily pregnant girl named Judy to accompany her to the back of the store. "Stand sideways," she told Judy, "and act like you're thumbing through the patterns." Using Judy's belly as a shield, Margaret quickly selected instructions for a baby jacket, hat, and booties from a metal rack. "Now come this way," she told Judy. "Stand there." Margaret plucked fine skeins of mint green wool and white satin ribbon from the racks. She raced to the counter with Judy in tow.

The fake wedding bands did little to obscure the reality presented by a group of obviously pregnant teenagers, who drew plenty of stares and judgment. Once, two men on the bus hissed at the girls as they got off. Margaret felt her cheeks flush with shame, her heavy coat now useless in hiding her pregnancy. As bad as things were inside Lakeview, outside, they were even worse.

As the weeks passed, Margaret, so accustomed to the televisions, languages, and wafts of dinner mingling in her building, felt particularly anxious amid the silence and the smell of only a single dull meal cooking. One quiet night while Margaret was in her room knitting her baby sweater, Pam burst through the door. "There's a phone call for you," she said. "It's a man."

It was Josef. He'd gotten off work early, he told her, and would be there soon. Margaret waited nervously in the common room, overjoyed by the surprise. When her father appeared in the foyer, she rose with her arms in front of her body, embarrassed for him to see her. She stood awkwardly before him and offered her cheek instead of their usual hug. He pecked it, and stroked her hair, carefully avoiding any glance at her body. "I brought something for you and the other girls," he said. He smiled, and handed her a big white box tied with a pink string bow. She opened it and breathed in the rich, buttery smell of chocolate and cinnamon rugelach. "Oh, thank you, Dad," she said. She popped one in her mouth, wiping the crumbs off her dress.

Then she laughed, and leaned closer to him. "They serve Jell-O for dessert here," she told her father. "Mom would be horrified!"

LITTLE AS MARGARET had known about how babies were conceived, she knew even less about how they were born. And Lakeview did little to prepare the girls for the process of giving birth. As concerned as they were about the need to keep up outside appearances, the administrators seemed to feel no obligation to educate the young women about the impending experience of labor and delivery. Some of the girls had older (married) sisters who whispered frightening details about labor pain. A doctor came every few weeks to weigh the women, measuring their bellies with a tape measure, and checking to see the position of the babies' heads. In the corner of his exam room was a small, fraying image of an infant making its way down the birth canal. But neither he nor anyone else at Lakeview ever explicitly discussed childbirth or birth control. The girls had little knowledge of their own reproductive cycles, and did not learn any more about them at Lakeview.

In most homes, prenatal care was minimal at best. Most girls typically only saw obstetricians when they neared their due date. Administrators seemed a great deal more worried with how the girls might look after they gave birth. In many homes, they had weekly weigh-ins and ate restricted diets in order to remain within the recommended weight gain of only fifteen pounds, a common prescription during pregnancy at the time, thought to ease delivery and "preserve the figure." In the 1967 memoir *The House of Tomorrow*, a young mother describes her experiences at a maternity home in California. If the nurse who weighed the girls each Monday discovered that they'd exceeded their fifteen-pound limit, she denied them the right to leave for shopping outings—or worse. The author viewed the nurse's castigations as a form of tough-love kindness. "When she restricts an overweight girl on passes, or sends her upstairs to sleep in Isolation or to eat in the diet kitchen, it is to help her," she wrote. (The book had many admirers: one reviewer called it "required reading for all parents of teen-age daughters," and another said it "should be read by all high school and college students.")

At Portland's White Shield home, Salvation Army sergeants showed women a film with a straightforward message: childbirth was looming, and it was going to hurt. There were no medical books to fill in the extensive gaps about the labor and delivery they would undergo in the small medical suite on the home's ground floor. It was staffed by obstetrical residents from a nearby hospital who did six-month stints there. In late 1968, thirty-two-year-old William Tarnasky was assigned to the home and remembers the clinic as little more than a "home delivery room" that was ill equipped to deal with any emergencies. He worked alone, assisted by a rotating nurse.

During his Thursday appointments, Dr. Tarnasky recalls trying to tell the girls what to expect as their pregnancies advanced, and how to cope with labor. He was direct and courteous but remained professionally reserved. Dr. Tarnasky knew that the women had been unfairly judged, and sometimes the sorrow of the mother-and-child separation weighed on him. "It was sad to see all these girls have to give their babies up for adoption," he recalls. "They were such nice girls."

One time, a teenage mother began hemorrhaging after a difficult, lengthy labor. Because of the bleeding, the girl's blood pressure plummeted to a dangerous low. One treatment is intravenous fluids, but the nurse couldn't insert the needle into the girl's caved-in veins. Dr. Tarnasky, fearing for the woman's life, removed his gloves and eventually inserted the needle into a vein on the back of her hand. Luckily, she began to recover and did not need a transfusion. "I don't even think we had blood there," he says.

He routinely showed the babies to their mothers after delivery, but did not allow them to hold them. "It wasn't procedure," he says. "We just accepted that this was the way it was."

Delores Swigert, a patient of Dr. Tarnasky's, recalls him as very approachable, and she asked him a lot of questions. Still, the whole process was confounding. The vast majority of girls had never had a gynecological exam, and didn't know how to act around a man who had more intimate knowledge of their bodies than they did. Perhaps most excruciating, he was also handsome—and the only other man on the premises besides the janitor. The shamed girls wanted to look their best for the doctor, and all set their hair in curlers the night before his weekly visits.

The home's staff also made sure the appointments were humiliating. They instructed the girls to take off their underpants as they waited in the hallway outside the exam room, apparently to save the doctor time. It underscored just how little control they had: the girls were pregnant and waiting to see how much their cervixes were effaced, but most knew little about sex other than that they'd said yes.

"We were lucky if we knew where our clitorises were," Swigert recalls. "Sex was something that you had *done* to you."

The final weeks of pregnancy, despite Dr. Tarnasky's kindnesses, felt like just another thing that *happened* to you. You had a metal speculum put in you. You had your membranes stripped to hasten labor. You got a spinal block during contractions. You had a baby.

And then the baby was taken away.

IF THE PHYSICAL PROCESS of becoming a mother was bewildering, to many, the legalities of closed adoption were hardly clearer.

At Lakeview, none of the Louise Wise social workers who showed up regularly to visit Margaret in the fall of 1961 explained the process of adoption itself, neither its finality nor the laws in New York that would make it all but impossible for birth mothers to reconnect with their children once they surrendered them. The courts favored adoptive parents and the agencies, leaving women with little to no legal recourse.

NEW YORK HAD BEEN among the first states to pass a law sealing the original birth certificates of adoptees. In 1936, Herbert Lehman, then governor of New York and an adoptive father of three, signed the first of a sequence of laws that attempted to create legal barriers that would minimize the odds that New York birth mothers and their surrendered sons and daughters would ever know each other's identities. The laws required the courts to file away the original birth certificates under seal, making them available only to state officials and licensed social workers or by court order. When adoptions were finalized, children received an amended birth certificate that substituted the names of the birth parents with the names of the adoptive parents; it also included the new name of the adopted child. This all but guaranteed that adopted people who did not know their original name, or had little information about their adoption, would hit significant hurdles when seeking information about their origins. Margaret knew none of this, since no one described the process to her, but she instinctively distrusted the near-daily lectures she and the other girls received that emphasized the importance of giving their babies "better lives."

Behind the scenes, though, at least some officials at Louise Wise were well aware that adoption was not just a simple transaction for either the supplier, the mother, or the product, an American baby. The agency recognized the act as a "major human event," calling the transfer of a child from its biological parents to adoptive parents a "crisis with enduring consequences." One agency document stated that "the human beings most closely involved are affected at the deepest levels, and what happens to them during the process will determine the course of their lives, in their attitude about themselves, and in the way they relate to the community around them." There was little indication that the agency ever demonstrated this privately expressed compassion toward its young providers.

Any emotional support offered to the girls during this wrenching period was likely to come from within its own ranks. Most nights, Margaret could hear sobs leaking through the floor or down the corridor. Sometimes she was the one crying herself. Among the girls, Margaret was quick to offer hugs and comfort. Another seventeen-year-old who said her name was Susan wondered why her young parents, only in their midthirties, couldn't just take her baby and pretend it was theirs. Susan knew from calculating the date between her parents' wedding anniversary and her birthday that her mother had been a pregnant teenager when she married. But when Susan pointed out to her mother the curious fact that she had been born at full weight after a pregnancy that seemingly lasted only six months, her mother dismissed the notion as absurd. "Are you nuts?" she asked her. "You're the only one in this family who is a *shonde*," she shouted, using the Yiddish word for "shame."

Another girl, who said her name was Naomi, was a sophomore in college. Late one night when she was crying, Margaret entered her room in her robe and put her arm around her. "It'll all be OK," she said. Naomi looked at Margaret with red-rimmed eyes and blew her nose. "What are you talking about?" she said. "It'll never be OK."

Others spoke of their plans to return to high school or college, and of "getting on" with their lives. Margaret could not understand why anyone would say such a thing. Disregarding everything she had heard from everyone since the day she'd first visited Dr. Grunstein, Margaret refused to believe that she could not keep her baby.

One social worker who came repeatedly to the house was a tall, pretty brunette in her late thirties. She wore pencil skirts, kitten heels, and sweater sets, and on humid days, her corkscrew curls escaped from what was clearly a losing battle to straighten and spray them. She had a reputation for being compassionate—a mother figure to women who'd been scorned by their own—and she was friendly to Margaret during their initial meetings in a small office, inquiring about her health, her feelings, and how she was getting along. Margaret liked her, and wondered if she might be an ally, but it didn't take her long to figure out that the social worker's motives were completely at odds with her own. Her job was to find out more about Margaret and the reasons for her pregnancy. She did this in order to convince Margaret that adoption was the only solution, since only the mother could legally relinquish custody even if she was still a minor. Although Gertrude had the legal right to give Louise Wise temporary custody of Margaret, only mothers could sign the relinquishment papers of their babies. Margaret didn't think anyone could be more coercive than Gertrude, but her social worker was coming close.

A Louise Wise brochure from the era describes the clear aims of the social workers' visits: "To try to make an out-of-wedlock pregnancy a positive turning point in the lives of the young mothers and to help them make the best decisions for their baby's future." There was, of course, only one possible choice.

Margaret's trust in the curly-haired social worker evaporated more and more at the end of each visit, when she would push adoption papers across the wooden desk and hand Margaret a metal ballpoint pen from which she dramatically removed the top. While Margaret wasn't sure what the papers were, she knew they couldn't be good—and she refused even to look at them. The social worker was precise in her impersonal language. "This child will go to a good home, Margaret," she said, kindly at first.

Margaret would only shake her head. "I'm not signing those," she said.

As the days wore on, the woman changed her tone. "What have you got to offer this child?" she snapped one day in mid-November. "You're a teenager." As usual, Margaret stammered that she and George planned to marry. The woman smirked, raising an eyebrow. Then she repeated: "This child is going to a good home.

"You," she said emphatically, "can have children of your own one day."

Margaret sat across from her, stone-faced, lacking the courage to blurt out what was on her mind: "Like the one inside me is someone else's?" Sometimes she felt her anger rise to the surface: "What do you think I am, an incubator?" she wanted to shout. Instead, she simply looked down, wordless. The social worker pursed her lips and impatiently tapped her pen on the desk. The disturbing noise put Margaret under the spell of painful memories. At first in slow motion she saw her mother's face as she threw the iron, and heard Fritz's screams, in German, over the living room receiver. Then they sped up: she felt the cold eyes of the taxi driver from the ferry, the hostile posture of the housemother, the hissing men on the bus.

But still, Margaret Erle, the good Jewish girl who'd "gone all the way," kept her resolve. Her mind raced with possibilities, and a desire, once again, to leave her faith. She'd been with her Catholic friends at church on their way home from school when they stopped by to make confession, their hearts guilty with transgressions they whispered to priests almost wholly visible through a wooden screen. Afterward, they seemed to emerge lighter, with concrete prescriptions of prayers and good deeds to remove their sins. I'm not a piece of garbage, Margaret thought. I can go talk to a priest. They seemed so kind, always doling out the sugared almonds left over from Italian American weddings to everybody in the neighborhood. As much as she was rooted in it, Judaism sometimes felt so black-and-white. She thought of her mother, and of Old Lady Rosen. What if they were right, and God had only punishment in store for her? If she were Catholic, she believed, she could go confess her sins and get to keep her baby. She already had a suggestion for her penance: she could take care of sick people.

But she knew this fantasy was absurd. She didn't know a single Catholic prayer, or for that matter, anything about Christianity other than Jesus's birthday at Christmas and his death at Easter. If she converted, she'd bring even more shame on her family, abandoning the traditions her ancestors had valiantly preserved. So she continued to say the Shema, the minute her eyes opened in the morning, and just before she closed them at night. "Hear, O Israel. The Lord is our God. The Lord is One," she would recite in Hebrew. She whispered prayers for the health of her baby, and for the long, healthy lives of the family she and George would create. "We're going to be a family," she'd whisper.

But she began to take note of the young women returning from the hospital without their babies. Their faces puffy, their breasts swollen, they came back to Lakeview for a few days to convalesce while their abdomens receded. Margaret's roommate Linda had returned from the hospital in early November. She said only that she'd had a boy, and turned her face to the wall when she slept, before returning to Chicago.

When Judy came back around Thanksgiving, her eyes were red and her face was blotchy from crying. "What did you have?" Margaret asked. "A girl," Judy said. "A beautiful girl."

"Are you all right?" Margaret asked.

"How do you think I am?" Judy snapped, and turned to the stairs, padding back up to her room.

By now heavily pregnant, Margaret continued to sing her German lullabies as she did her chores or sat at the sewing machine. Once, a woman asked what she was doing. "Oh, just singing folk songs," she replied. "They calm me down." A few days later, George arrived late on the afternoon of December 3. It was a few hours before the first night of Hanukkah, and he brought Margaret a bag of gold foil–wrapped chocolate, or gelt. Margaret opened the net bag and divided them equally. They each ate one, but then George stacked his like coins in a poker game, and pushed them over the coffee table to Margaret. "You," he said, "are eating for two." He kissed her goodbye.

As dusk fell, an administrator flipped the switch on the first blue light bulb of an electric menorah. Normally, Margaret would have chanted the prayer marking the beginning of the holiday, but all of the other girls were silent. So she whispered it to herself, thinking of how the ancient Jewish warriors the Maccabees had defeated the far-mightier Greeks, and promptly burst into tears. She was strong, she knew. But what if, like Linda, Judy, and so many before her, she couldn't win the battle against the enemy that was starting to feel like Goliath?

6.

"You Don't Get to Hold Your Baby"

L ate on the frigid night of December 16, Margaret felt a contraction. She wondered if she was just having cramps from eating
ice cream. All she knew about childbirth was that it hurt, but
this just felt like a band tightening around her lower abdomen. Then she
realized the pains were coming at regular intervals, and knew it was
labor. "I think I'm about to have the baby," she told Pam.

Pam ran downstairs to get the housemother, who didn't bother to
leave her room. "Go back to sleep," she instructed. Margaret's contractions intensified, and she buried her face in her pillow to stifle her cries
so as not to bother Pam, or the new girl, Faith. She got up the next
morning, having had only an hour or two of sleep, but that was no excuse for skipping chores. After breakfast, the housemother ordered
Margaret to sweep the dining room floor. The pains were six, then five
minutes apart, and finally, after lunch, the woman called a cab. As often
as possible, administrators coordinated the taxis going from Lakeview
to the hospital so they could pick up the girls who were being discharged.
This way, the agency could save on fares.

"This will all be over soon," the housemother said as she watched
Margaret stagger down the icy brick steps, clutching the metal handrail
with her right hand, her suitcase with the other. She stepped into the
cab, terrified her water would break. That had happened to one of the
other girls on the way to the hospital, she'd heard, and the driver had

asked for extra money to clean it up. Some girls brought towels with them, just in case.

When she arrived at the hospital—seventeen, alone, and laboring—the nurse at the front desk barely looked up. "Get a wheelchair," she instructed an orderly. "It's one of the girls from Lakeview."

The young man wheeled Margaret to a bright room where he deposited her in the care of a nurse. "Undress and put this on," she said, handing her a hospital gown. Margaret stepped out of her clothes behind a curtain and emerged wearing the blue gown. "Lie down here," the nurse said, without offering her hand. Margaret struggled to climb onto the examining table, alarmed by what she saw on the table next to her: shaving cream, a razor, and a strange device with a nozzle. The woman administered an enema, to Margaret's horror. Once it was over, she lathered her pubic hair with shaving cream and began to shave it off. What is happening to me? Margaret wondered. After all her humiliation, now *this*? None of the girls at Lakewood had ever mentioned it.

Margaret spent the next few hours alone, traveling from her gurney to the bathroom, doubled over with cramps—and terrified that she was going to have her baby in the toilet.

She was thirsty and hungry, and no one checked on her progress for hours. Late in the afternoon, a nurse came into her room to take her pulse and time the length between her contractions. "How much longer?" Margaret asked, fearful. "When we tell you," the woman replied.

As the day's light waned, Margaret looked at the giant wall clock near the door. "Please," she called out to a nurse. "These really hurt now." She kept trying to take deep breaths, visualizing a beautiful baby in a tidy apartment with George. But as the pains increased, so did her fears. A nurse came in to check on her pulse, accompanied by a social worker. The nurse left, and the social worker passed Margaret a set of papers on a metal clipboard.

"I'm not signing *anything*," Margaret shouted. "Leave me alone!"

"Sign them," the woman insisted as Margaret winced from the pain.

"I said, leave me alone!"

Margaret began to shake—with rage, with pain, she couldn't tell which. "We've got a thrasher in here," the social worker called. Two nurses and a male orderly instantly appeared, moved Margaret onto a gurney, and slipped her arms and legs into restraints. As they wheeled her into the delivery room, she shouted: "Don't knock me out! I want to be awake!"

Fluorescent lights blazed overhead, so blinding they gave Margaret a headache. She tried to raise her hand to shield her eyes, but her hands were as captive as she was. The next thing she knew, she saw a green glass mask descend over her face, and she didn't know whether she was going to live or die. She didn't have time even to pray. But for the split second before she lost consciousness, she wondered, Does God even exist?

She woke, dazed, sometime later, when a masked doctor barked gruffly at her to push. A few moments later, she heard a baby's loud cry. Thank God, she told herself. It's healthy. She looked at the clock. It was 6:34 p.m., a Sunday. She closed her eyes for a moment, hazy in a scopolamine-and-morphine fog, a combination of drugs that was commonly administered during childbirth at the time. Called twilight sleep, it was anything but: it sometimes induced hallucinations, and often left women with amnesia about what they'd experienced. Margaret forced herself awake. She wanted to remember everything.

She sat herself upright in order to see, and asked a nurse the sex of her child. "A boy," one replied wanly as she washed and weighed him: "Seven pounds, one-half ounces," she announced to another nurse, who recorded the information. "Excellent vitals." They spoke about the baby boy she had just delivered as if Margaret wasn't even in the room.

One nurse held Margaret's son up before putting him in a diaper and swaddling him in a white-and-blue hospital blanket. As they covered his head with a small cotton cap, Margaret could see from her hospital bed that he had a fine coating of black down on his head. In a quick glimpse of his crying face, she noted that he had a tiny dimple in his chin, just like her and George.

"Can I hold him?" Margaret asked. The nurse didn't answer.

"Can I see him?" she asked again, pleadingly.

The woman shot Margaret a cold look. "Of course not."

"Why not?" Margaret asked testily. At first, the nurse ignored her.

"He's my baby!" she cried. "Let me hold him!"

"Look," the second woman finally said. "You're one of the girls from Lakeview. You don't get to hold your baby."

Margaret, released from her restraints, pushed her legs over the side of the bed as if to walk toward her son. "He's my baby!" she said, her voice on the edge of tears. "I want to hold him!"

The first nurse stood in front of the baby's plastic cot, blocking Margaret's view.

"I'll call the police if you don't let me hold him!" Margaret shouted.

The nurses both laughed. The first one looked on with a sneer.

"You go right ahead," she said icily. She summoned an orderly from the hallway. "Get this one out of here," she commanded, nodding at Margaret. "She's hysterical."

THE YOUNG MAN WHEELED Margaret back to a room occupied by another young woman who lay in her bed weeping softly. She said her name was Mary. She had come from a Catholic maternity home nearby, and had also given birth to a boy that afternoon. Margaret noticed Mary's plaid suitcase at the foot of the bed by the window and fog in the nighttime sky. The man cranked the bed down so Margaret could easily step into it. Still in the cotton gown in which she'd delivered—the nurses had given her paper underpants, a giant pad, and an elastic Kotex belt—she reached her hands behind herself so as not to expose her backside. She was shaking and shivering uncontrollably—typical aftereffects of delivery—and wanted to wail in psychic, bewildered pain. It was past 8:00 p.m., long after dinner had been served, but she hadn't had food all day, and she was starving. She asked the orderly if she could eat something.

"Dinner's over," he said.

"I'm so hungry," she said pleadingly. "Could you please bring me something?"

Sometime later, he came with a tray holding a glass of orange juice, a piece of toast with butter, and a hard-boiled egg. She devoured them, and she burst into tears. The orderly looked at her impassively. "You'd better get ahold of yourself," he advised. "Your behavior isn't going to get you anywhere. Believe me."

She went into the bathroom and splashed her face with cold water. It was puffy from the delivery. She looked down at her belly, which hardly appeared as if she'd given birth. When she reached down to touch it, it felt as spongy as bread dough, and empty. She took a quick shower and then put on her own nightgown and robe.

She padded to the hallway pay phone to call George. It was almost 9:00 p.m., and she knew the family would be watching television, and she braced herself in case Fritz picked up. Luckily, George answered.

"Georgie," she said, sobbing, "we had a boy. We had a boy. A beautiful boy. But they won't let me hold him. You've got to help."

She could hear laughter coming from *The Ed Sullivan Show* in the background.

"I'll come as soon as I can," he whispered. "We'll sort it all out."

She went back to her room and fell into a deep sleep. But at two in the morning, she woke up feeling as if she'd been caught in a rainstorm: her hair, nightgown, and bed were soaked with postpartum sweat. No one, of course, had warned her that this, too, was common.

It felt as if her entire body was crying.

BEFORE THE SUN WAS UP THE NEXT morning, a nurse came in and turned on the overhead lights. Margaret was dozing in her damp nightgown.

"You can't wear that," she scolded. "Take it off."

"What for?" Margaret asked.

"You have to wear a hospital gown so we can bandage you." Margaret looked pleadingly at Mary, who pointed to her own flattened chest. Margaret had no idea what the nurse was talking about, and asked to take a shower first so she could wash off her sticky skin. The nurse pursed her lips and agreed. "But hurry while I fix Mary." When Margaret stepped out of the bathroom, the nurse began wrapping her hard, engorging breasts with tight Ace bandages she claimed would help to discourage the swelling from lactation. Then she handed her a small white cup with two small pills. She turned to Mary and gave her the same.

"Now take them," she commanded.

"What are they?" asked Margaret.

"Lactation suppressants and sedatives," she said curtly. "We don't want you carrying on."

Then she stood watch to make sure girls swallowed the medicine. Mary put the pills in her mouth and tilted her head back when she drank, but Margaret pushed hers into her cheek with her tongue and pretended to gulp them down. When the nurse left, she spat them out and flushed them down the toilet. If she kept her head clear, she reasoned, she would manage to nurse, and keep, her son.

She would find little support for such an idea when she left the hospital. In a 1954 book Sara Edlin wrote after her forty-year term as Lakeview's director, she described little sympathy for the "average American-born girl at Lakeview who had been overprotected and hopes to solve her problem by wishful thinking."

ASIDE FROM GEORGE, Margaret knew she had no allies—at the hospital or anywhere else. Since her anger had seemed to backfire, she decided to behave more submissively, but that didn't mean not seeing her son. The next day, she repeatedly slipped into her robe and crept down the stairs to the glass-sealed nursery a floor below. When she passed other rooms, they were full of visiting grandparents and dazzling bouquets of roses and chrysanthemums. Rows of couples—happy mothers, pushed in wheelchairs by their proud husbands—parked outside the nursery door. Smiling nurses delivered them their pink- or blue-swaddled infants.

"Which baby is mine?" Margaret sweetly asked, first one nurse and then another. Some ignored her; others ordered her back to her room. "Why?" she said. "I have a son in there, and I want to see him." Again and again, they told her: "You're not allowed."

Fog, snow, and rain snarled New York City the week her son was born, but the trying conditions did not stop two social workers from showing up at the hospital with adoption papers the day after she gave birth. "Sign these," one told Margaret. "Your child will have no life with you," the other insisted. "You are a minor, and will be destitute."

Still, Margaret left the papers untouched. "Why do you keep badgering me?" she finally asked one day. "Because a nice married couple can give your baby a better life," one woman told her. "But I'm marrying his father, and we'll love him," Margaret said.

The social workers looked at one another and smirked. One of them said, "Look at you."

Margaret had only gained twenty pounds, most of which she'd lost in delivery. She had washed and curled her hair, and had brushed her lashes with mascara. She may have been in her robe, but she had enough self-respect to look decent. What were they talking about?

One of the women peered over her glasses to check her name. "Margaret," she said declaratively. "That guy you're talking about is not going to be there. Nobody's going to want you when they know about this. You'll have a new life, the baby will have a new life. Just sign these papers—and this whole thing will be like it never happened."

Margaret's first-born child lay in a cot only a floor away. Her breasts were leaking milk and she was still bleeding from childbirth. What kind of advice was this, to tell her to pretend it had never happened?

THE NIGHT AFTER THE BIRTH George came to the hospital, and the two made their way to the nursery. George, who stood a head taller than Margaret, was able to spot their son's name on a bassinette in the distant corner. "ERLE Boy," it said. Margaret, at five feet four, couldn't see past the first row of babies. She wanted George to lift her up, but they decided it would make too much of a scene—and might be dangerous.

The next day, social workers summoned Margaret again, and asked her what name she wanted to put on her son's birth certificate. Her hopes soared—could this be a sign that they cared about her after all? She told them that she and George had chosen the name Stephen, in keeping with the Ashkenazi Jewish tradition of naming a child after a deceased relative, or, in the New World, substituting his first initial, after her great-grandfather Solomon. His middle name, Mark, would be in honor of Moses, her grandfather, and Mark, her kind friend in Queens. The women nodded in agreement, which Margaret found comforting. She made another request: Could her son have a ritual circumcision, or *bris*? "Fine," a social worker assured her, not looking up from her paperwork. She felt doubly reassured. Surely a Jewish organization that agreed to perform this ceremonial act would do everything it could to help her and George raise their son.

Every day, Margaret would go to the nursery and peer in to see her baby, kept far out of view. It comforted her just to know they were in the same building.

On December 22, the day Margaret was to return to Lakeview from the hospital, she stole downstairs to peek at Stephen, who was still sleeping in the back of the nursery. She blew him a kiss and returned to her room, where she pulled on her loosened stretch pants and buttoned her giant blouse. A nurse came in to tell her to hurry; there was a taxi waiting downstairs to return her to Lakeview. Amid Christmas carolers and families posing for photos, seventeen-year-old Margaret Erle signed herself out of the hospital. She stepped into the cab with a driver who didn't acknowledge her presence and didn't need to be told where to go. She peered from the rear window as the hospital where her son lay disappeared from her tear-streamed view.

SURPRISINGLY, SHE WOKE UP hopeful on the morning of December 25, the day she was scheduled to move back to her family's apartment. It was the eighth day of Stephen's life, under Jewish custom the one reserved for circumcision. She dressed, applied her black eyeliner, and put on pink lipstick, convinced that the hospital would call her to witness the ceremony, and wondered who would make up the minyan, the quorum of ten Jewish men who would customarily be present. Once the bris was over, she reasoned, she could take her son home: She hadn't signed any papers—and how could her parents turn their backs on their first-born grandchild?

But when Gertrude arrived at Lakeview to pick her up, she slipped into the administrative office and signed papers that allowed Stephen to go into temporary foster care. It was a necessary legal step toward Stephen's adoption, and one of which Margaret was unaware. This wasn't common practice, but since Margaret was still a minor, Gertrude had the right to do this. Procedurally Margaret, as the mother, should have been the one to sign this document, but Louise Wise officials were known to skirt the rules on this matter with the irate parents of under-age daughters.

Margaret's ordeal had done nothing to soften Gertrude's attitude. She stood in the lobby in her overcoat, gloved hands clutching her handbag when Margaret descended the stairs with her suitcase. "Stephen is having his bris today," Margaret declared. "I want to go to the hospital."

"You're not going to any bris," Gertrude told her. "He's not your baby. Put that out of your head. Pretend it's not happening." (Gertrude was more correct than she knew: The agency only rarely arranged religious circumcisions. Far more often, it simply had doctors perform the proce-dure at some convenient moment in the hospital.)

Margaret stared at her in disbelief.

"Let's go," Gertrude snapped. "Get your things."

Once they were back in the lobby of their apartment building, though, she smiled at their Catholic neighbors as if nothing at all was amiss. Margaret wondered how the two of them must have looked. Under her coat, her breasts were seeping milk through the constricting elastic. Still weak from childbirth, she lugged her suitcase up two tall flights of stairs and into her old bedroom. Her father and brother were watching televi-sion, and she wandered into the kitchen wordlessly to make herself a sandwich.

Then she collapsed on her bed and sobbed herself to sleep. The next morning she stared at herself in the bathroom mirror. Her soft, fleshy belly was marbled with purple stretch marks. Her youthful figure, she thought, was gone forever. Was her baby too?

7.

"This Never Happened"

Eleven days after he was born, Stephen was moved from the hospital to a temporary foster home, a typical practice. During the 1950s and '60s, babies were not placed directly with adoptive families upon birth, but stayed in what era records called "boarding homes." A brochure for Louise Wise's fundraising said the time babies spent in foster care was typically three months. Louise Wise Services told its clients that professionals often watched babies and toddlers from behind mirrored one-way glass as they played alone with toys and games in a cold white room. The nervous would-be parents were undoubtedly reassured by the agency's implicit message: Our methodology can give you what nature could not. And ensure perfection—or a perfect match.

The prolonged process also allowed Louise Wise and other agencies to collect more fees from adoptive parents, who had to pay to remain on the organizations' waiting lists. This enabled the agencies, which operated as nonprofits, to expand both their bankrolls—and their reputations. Between 1950 and 1966, Louise Wise's budget, which was funded by both large Jewish philanthropic organizations and adoptive parents, rose more than 600 percent, from $190,000 to $1.34 million.

STEPHEN'S BOARDING "MOTHER," who was paid a modest fee to care for him, dutifully recorded his feedings, his disposition, his behaviors, and his two hours of crying between 11:00 p.m. and 1:00 a.m. The foster mother, who is not named in his file, altered her bedtime to try to stay up with him, but by the time he was six weeks old, his pediatrician prescribed phenobarbital, a powerful narcotic, so he would sleep. (The drug, which is addictive, was casually dispensed for colicky infants in the 1950s and 1960s.) The first social worker to visit Stephen dropped by his foster home to observe him when he was just a few weeks old and visited regularly, monitoring his integration into the boarding family, who, along with their grown children and grandchildren, doted on him.

In January, when Stephen was just a few weeks old, the social worker commented on his darkening skin and "masculine Jewish features." In February, she noted his hearty appetite for whole milk and rice cereal. She also described his behavior in a document that was written for his adoptive parents, and perhaps Stephen, to read someday: "You were a very shy little boy, crying when a stranger came too close, and clinging to your boarding mother, who you simply adored. You would smile at her when she held and spoke to you. She felt she had possibly spoiled you a bit." In March, she noted the baby's "husky voice," "dark olive complexion," and his "attachment to the boarding mother." She described him as "alert." "You loved to coo and 'talk' to people around you, your toys, and pictures on the wall," she wrote.

IN THE MONTHS AFTER Stephen's birth, Margaret moved out of her parents' apartment and rented a room at the YWCA in midtown Manhattan. She found a job as a clerk at the headquarters of a department store, learning how to make entries into big data processing machines. George relinquished his scholarship at Ohio State in order to stay close to Margaret, and began doing office work at a collections agency. At night, he took classes at Bronx Community College. Together, they could salt away enough money to put down a security deposit for a modest apartment.

They also started making plans to elope. In New York they were still considered minors, but they hoped to move faster by marrying outside the state. Girls at Lakeview had told Margaret that adoptions could take many months to finalize, and since Margaret didn't know that Gertrude had signed papers granting Louise Wise temporary legal custody of Stephen, they thought they could still get him back. On Saturdays, Margaret pored over information at the main branch of the New York Public Library on Forty-Second Street to find which East Coast states had the most relaxed marriage rules.

The nearest state with the lowest age requirement was Maryland, but it required blood tests from both partners. This was out of the question: George hated needles, and they were anxious enough already. In South Carolina, on the other hand, they were both legal adults, and the state required no tests whatsoever—you just showed up at a courthouse with proof of age.

The couple reasoned that if they were married, their parents would have to accept them as a family—and surely then they could convince social workers they were qualified to be parents. They even had all their kitchenware. By this time, George's arm had won a set of new orange Melmac dishes, Oneida cutlery for eight, and a silver-plated cake knife.

MARGARET REPEATEDLY CALLED Louise Wise to ask when she and George could see their son. Such visits were atypical, but not unheard-of. Birth parents would never be allowed to visit the child in his foster home, but the foster mothers had to make monthly outings to social service departments and adoption agencies so that the babies could be weighed and measured—and, in the days before direct deposit, so that they could receive payment for their care. While the vast majority of unwed mothers signed surrender papers soon after giving birth and never saw their babies again, Margaret had heard that those who did not could occasionally see their infants for brief visits. The encounters had another purpose for the agency: they also gave social workers the opportunity to pressure birth mothers into signing the documents.

In March, an unsuspecting Margaret and George were granted permission to see Stephen for a brief meeting. They were giddy with excitement, thinking it was a step in the direction of custody, and they each arranged for the afternoon off. Margaret wrapped the green sweater and hat set she had secretly knit for Stephen at Lakeview and put them in a bag with a rattle and some small toys they'd picked out for him at a baby store. George brought along his Polaroid.

It was a chilly day, and Margaret, who had shed almost all of her pregnancy weight, carefully dressed in a pleated wool skirt, a sweater set, and her heavy winter coat. George wore a suit, a freshly ironed white shirt, and a tie. The young couple surmised that Stephen was being evaluated, but they were sure they were too. George had the pictures he'd taken of all the home goods he had won that were hiding under his bed at home. They had nearly enough to stock an entire kitchen. George and Margaret wanted to appear as a respectable couple, the sort of young people to whom a baby could be entrusted.

They held hands on the subway downtown, but stopped touching each other the minute they entered the imposing gray city building. A secretary ushered them into a cold room with nothing but chairs and a table.

Finally, they heard a baby's cry, and the click of heels coming down the corridor. Margaret and George leapt to their feet. A social worker came through the door, holding an infant carrier in the crook of her arm. A fussy three-month-old Stephen sat inside. Margaret rushed to her baby with outstretched arms, not caring who was watching. She unbuckled her son from his plastic chair and held him in her arms for the first time. She kissed his cheeks a dozen times before handing him to George, who had never held a baby. "Am I doing this right?" he asked her, as he balanced Stephen's head in his elbow. Aware of the clock, Margaret reached back for her son. Instinctively, she removed his shoes, his socks, his shirt and trousers, his rubber pants, and unpinned his diaper so that she could reassure herself that he had been circumcised, as she had been promised. "Look," she said to George. "He had a bris!" Her eyes welled with tears as she thought of the milestone she had missed in the beginning of her son's Jewish life.

Then she inspected his hands and feet and kissed each digit. They exclaimed over his resemblance to George, from his eye color to his large ears, as they passed their son between them. When the social worker turned away from the couple—perhaps out of compassion, perhaps out of boredom—George sneaked his camera out of the bag they'd brought carrying the gifts. With their backs to the social worker, Margaret began singing German lullabies to Stephen to cover the noise of the snapping camera and the photo it spat out. As soon as the damp image emerged, George quickly waved it dry as Margaret turned toward the social worker. George tucked the clandestine picture of the couple's son back into the empty toy bag.

Then, abruptly, the social worker said, "OK now," and took Stephen from Margaret's arms. Another entered with a clipboard and addressed Margaret with the routine diatribe. George began to fan out the photos he'd taken of the couple's kitchen goods, but the woman waved him away. "Go wait for her outside," she snapped.

"Sign these," she commanded Margaret.

"Please," Margaret said, "you just took my baby away again. Leave me alone."

"What kind of life can you give him?" the social worker asked.

"We love each other, and we're going to get married," Margaret said.

The woman smirked. "When are you going to understand that it will be better for everyone if you just accept this never happened?" she demanded.

"He's my baby," said Margaret, in tears, as she rose to leave. She met George outside, and they pushed open the doors into the windy March day. As they got on the subway to go back uptown, Margaret began to cry. "We'll get him back, won't we?" she asked. "Of course we will," George told her. He took the bag on his lap and withdrew the only tangible thing they had of their child: a celluloid image of an infant boy, staring solemnly, like a little old man, at his own parents.

Who were also, by then, perfect strangers.

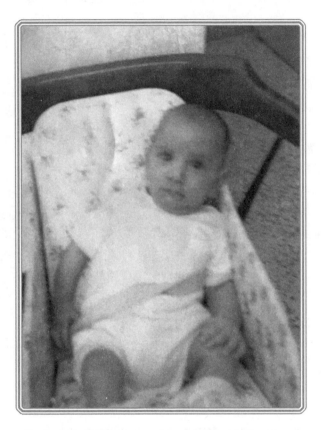

Stephen Mark Erle during a March 1962 visit George and Margaret made to city welfare officials. George snapped the photo while Margaret tried to distract the social worker.

MARGARET WENT TO BED at night anxious, and she woke up anxious. Prayers didn't calm her down no matter how much she repeated them. She kept one copy of Stephen's picture in her purse, and another on the small mirror in her room. If anyone ever asked about it, she'd say he was a baby nephew. But she didn't make friends. No one ever entered her room, so no one ever asked.

She and George hoped to make the trip to South Carolina in a few months, and they were saving every penny they could. Margaret visited the hulking Port Authority bus terminal on Forty-First Street for schedules of Trailways routes that would take them to Dillon, a small border town that was also a county seat, so that she and George could marry quickly and leave as soon as possible. They had to budget for several nights in a motel, and come up with a story that would fool their parents. Margaret, who would turn eighteen in June of 1963, would soon be a legal adult in New York. But the legal age for males was twenty-one, so at nineteen, George was still a minor under New York law, and Margaret was afraid that in an ironic twist Fritz would press charges against her for kidnapping George. Gertrude, not wishing to draw attention to Margaret's pregnancy and baby, had long since dropped the threat of prosecuting George for statutory rape.

Margaret planned for them to leave on separate buses, and on the outside chance anyone they knew in Port Authority was watching them, they hatched a story that they would be going to Washington, DC, on a sightseeing trip. She took a second job as an usherette on Broadway during nights and weekends to keep busy while George was taking classes. She was elated—as a perk for handing out playbills and showing people to their seats, she would also be able to watch some of the city's greatest plays. But the point was that her extra money got the couple closer to their goal.

IN THE LATE SPRING OF 1962, Stephen's caseworker visited him at the home of his boarding mother and observed that he had grown out of his shyness and loved to spend the day outdoors in the garden. He was beginning to teethe, and enjoyed going on stroller rides when she went to visit friends. His boarding mother noticed his "black, sparkling eyes," dark hair, and dark complexion, and described him as thriving, saying he got a lot of attention, love, and cuddling. He was desperately trying to form his first words.

A few miles away, Margaret could only think about her baby. She called the city welfare office on her break at work, asking to see Stephen again, and began knitting another sweater. This time, she chose a sturdy white cotton pattern adorned with blue ribbons for summer. Alone in her room at night, she pored over the intricate rows of yarn, intent on making every stitch perfect. One night, she told George about her project, but he gently changed the subject. "What can we do, Margaret?" he'd ask her, his eyes sad. They didn't yet have money to go to South Carolina, and Margaret's worries grew. When she felt hopeless or angry, she would pull out Stephen's blurry little picture and kiss it.

Her job at the Cort Theatre, on Forty-Eighth Street, came as a welcome respite from reality. She was working there one spring evening when Joanne Woodward was starring in *Long Day's Journey Into Night*. Margaret had seen the play twice already during its brief revival, and wanted to be alone with her thoughts once the doors closed.

Near the end of the first act, the door to the street opened, and a man walked in. She stood up, about to tell him that he couldn't enter until intermission, but then stopped herself. It was Paul Newman, coming to watch his wife. "I'm not supposed to . . ." Margaret started to say, but Newman put up his hand and said, "No, I'm late from rehearsal—I know the rules. Don't let me disturb anyone else!" He was even more handsome in real life than he'd been as the hero in *Exodus*. Margaret struggled to think of what to say. But Newman immediately put her at ease. "I'll just wait here," he said, and motioned to the steps where Margaret had just been sitting. "Mind if I join you?" he asked, and perched on the stair below her. They chatted briefly, and he inquired about her future. Just as the doors opened for intermission, he told her: "Go to college. Do what it takes to get an education." He reached out his hand to shake hers. She forced a smile, her mind on a very different dream.

꩜

AFTER REPEATED CALLS TO the city office, a secretary finally granted a visiting slot in late May 1962, after Margaret's first, rootless Mother's Day. Just weeks shy of her eighteenth birthday, Margaret wore a new pinstripe pantsuit she had sewn herself. George, too, now nineteen, wore his suit. He carried a large bag filled with his Polaroid; the immaculate white sweater, hat, and booties Margaret had knitted; a stuffed dog rattle and a teething ring. They again brought photos of their trousseau, such as it was. It was a cloudy, humid day, and once again, the couple spent more than an hour in an airless room as they waited to see their five-and-a-half-month-old baby.

When Margaret heard his cries in the hallway, she jumped up to meet the woman who carried Stephen in his plastic seat. Margaret rushed to him, exclaiming how handsome and happy he was. She and George cooed to their baby as he grinned, giggled, and grabbed his feet. Margaret peppered the social worker with a series of questions about Stephen's developmental highlights. She asked what he was eating, and how much. It was impossible not to notice his resemblance to George.

A moment later, another social worker briskly opened the door. "Come with me," she commanded. Margaret obeyed, her heart racing as she followed the woman into a separate room. The woman shut the door behind her, sat in a large wooden chair behind the desk, and motioned for Margaret to take a seat in the small one in front of it. She swallowed hard, trying to calm herself with the thought that at least George was with Stephen—he had to be safe with his father. The woman withdrew a cigarette from a pack of Pall Malls and lit it with a brass lighter she kept in a drawer. She exhaled streams of smoke out her nostrils and surveyed Margaret, who squinted under bands of buzzing fluorescent lights overhead. "A diplomat wants to adopt your son—this week," the woman told her. For the umpteenth time, Margaret stammered that she and George were in love, that they were marrying within months, and that they planned to raise their son themselves. She felt perspiration gather on her upper lip and under the arms of her blue suit. The woman pushed some forms across the desk and looked Margaret in the eye. "If you don't sign these right now, your child will stay in foster care for God knows how long." Margaret shook her head.

"You've got nothing to offer him," the social worker said. "This nice Jewish family will give him a wonderful life with every comfort."

Still, Margaret refused.

"You're a minor," the woman insisted. "You've got nothing to offer him."

The more Margaret resisted, the more dire the social worker's threats became. She sat for what felt like hours, but the clock on the wall above the woman's head revealed she'd only been in the office for ten minutes. "I'm not signing anything," she said repeatedly, shaking her head. She crossed her arms in front of her chest. "I'm keeping my baby."

The woman took a deep draw on her cigarette, and blew smoke directly toward Margaret. She smiled a pursed-lip smile.

"Oh, really?" she said. "You go right ahead and refuse." She glanced down at Margaret's file, leaned across the desk, and changed tactics.

"Would you like to know what can happen to you, Miss . . . Erle?" She inhaled again. "If you don't sign these papers we'll make you a ward of the state." She crushed out her cigarette in her heavy glass ashtray.

"We can put you in juvenile hall," she said, narrowing her eyes. "Think of how that will look for your parents. First the pregnancy. Want to get locked up now too?"

The threat was not idle: Under nineteenth-century laws known as the wayward minor codes, juveniles whose actions fell under the general rubric of "deviant" were often committed to reformatory institutions. The long list of vague, punishable offenses included deliberate disobedience to the "reasonable and lawful commands" of a parent; associating with "disorderly persons"; and "moral depravity," under which willful premarital intercourse most certainly fell.

The social worker stared at Margaret as she pulled out another cigarette and flicked her brass lighter open again. Then she clicked the top of her heavy ballpoint pen, and inched the papers even closer to Margaret's side of the desk.

Margaret felt like she was going to be sick. It was bad enough to have shamed her family, and herself, with the baby. But the threat of juvie— where the authorities sent serial shoplifters, young prostitutes, and kids in gangs—was too terrible to contemplate. After everything she'd been through, this one hit home: What good could she be to her son if she was locked away?

She felt the tears come—a year's worth of humiliation, guilt, and fear. Then she took the ballpoint pen from the social worker and scrawled her signature.

Although Margaret understood, fundamentally, that she was surrendering custody of her son, she did not, could not, imagine that with the stroke of the pen she was irreversibly severing all legal claims as Stephen's mother. She clung to her fantasy that the decision could be changed. Stephen would spend a few months with the diplomat's family and could then be returned to her and George once they were married. She did not read the dreaded document carefully—tears flooded so profusely she couldn't see the words, and no one, certainly not the social worker, certainly not an attorney, explained that it was irrevocable. She was not even given a copy of what she had agreed to.

Margaret's scribbled signature set in motion a series of legal processes that made it all but impossible to reconnect with her son. Children adopted in New York at the time were issued amended birth certificates that listed only their new, adoptive names and their adoptive parents as their only mother and father, and in no way indicated it was not the original. The original birth documents were sealed, available only to adoption agencies and state officials. Stephen had a right under New York law to ask a court to release the closed records for "good cause," but such legal actions hardly ever succeeded. The name Stephen Erle was gone, erased from public records as thoroughly as if he had vanished into witness protection.

It wasn't just Stephen who disappeared. He was to join millions of other babies adopted at this time, for in the United States, this systemic secrecy was near universal.

Even Margaret's own history would come to be rewritten. When she left Dr. Grunstein's office with Gertrude, the elderly gentleman had promised her that if she returned to him to deliver her next baby as a married woman, he would falsify that baby's birth certificate—an official state and personal record—so that it described Margaret as a first-time mother.

MARGARET HAD BEEN RAISED to believe that God would take care of her if she did the right thing. And until that moment, she believed the Jewish adoption agency—her own community, her own people—would help her and George to raise their own baby—a gift from God himself. Suddenly she found herself asking, "Where is he?" Looking down at the papers she had signed, she felt the stubborn optimism to which she had clung cratering underneath her.

"What if there's an emergency?" she asked the woman, her face flushing.

"If there's anything medical," the social worker answered, "tell the agency, and they'll tell his parents." She snuffed out her cigarette, and moved the papers Margaret had signed to her side of the desk.

The social worker stood up, the heels of her pumps clicking on the tiles. She opened the door and waved her hand for Margaret to leave.

Stephen had long since been delivered back to his foster mother and George was waiting for her in the hallway. As soon as Margaret saw him, she buried her face in his broad chest, crying so hard she got his shirt wet. He pulled out a handkerchief.

"What is it, Margaret?" he implored.

She could hardly get the words out.

"They made me sign the papers," she said. "They told me if I didn't, they'd send me to juvie."

George took her by the hand to the subway, and wrapped his arms around her.

His own hand shaking, he withdrew a new Polaroid he'd taken of Stephen while Margaret was signing away her parental rights. In it, the five-month-old baby looks up at his father, grinning toothlessly as he grabs his feet. A shock of black hair covers his head, and his black eyes dance, delighted.

George stroked her hair, and murmured that everything would be all right.

"How?" she exclaimed. "They're taking him."

George Katz took this snapshot of Stephen, five months old, at a social service agency in May 1962, while Margaret was in a separate room being coerced into signing away her rights as his mother. The hope, not realized, was that he and Margaret could build a case for their fitness as parents.

8.

Blue-Ribbon Babies

There was, in fact, no hurry. There was no family awaiting Stephen. The diplomat eager to adopt was an invention, a ploy to manipulate Margaret into finally giving up her baby. That story was no more factual than the agency's portrayal of Margaret and George for prospective adoptive parents. Margaret was accurately described as a "very attractive" brunette, noting her light olive skin, dark eyes, and "very dark hair." But the agency fictionalized her academic interests, claiming she'd been accepted to a prestigious high school for aspiring scientists. The agency also claimed that a social worker had met with George, who was described as a nineteen-year-old college student with light brown hair, light eyes, and fair, freckled complexion. It made no mention of his athletic prowess, and said his father ran a trucking business, not an army-navy surplus store. The agency said that Margaret was ambivalent about the adoption, but felt she needed to continue her education. Nearly all of this was untrue. George was not in college, and he was eighteen when this document was written. No one from Louise Wise had ever laid eyes on George. He was neither fair nor freckled. Margaret had no interest in science and was in no way uncertain about surrendering her son. The only choice she was offered—signing the papers or going to jail—was in fact no choice at all. Among agencies nationwide, this strong-armed strategy toward unmarried mothers—along with the deceptive marketing of both sets of parents—was widespread.

Until July of 1962, social workers continued to observe Stephen Erle at his foster home. This time frame was normal. While some adoption officials favored swift placement, others argued that prolonged, detailed observation of babies in various environments was the only way to assure the best "match" with adoptive parents. Doctors and social workers at Louise Wise and other agencies played a crucial role in this process, studying the children as they moved from infancy to toddlerhood. The professed idea was that if they had time to observe the infant, they could better create new families in which the children could appear to have been conceived by their new parents. Adoption experts believed that if they collected enough data on appearance, temperament, demeanor, and intellect, they could seamlessly blend a child into a family not his own, socially engineering a bond every bit as enduring as a biological one. There was little or no evidence to support this proposition. And the effort to find "matches" presented a real problem for children whose looks differed from what the majority of American adoptive parents wanted: white babies who could pass as their own. (Redheads, who make up a fraction of the population, were so difficult to place they were considered children with "special needs.")

The science of genetics was in its infancy. While there was a consciousness that both nature and nurture played a role in a child's development, the prevailing view at the time was that the best outcomes would occur when the parents doing the nurturing were optimally matched with offspring. As the number of couples waiting to adopt grew, the agencies' unstated mission became clear. Premium parents deserved premium babies, while ordinary parents were best paired with ordinary children. It wasn't only looks that mattered: the baby's potential cleverness mattered too. Adoption agencies, particularly Louise Wise, tried to do everything they could to match the right baby with what they deemed to be the right family, and they were confident in their scientific ability to assess children's characters and predict their capabilities.

This posed a conundrum for the adoption officials making these consequential decisions: How to assess the potential of preverbal infants who were many years away from being able to take an IQ test?

SAMUEL KARELITZ, A PEDIATRICIAN who served on Louise Wise's board for decades, was fixated on finding a way to evaluate infants' capabilities in order to match them with the proper parents. Karelitz argued that the swift placement of infants was problematic, and insisted that both adoptive parents and children undergo extensive testing and observation over many months before deciding which baby would go where.

In addition to submitting financial statements, medical records, and character recommendation letters, couples had to prove their psychological fitness to become parents. Therapists made them come in for a battery of exams that judged everything from their perceptions of inkblots to the quality of the sketches they could produce on command. The goal was to determine why a couple wanted to adopt: Were they wishing to create a family after failing to conceive? Had they reconciled their own infertility? Were they driven by more painful intentions, such as filling the void left by a dead child? Or, as one adoption worker put it, were they hoping to "keep up with the Joneses in children as well as ranch houses, fur coats, and the current year's model of automobile"? The subjective analyses—if one could even call them that—bordered on the absurd. Yet the tests, along with home studies and interviews, determined whether the applicants could proceed to become parents. One woman said the power invested in the young social workers made them feel as if they were on the "admissions team at Harvard."

Like elite colleges, Louise Wise rejected far more couples than it accepted. To prospective parents, the mysterious decision-making process about who would get a baby—a "good" baby—seemed just about as arbitrary.

If the files can be believed, at least in some cases their verdicts seemed understandable. Take the case of the L.'s, a well-connected couple who sought to adopt in the early 1960s. A close relative had adopted a baby from Louise Wise, so the L.'s had high hopes that they would be selected too. The couple's income impressed the agency, but their personalities provoked only contempt. They had poorly concealed marital tensions, and disparate aims as parents. The social workers described Mrs. L. as a narcissist: she didn't want a baby to interfere with her active social life, and described the ideal child as one who was neat, well behaved, and perfectly dressed. Mr. L., on the other hand, thought kids should be free and have fun, but he didn't like to disagree openly with his wife. "Why make a fuss?" he asked.

When they received the letter informing them that their application had been turned down, Mrs. L. called her social worker. Crying uncontrollably, she said: "How much *I* need a child, *I* want a child, *I* am something special." The social worker responded by offering to have the couple come in to discuss their feelings a few weeks later.

In the interim, influential friends of the L.'s weighed in on their behalf, asking the agency to reconsider. The agency workers remained unconvinced—and their opinion of the couple only worsened after they showed up for their appointed meeting. Mr. L. angrily insisted that only couples who exerted community pressure on Louise Wise got babies. Then Mrs. L. began screaming at her husband, and blamed him for answers he'd given in their first interview. They should have offered to take a handicapped child, she cried. It would match her husband, who she said was "handicapped" because he had a scar on his arm. Perhaps her humiliating dig had a more malicious aim: it was Mr. L. who had been diagnosed as infertile.

While Mrs. L. seemed unrepentant in her entitlement, she did seem to understand the social stratifications of the matching process. "I was not asking for a blue-ribbon baby," she cried. "You can see I did not marry a blue-ribbon husband."

Other couples were far more deferential and open-minded. But judgments about them were no less harsh. In one assessment, a psychologist contracted by Louise Wise Services wrote that an anxious young wife who saw "trees and withered trees" in a Rorschach image clearly had disturbing thoughts about fertility. And since she saw "snow" in the white spaces on another, she was no doubt "frigid."

Another psychologist was vicious in her appraisal of a worried twenty-eight-year-old man who seemed perfectly intelligent, but was nothing much in the looks department. The psychologist described him as a "short, balding man with a few desperate strands combed over the top," and eviscerated his character for what appeared to be his below-average artistic abilities. She found his renderings of men and women "disturbing," with "gross disproportions" and "bizarrity [sic]." She carried on at length about his drawing of a man whose "chicken-like head rests on an odd-formed body with bumps in front and back" and who left the figure's crotch blank: "Where there should be genitals is a gaping vast emptiness." His female character fared no better: it, too, lacked genitals, and had an "enlarged bosom but no arms."

The intent of the tests was to create a quantitative measure of each couple's suitability as parents, helping the agency make the best choices identifying what Karelitz described as the "healthy nutritive soil in which new life can develop."

As preposterous as these pseudoscientific exams of parents were, they were exacting when compared with what Karelitz came up with to test infants' abilities. He had plenty of leeway. Male doctors in the 1950s enjoyed a godlike status, and Karelitz was no exception—even though no one much liked him. A national authority on childhood diseases, Karelitz wore glasses, had a thick gray mustache, and spoke in a haughty, clipped voice. Board members at Louise Wise privately disparaged him, with one calling him "downright nasty" after he unleashed a racist tirade while he was driving her home. He had a strange idea of what people would find impressive, boasting to an interviewer that he had honed his interest in medicine as a teenager by buying hearts, kidneys, and eyes at the local meat market and dissecting them in his backyard.

Karelitz offered himself as an avuncular authority on infant crying. The source of his data on this subject is nothing short of sinister. A few miles away from the Wise agency's Manhattan offices, he conducted a series of experiments at Long Island Jewish Hospital, in which he inflicted pain on babies and measured their cries. Karelitz and Vincent Fisichelli, a psychologist at Lehman College of the City University of New York, theorized that differences in the babies' wails were linked to their level of intelligence. To gauge this, Karelitz and Fisichelli used a specially designed gun that shot rubber bands at the feet of newborns. Some were only ten minutes old. The researchers then rated the length and quality of the crying that resulted from the snap of the elastic on their tender new flesh. The most vocal infants, the researchers believed, would become the smartest children. The studies of what the authors euphemistically called "induced crying" were published in leading scientific publications, including the *Journal of the American Medical Association* and the *Journal of Pediatrics*.

Putting aside for one moment how deeply horrifying this whole endeavor was, conducting such research posed an obvious problem: Where would researchers find parents willing to let doctors intentionally subject their newborns to pain? And so Karelitz and Fisichelli tapped a population with no real rights or protectors: babies awaiting adoption while in the custody of adoption agencies.

The details of the experiments, spelled out in the dry, scientific language of medical journals, are chilling. Researchers placed the infants on an examining table and commanded, "Down." Then they said, "Pick up foot," and "Touch," as they aimed the gun, which had stretched a fresh, seven-centimeter rubber band to three times its original size, at the center of the baby's bare sole. Next they said, "One," shot the newborn's foot, and recorded the child's cry. If the baby didn't react, researchers took a ten-second break before they repeated the procedure as many as seven times to produce at least a sustained sixty seconds of crying. If the baby didn't cry after seven shots with the rubber-band gun, Karelitz directed researchers to scrape the infant's foot with three clusters of five scratches with a fingernail. If that didn't prompt howls of discomfort, the researchers were told to flick the baby's sole with an index finger. Nearly all experiments were made deliberately before feedings, when the babies were hungry. Babies who cried violently and vigorously without being snapped in the foot did not receive the "full program of stimulation." In a 1962 study in the *Journal of Pediatrics*, Karelitz and Fisichelli explained that they had considered and decided against using electric shock and heat, as such stimuli seemed "too severe for use on very young infants." The rubber-band gun, they wrote, was effective and simple.

The researchers snapped babies awaiting adoption throughout their hospital stays, and continued to do so regularly during the first three months of their lives. In 1962, Karelitz and Fisichelli wrote that they found their infants in the clinic of Louise Wise Services, in the wards of a second adoption agency, the New York Foundling, as well as in the clinic of Karelitz's Long Island Jewish Hospital. The federal government was an important source of funding for these studies. The National Institutes of Health and the National Institute of Mental Health issued research grants totaling at least $150,000—roughly $1.6 million in today's dollars—from 1957 to 1967; findings were published until 1975.

Karelitz, who was president of a New York chapter of the American Academy of Pediatrics and was honored in its hall of fame, was very much in the public eye. His experiments raised neither ethical questions nor concerns about the potential harm to newborns. Instead, they were praised as providing a quantitative measure of a child's future intelligence. In subsequent studies, Karelitz claimed his hypothesis was confirmed by three-year follow-ups: he found that the powerful criers mildly outscored the slow criers on IQ tests administered to them as toddlers. Dr. Joyce Brothers, a psychologist who appeared regularly on television as a family expert and wrote a syndicated newspaper column, commended Karelitz's experiments. "Having made thousands of recordings of babies' crying," she wrote, "Dr. Karelitz claims to distinguish

easily between cries for hunger, for tiredness, or discomfort, or for delight." Karelitz reported, she added, that "brighter infants passed through
the stages of crying, gibberish, and speech more quickly than one that
ultimately measures a lower IQ." The aim of the research was well understood. "It is hoped that ultimately these investigations will help in
the screening of babies for adoption," Brothers wrote. Dr. Walter Alvarez, the author of a syndicated medical column, praised Karelitz for giving pediatricians a valuable new diagnostic tool. "Doctors can recognize
those babies whom they had better not put out for adoption, because
there is something wrong with them mentally," he wrote. "Later, as the
child develops, the doctors usually find that their fear was justified and
that there was some brain damage."

Today Karelitz's theories seem as plausible as the medieval ideas
about the four humors, and his experimental methodology was barbaric.
Postwar standards for studies on human subjects were less clear than
they are today. But it is notable how willing medical professionals and
adoption agencies were to participate in research on defenseless infants,
all in the name of finding the perfect match.

AND THEN THERE WAS the issue of race. New mothers might provide
specific details about the fathers' identities, but because the girls had
already made the morally reprehensible decision to have sex outside
marriage, nothing they said could be believed—especially this. Adoption officials favored the term Louise Wise caseworkers used with Margaret when talking about George—"putative father." Of particular
concern to Louise Wise officials were the Jewish women who had become involved in the civil rights struggles of the 1950s and 1960s. Many
had become romantically involved with African American men, and
many became pregnant. Under Jewish law, babies are Jewish if their
mothers are, but they still might be dark-skinned and considered black
in the eyes of a deeply racist society. And making them "legitimate"

through marriage was not an option. Interracial marriage—prohibited in many states until the Supreme Court's 1967 landmark ruling, *Loving v. Virginia,* legalized it—was an even bigger taboo than unwed motherhood. Society was scarcely less hostile toward biracial children. Considered "unadoptable" by most agencies, many—especially those who were dark-skinned—languished in foster care, often till adulthood.

To address this issue about how to determine race, and to avoid placing a dark child in a white household, the Louise Wise agency worked closely with Harry Shapiro, a forensic anthropologist at the American Museum of Natural History. Trained at Harvard in the 1920s, the Boston-born Shapiro served as president of the American Eugenics Society for seven years beginning in 1956, the same year he joined Louise Wise's professional advisory committee, and later, its board.

Shapiro, who wore his thick salt-and-pepper hair in a crew cut and looked out from behind thick, clear-framed round glasses, was well known in New York for his supposed expertise in identifying racial characteristics. Early in his career, Shapiro had studied mixed populations in Polynesia, and after World War II, helped establish a system to identify the remains of unknown soldiers. At some point, someone at an adoption agency sought his advice about determining the racial identity of surrendered babies, and soon major agencies in the city were turning to him as an expert about what the children would look like as they grew. Over the course of two decades, he evaluated thousands of infants. And while he was not a physician, he carried enough authority in New York to be able to alter the birth certificate of a surrendered biracial baby who'd been marked "Negro" at birth. The blond, blue-eyed baby looked so sufficiently Caucasian, Shapiro changed his racial category to "white," apparently in order to offer the boy life in a white family. Shapiro even offered guarantees about the white appearance of the future children of biracial babies, provided the "Negro strain has been diluted out." These declarations were based wholly on Shapiro's instinct, as well as the nineteenth-century principles of physiognomy, the practice of assessing a person's personality and character from his or her features.

The work was tricky, since, as Louise Wise officials noted, the looks of interracial children could "run the gamut." This was a conundrum for the agency—and waiting parents. Transracial adoption, in the conservative postwar era, was a radical—and mostly undesirable—concept. While black families wanted to adopt black or biracial babies, they were often discouraged from becoming adoptive parents because of the income and housing specifications many adoption agencies had set. But with its waiting lists of white parents still long, in the early 1960s, Louise Wise began offering to place children of color with white parents, who, for example, exceeded the age limits they had set on prospective parents—thirty-six for women; forty-two for men. It also took part in a national program called the Indian Adoption Project, which took Native American children from their families and tribal lands and placed them in white homes. No one really knows how Louise Wise bypassed the New York law about matching religion, but it is possible that the agency argued, and the courts accepted, that no families of the same faith were "practicably" available.

Some news reports equated the agency's attempts to place biracial and black children with the civil rights effort. Often, this undertaking looked a lot more like advertising: In a front-page article in 1963, *New York Newsday* ran a large photo of five brown babies underneath the headline "'Unadoptable' Babies Want Homes with Loving Hearts." The reporter described the "orphaned or unwanted babies" as "too little to march, too young to vote, and too important to be forgotten."

BUT WHAT ABOUT CHILDREN who might be able to "pass" as white? Was the agency under obligation to disclose the child's background to its long list of waiting parents? In their private meetings, Louise Wise agency's leaders wondered: "Where then can we draw the line? Biologically there is no way to draw the line, as there is [*sic*] no criteria."

By contrast, Shapiro was confident in his determinations. He seemed to have no trouble finding physical clues to race, and he acted as Wise's scientific authority on the matter from the mid-1950s through the early 1970s. His office was in the American Museum of Natural History, a Beaux-Arts building on Manhattan's Upper West Side that famously draws children excited to see its hulking dinosaur skeletons and giant meteorites. But the tiny visitors brought to the fifth floor for Shapiro's perusal were specimens themselves. Social workers lined up babies in their strollers outside his paned doors, waiting for his evaluation. Shapiro, who was Jewish, made his rulings by judging skulls, nail beds, and birthmarks known as Mongolian spots that are more common among babies of African and Asian descent. The Nazis, of course, employed this same sort of "race biology," rooted in the eugenics movement of the late nineteenth century, to identify Jews.

Shapiro was a practitioner of a scientific system that was both authoritarian and uninformed by twentieth-century science. Despite the groundbreaking discovery of the structure of DNA in the 1950s and its implications for the importance of nature, Shapiro remained rooted in the beliefs of the past. In fact, he was indifferent to the harms that might result for the children as the result of his perverse pseudoscience, either from his random rulings on race, or from the prolonged stays he urged that they spend in foster care. In fact, Shapiro refused to render his opinion regarding a child's physical characteristics until he or she was at least six months old. He understood that this precaution might complicate issues for adoption agencies. But, he told Louise Wise officials, the time was necessary in order to prevent "mistakes."

If Karelitz and Fisichelli could promise a baby's intellectual future, Shapiro could deliver guarantees on his skin tone. Their combined reassurance helped adoption agencies give prospective parents a clear message. Nature had disappointed them with infertility. But state-of-the-art expertise—however far it actually was from true scientific inquiry—could offer them confidence about the babies of strangers.

෪

ANOTHER PROMINENT child advocate played a central—and disturbing—role at Louise Wise Services. Viola Bernard, a Columbia University psychiatrist, joined the agency as its principal consulting psychiatrist in the 1930s, and was a board member for a half century. Like Karelitz and Shapiro, Bernard was a nationally respected scientist considered so unstinting in her devotion to children, the headline of her 1998 obituary in the *New York Times* would describe her as a psychiatrist who "eased young fears." Her research explored many aspects of adoption, from the psychology of unwed mothers to how adopting a child might help heal an infertile couple's grief. She was instrumental in the development of "matching" techniques, and was an early promoter of transracial adoptions.

Behind the scenes, Bernard had more complicated aims. Bernard and Peter Neubauer, a New York University psychiatrist who was a protégé of Anna Freud's, devised a study they believed would yield the greatest clues for weighing the influence of nurture over nature. They wanted to separate identical twins and triplets who had been surrendered for adoption, place them with different families, and track their development over many years.

Not surprisingly, Bernard and Neubauer had great difficulty finding babies who could be the subject of this experiment. Neubauer initially approached Catholic Charities, which handled the greatest volume of adoptions in the New York area, with the idea of splitting up twins or triplets born to unwed mothers. A nun turned him down, saying the church could not tear asunder what God had created. This amused Neubauer, who noted that adoption was already doing just that.

Louise Wise Services agreed to what the nun refused. Beginning in 1961, the agency turned over the files for at least eleven sets of identical twins and one set of identical triplets and arranged to have the children adopted into separate families. (The triplets were particularly valuable, since they occurred in only one of every one million births.) The researchers then arranged to observe and follow them over the next several years. The birth mothers were not told that their children would be sent to different families, and the adoptive parents were never informed that the baby they were adopting had an identical twin (or triplet) sibling.

The Bernard/Neubauer study, which has come under considerable scrutiny in recent times, is a particularly haunting instance in which the children of unwed mothers were exceptions to the emerging rules on human experimentation. At the time, Bernard seemed unperturbed by the ethical issues raised by separating siblings, pressing administrators at Lakeview to come up with more investigative subjects. A 1961 letter from a Lakeview official to Bernard reflects the intensity of that search. "PS: Hold your breath! . . . We are going to [get] some more twins. . . . It is my understanding . . . that the girl is in her eighth month. And now will you please stop it! We have enough twins!"

It seems implausible that experienced scientists like Karelitz, Bernard, and Neubauer were unaware of the ethical lines they were skirting. In the wake of the Nazis' horrific experiments on Jewish concentration camp prisoners, many countries, including the United States, had signed the Nuremberg Code, which required doctors to obtain "informed consent." (It was further codified with the Declaration of Helsinki in 1964.) The principle could not have been simpler: no human being was to be the subject of medical research without his or her permission and a full understanding of the risks. The scientific papers published by Karelitz and his colleagues throughout the 1960s do not address how babies could have consented to the experiments. Legally, surrendered children in foster care were wards of the state, their teenage mothers potential criminals under wayward minor laws. The consent, such as it was, appears to have been granted by adoption agency executives and social workers, including the agency on whose board Karelitz served. One might have expected Louise Wise Services—as well as Bernard and Neubauer, who were both Jewish—to be particularly sensitive to such matters. In fact, the opposite occurred.

Bernard asserted that the study was actually improving the babies' lives, since the twins would get more individual attention once they were placed with separate mothers. She insisted that the twins be kept apart after birth so they would not develop an attachment to each other, and described the study as a perfect "natural laboratory situation" in which to evaluate the effects of nature and nurture. That guideline was ignored repeatedly: the triplets Eddy Galland, David Kellman, and Bobby Shafran, who went on to have brief fame after their improbable reunion in the 1980s, were separated only after they had spent six months together in foster care. Twins in the study were similarly kept together for months before being dispatched to different families.

The records for the Bernard/Neubauer study are sealed until 2065, so it's impossible to know the study's design or aims, let alone whether researchers even considered the damage the separation and secrecy might do to the development of their subjects. But the triplets and their respective adoptive parents understood the extent of the harm to the men, and sought to sue Louise Wise Services for damages. (The reactions of the birth mother, who remains anonymous, are undisclosed.) Yet despite the questions the experiment raised, the agency's influence remained formidable. When the parents interviewed attorneys for a potential lawsuit against Louise Wise, firm after firm turned them away. Each was concerned that filing a complaint against Louise Wise would diminish the chances of any lawyer in the firm who hoped to adopt through the agency.

Fifteen years after the triplets reunited, Eddy Galland took his own life. Like his brothers, he had long struggled with profound depression. Other twins from the study also displayed worrisome behavior when they were children. Their adoptive parents reported that they banged their heads, were unable to soothe themselves, and held their breath until they passed out. Most describe a lifelong sadness. In addition to Galland, two other twins have killed themselves.

It has long been understood that twins, particularly those who are identical, have an extreme level of closeness and mutual understanding that may prove protective over the course of their lives. Neither now nor at any time has any research supported the idea that deliberately separating them is beneficial. Yet not only did the agency allow it, it also permitted the researchers to withhold from adoptive parents the true purpose of the study. Instead, Louise Wise merely told the parents that their children needed to be "observed periodically" for the first several years of their lives. Prospective parents, who had been on the waiting list for years, were offered the chance of a baby—along with a caveat. The coercive pressure was hard to miss. One adoptive father put it this way: "You can have the baby, but only if we get the chance to study it."

THE IDEA THAT BABIES awaiting adoption were model subjects for study was not restricted to medicine. For a half century, surrendered children served as human dolls for thousands of home economics students who used them to hone their mothering skills. Supervised by university officials, these "practice homes," where young women learned to keep house and raise children, initiated at Cornell University in 1919 and spread to as many as fifty other campuses nationwide. Students learned to cook, manage finances, and care for infants who were awaiting adoption. Orphanages originally supplied the infants for these homes, but by the late 1940s adoption agencies were providing most of the babies, often just a few days old.

In some cases, the "practice mothers" switched hour to hour. They kept meticulous records of the babies in their care, noting their sleep schedules, the ounces of milk they drank, and their preferences for strained pears over spinach, but there is no evidence that anyone paused to consider the long-term consequences this carousel of caregivers might have on the babies' emotional development. At Cornell, the make-believe houses endured until 1969. While the programs varied from campus to campus, the babies typically lived in the homes until they were toddlers, and were considered to have an advantage in adoption because of their participation—they had, after all, been brought up under the most disciplined methods possible.

At Oregon State University in Corvallis, the home economics department ran two practice houses from 1926 until 1950 in which 1,515 "mothers" looked after fifty babies. Home economics majors who were seniors moved from their dormitories into the stately homes for six-week stints, where they took weekly turns cooking, cleaning, sewing, and caring for loaned-out infants. At Withycombe House, the library, ironically, was stocked with Dickens's entire canon.

Aya Fujii was a twenty-two-year-old senior at Oregon State University in 1949. She warmly recalls the week it was her turn to care for a wide-eyed little girl with light brown hair. Her tasks included feeding, changing, bathing, putting her to sleep, and even ironing the baby's diapers in a giant mangle. "I thought to myself, My God, why would you ever need to iron a baby's diaper?"

All the girls were fond of the baby, but there was little time, let alone encouragement, for them to become attached to her during a weeklong shift. Fujii enjoyed her stay in the house, and her experience there gave her confidence when it came to bathing, feeding, and tending her own three children. The house supervisor, a woman in her early thirties, instructed the girls to remain businesslike when it came to caring for the baby—especially when it came to her sleep schedule. The baby had a crib in her own separate room, and the supervisor directed the girls to put her to bed with calm firmness. Yet one day, when Fujii ran upstairs to her room to collect a forgotten item, she noticed the supervisor's door ajar. When she passed the room, she saw the young woman on her bed, the little girl resting in her arms. The two of them were napping peacefully, their chests rising and falling in tandem. "She was very fond of that baby," Fujii recalls. "She just cuddled it."

From all available evidence, it seems that the practice mothers behaved with warmth and compassion. But it's impossible to imagine the same of Karelitz, Shapiro, Neubauer, and Bernard. For all their education, and for all their public personae as respected child experts, there is no indication of any tenderness or regard for the objects of their study: the relinquished infants themselves.

ALL THIS EXPERIMENTATION PLAYED out against the backdrop of a very different type of study of children. In the 1940s, researchers had begun to investigate the importance of the deep connection between babies and their mothers or caregivers in the first years of their lives. Unlike the sinister experiments that deliberately *inflicted* psychic and physical pain on vulnerable infants, this research attempted to explain how mental suffering originated—and could be prevented. Their findings were unequivocal: babies could suffer lifelong emotional damage if they did not develop strong, secure bonds with the primary adult in their lives. The implications for the adoption professionals were huge, affecting both their timetables and their matching techniques.

Among the most notable of the researchers was John Bowlby, a British psychiatrist and psychoanalyst. In 1951, he wrote a book for the World Health Organization called *Maternal Care and Mental Health*, in which he developed a theory he called the "maternal deprivation hypothesis." Bowlby examined the work of researchers who had observed children who had been separated from their mothers in a variety of settings in Europe and the United States, including those in displaced persons camps, those hospitalized for long periods, and those in extended foster care. In the book, Bowlby asserted that "what is believed to be essential for mental health is that the infant and young child should experience a warm, intimate, and continuous relationship with his mother (or permanent mother substitute) in which both find satisfaction and enjoyment." While a gifted research scientist, Bowlby also likely drew on his own childhood experiences in an upper-class British home. Customarily for the time, Bowlby rarely saw his parents, and was allowed to visit his mother in her drawing room for only an hour a day. He was raised by a beloved nanny who left the household when he was four, and Bowlby was heartbroken by her departure. At age seven, he was sent to boarding school, an experience he later said he wouldn't wish on a dog.

At a time when affluent parents tended to believe affection could "spoil" a child, Bowlby argued that a caregiver's attention to an infant's needs was an essential element in the development of a child's emotional well-being—as crucial for the soul as vitamin D was for the development of strong bones. And if a child in the first three years of life was deprived of reassurance and maternal love, either from his mother or a mother substitute, he would grow to develop anxiety, depression, and enduring difficulty in cultivating healthy relationships with others. This could happen if for any reason a child was removed from his mother's care, Bowlby wrote. "This deprivation will be relatively mild if he is then looked after by someone whom he has already learned to know and trust, but may be considerable if the foster-mother, even though loving, is a stranger."

He compared the intentional deprivation of mother love to deliberately exposing a child to tuberculosis-infected milk or polio. "In both these cases a sufficient proportion of children is so severely damaged that no one would dream of intentionally exposing a child to such hazards. Deprivation of maternal care in early childhood falls into the same category of dangers." The book was translated into fourteen languages, with English-language sales totaling 400,000. It was influential, prompting hospitals to introduce the new policy of visiting hours for the families and friends of young patients. Bowlby's findings, while controversial, circulated widely among psychologists in the West. He further refined it with the development of "attachment theory" in later decades.

During the same time period, officials at Louise Wise continued to uphold its "waiting period," which it claimed in promotional materials was three months. This was an understatement—the delay was often much longer—and the time lag was controversial even within the agency.

Outside it, some challenged it openly. One doctor who had studied adoptees wrote that the optimum time to place a baby from the *"baby's point of view"* (italics in original) was as close as possible to the day of his birth. The sooner the placement, "the better off he will be—physically, intellectually, and emotionally," he argued. "It prevents the destructive, and sometimes lifelong and irreversible, emotional scarring that may result, both from the difficulty in achieving a smooth transition from one kind of mothering and from the effects of the separation itself . . . Early adoption tends to provide the child with that all-important, consistent, uninterrupted, continuous mothering experience that lays the essential foundation for a sound mind and body."

BEFORE THE INTERNET, news of research studies traveled slowly, arriving in journals and at distant conferences that in the days before modern plane travel were often prohibitively expensive, and difficult, to attend. But it is hard to imagine that an organization devoted to child welfare—with board members who were scholars at some of the country's most revered research institutions—was fully in the dark about the emotional impact of keeping babies in foster care for prolonged periods, no matter how caring the foster mothers were. Certainly if Louise Wise was aware of the research, its policies did not reflect it. Indeed, Stephen's early months seemed like a case study in how to create disruption instead of attachment. Margaret had continually sung and spoken to her unborn baby, gestures now understood to play a role in building the first bonds between mother and child. But after Stephen was born, hospital nurses did not allow her to touch him, and they would only have held him when they changed or fed him. His boarding family, experienced grandparents who had two dogs, welcomed him affectionately when he was eleven days old.

Yet the social worker who came to check on him seemed fixated on his looks, not his emotional development. In addition to describing his appearance as "Jewish" and "masculine," she noted his dark brown hair, slightly slanted eyes, pronounced chin, and large ears, hands, and feet; and that his boarding mother predicted he would grow to be a "big man."

As the weeks progressed, Stephen clung to her; the social worker wrote that he "adored" her. The unnamed woman confessed that she had pampered him.

In the care of his foster family, Stephen progressed completely normally. When he was three months old, he began to coo to his boarding parents, to toys, and even to pictures on the wall. He also liked to "talk" to another infant boy in the family's care. At naptime, he would reach out and hold his hand as they lay side by side. At that age, most babies are just beginning to master rolling from their stomachs to their backs. But Stephen was physically precocious. He used the slats of his crib to support himself while standing, and was beginning to tug at the bar of his cradle gym as if he was attempting to do pull-ups. By May, the caseworker again noted his dark complexion and outgoing personality, and mentioned a "deep attachment" to his boarding mother.

That was all perfectly in keeping with normal infant development. At about six months, babies start to differentiate one person from another, and form intense emotional connections to their parents and caregivers. They also begin to experience separation anxiety, understanding when a caregiver has gone out of sight, and wondering when she or he will return. This worry is most acute for youngsters until they are about two years old. According to Bowlby's research, it is a particularly sensitive time for infants developing attachments. And it was at just that age that Stephen was about to be separated from his caregiver—again.

When Stephen was almost eight months old, a caseworker and his boarding mother took him to meet a couple who were interested in adopting him. A few days later, on the muggy afternoon of August 2, 1962, a caseworker handed him to the third mother figure of his young life. It didn't go well. Perhaps Stephen experienced extreme separation anxiety. Perhaps the prospective parents, new to infants, were at a loss for how to handle a baby. Or perhaps the couple decided, quite simply, that Stephen was not a "good fit" for them in temperament or looks.

There is no record of what happened when they took him home, but just eleven days later, social workers, a nurse, and a city adoption worker decided simply that the home "wasn't working out"—no other explanation was given in the records—and Stephen returned to his boarding home. His concerned foster mother reported that for days afterward, he was upset, and seemed troubled by nightmares.

MEANWHILE, MARGARET AND GEORGE were pushing ahead with their plans to marry and regain custody of their baby. Margaret convinced herself that the imaginary genteel diplomats described to her by city officials had merely taken her baby on a long trip. Surely his parents would be entitled to his return once they were married.

Instead, later that autumn Stephen Erle's foster mother brought him to meet a couple the Wise agency had identified as a potential match. They were Esther and Ephraim Rosenberg, childless Holocaust survivors from Romania who had immigrated to New York in the early 1950s. Ephraim Fishel Rosenberg was a gifted cantor trained in the passionate liturgical music of European Jewry; he was a member of a rabbinic dynasty called the Vizhnitz Hasidim. In 1941, he had married his second cousin Esther when she was eighteen and he was twenty-four. They had survived the war, in part by wit, in part by luck, in Bucharest. It was one of the few cities in Nazi-occupied Europe where many Jews survived, and the Rosenbergs helped hide in their synagogue many Jews fleeing terror. Later, they moved to London and to Israel, and had been trying to conceive a baby since they wed.

No doctor anywhere could determine a cause for their infertility, and for many years Esther devoted her maternal energies to her younger sister Yafa's three children in Israel. Whenever she arrived to visit from New York, she came loaded with extra luggage so heavy she always had to pay a special fee. It was expensive to fly across the Atlantic, and Ephraim, as a cantor, wasn't a wealthy man. Despite the conclusions of their doctors, Esther blamed herself for what she called her "barrenness."

While she always did her best to celebrate the arrival of friends' and relatives' babies, she also mourned the ones she could never carry herself. Sometimes she told her sister that her infertility seemed like such a curse, she wondered if she'd done something to anger God. At some point in the late 1950s, Esther and Ephraim had tried to arrange a private adoption, but it fell through at the last moment. Esther was crushed.

By the time they met Stephen, they were beginning to lose hope of ever becoming parents. They were slipping further and further outside the guidelines for adoptive parents set by Louise Wise, where they had applied for a baby. No doubt Ephraim's status as a highly revered cantor—he had served as the head cantor in the Great Synagogue of Bucharest, the chief cantor of Israel for three years after its founding, and taught young cantors at New York's Jewish Theological Seminary—made an impression on the Wise agency. Still, the rules were clear, and the Rosenbergs only fit some of them. To be considered for a child younger than six years old, prospective parents had to be childless after three years of marriage, live in New York City or its surrounding counties, and fit within its age limits of thirty-six and forty-two. These rules appear to have been relaxed for the Rosenbergs: in late 1962, Esther was thirty-nine; Ephraim, forty-five.

When they got the call that a boy was available, they were overjoyed. The couple asked many questions about his unnamed parents, and were deeply impressed that both had come from kosher homes. They came often to see Stephen at his foster home in the following days, changing his diaper, playing with him, and putting him to sleep. He was moved permanently to the Rosenbergs' Bronx apartment on November 5, 1962, embraced and comforted by his fourth set of caregivers. Esther was so thrilled, she paid the exorbitant international long-distance fees to call Yafa in Israel. "I'm a mother," Esther said, her voice breaking. She held the phone up to the baby's ear so that he could hear the voice of his young aunt in Israel. Yafa spoke to him in Yiddish and in Hebrew. He was ten and a half months old.

9

"Better" Families

S tephen was part of a vast exercise in social engineering unlike any other in American history. In the years between 1950, the peak of the baby boom, and 1975, untold numbers of young, mostly unwed mothers like Margaret surrendered their newborns to strangers, often without fully understanding that they would never see their children again. This is why many adoption reformers, adopted children, and birth mothers have taken to calling these years the Baby Scoop Era. Although adoption and agencies were not new, in these years, adoption had become a big business.

An accurate accounting of how many mothers and children were involved is impossible. The federal government attempted to collect data on adoptions between 1944 and 1975, but since not all states and territories participated, the data are incomplete. Federal statistics show 2.7 million adoptions during that period, with a steady increase from an estimated 50,000 adoptions in 1944 to a peak of 175,000 in 1970. By 1975, that number had dropped to 129,000. The total of 2.7 million is a significant underestimate, since it did not include the so-called gray or black market, private cases in which attorneys or obstetricians arranged for adoptive parents to cover a pregnant woman's obstetrical care and living expenses, as well as pay an extra fee in exchange for the baby. One researcher estimates that nearly 39 percent of adoptions fell into this category. That would bring the number of postwar adoptions to well over 3 million.

An array of demographic and social forces propelled the explosion in adoptions. The Erles were just one family among millions that had been catapulted into a growing white middle class. Back when they were young, the solution to an unexpected pregnancy was to marry quickly and keep the baby. But even if the Erles had been on friendly terms with the Katzes, a shotgun wedding for Margaret and George was out of the question. Both families believed their children's mistake jeopardized the new lives they had built in America. The Erles were caught up in the pressures on their generation as much as Margaret was. Their daughter's surprise pregnancy was an obstacle to a better life that needed to "go away." And for the millions of white couples who could not conceive and were longing to join the baby boom, the plight of women like Margaret was an opportunity, the ideal solution to a painful problem.

The kind of arrangement the Wise agency offered—a discreet transaction, a one-time fix—repackaged the obvious: to create one family, another had to be disintegrated. The process of adoption was neither casual nor spontaneous. There had always been adoptions and facilitators, but now a full-scale and complicated bureaucracy—think of it as an "adoption-industrial complex"—came to fruition after World War II under a system of laws and policies crafted to serve the interests (and privacy) of the upper class and emerging middle class. It was the work of an array of institutions, from researchers whose pseudoscience justified the advantages of unproven practices, to adoption agencies that stood to profit from each woman who was persuaded to relinquish a child by their social workers. Good intentions often masked colder calculations.

LEGAL ADOPTION ITSELF was a relatively new phenomenon in twentieth-century United States. To understand how and why secrecy came to be its defining feature, one must understand Americans' shifting understanding of what makes a family.

In the colonial era, the vast majority of settlers lived in rural areas, and children whose parents died were typically cared for by relatives, friends, or neighbors. White families were an economic unit, and youngsters of the era shared household and farming duties. Extra mouths also meant extra hands to chop wood, to harvest crops, to sew, spin, cook, and weave. To the extent it existed, adoption was informal and open. If an unmarried woman got pregnant, she typically married, or nearby relatives took the child in as their own.

By the mid-nineteenth century, demographic shifts changed the entire landscape. The industrial revolution had transformed the nation's largely Protestant agricultural society to an industrial one whose explosion of jobs attracted millions of immigrants from Ireland, Italy, Germany, and Poland, and Jews from the Pale of Settlement, all looking for a way up the economic ladder. Between 1850 and 1900, the US population grew from 23 million to 76 million, due mainly to the new arrivals. More established white Americans viewed the newcomers, mostly Catholic and with large families, as threats to the national fabric.

The new economy changed how families functioned. Farmers and tradesmen who had worked alongside their wives and children in rural communities now lived separate lives. The men worked in factories, while women tended the home. Families crowded into tenement apartments, far from fresh air, fresh food, and clean water. Tuberculosis, typhoid fever, cholera, and other illnesses were rampant, especially in factories, and the diseases claimed the lives of more men than women. When breadwinners died, families were left destitute.

Where rural communities had ample resources to absorb children whose parents could not care for them for whatever reason, urban ones had a harder time marshaling resources. Cities and religious organizations constructed poorhouses for surviving widows and children, but those institutions were riddled with the sick and dying, as well as thieves and pimps. To shield children from such dangers, some religious leaders opened orphanages to house the rapidly growing number of children left parentless or fatherless by disease. They provided a piece of bread in the morning, a bowl of soup in the evening, and vermin-infested cots in which to sleep. Lacking guidance, stability, and education, tens of thousands of hungry children roamed the streets of the dirty cities, with threadbare coats, bare feet, and lice-ridden heads. Some sang as buskers. Others sold matches, or their bodies, and many formed gangs to protect themselves. The children were believed to possess the "bad blood" and voracious libidos attributed to their immigrant parents— negative traits to be eradicated.

But one clergyman who observed the aimless children devised a different plan for their futures. Charles Loring Brace, a Connecticut-born minister who had founded a mission for impoverished men in the 1850s, noticed groups of children from the orphanages smoking and selling cigarettes. Brace, a bearded man with ice-blue eyes, called them "street arabs" and "street rats."

He asked to tour the orphanages and denounced them as "human factories." To combat the "backwardness" he was certain such living conditions were spawning, he founded a private group called the Children's Aid Society. Its aim was to transport as many of the children as possible to work for farm families in the Midwest. The fresh air and space offered a healthier environment than urban slums, but the children could also provide free labor. Between 1854 and 1929, the CAS and its imitators sent an estimated 250,000 children to midwestern towns on what it called "Orphan Trains."

The children weren't all orphans. It's now estimated that about half had one parent still living, but to Brace and his peers, the children would be better off without them and their old-world religions.

Few of the children were consulted about this arrangement, and many did not view the separation from their familiar surroundings as a blessing. Most had no idea where they were going. They traveled for several days, sleeping on wooden seats with only dry biscuits to eat.

When they arrived at their small-town destinations, CAS officials met them at the train stations and marched them to their local headquarters to wash their faces and change their clothes. Then they took them to churches and town halls, where hundreds of locals gathered to gawk as prospective "guardians" inspected the sturdiness of their muscles, the luster of their hair, and the health of their teeth.

The Orphan Trains' child-transferring system was casual at best, and at worst, it resembled slavery. The contracts varied, but when families selected a child, they signed an agreement with the CAS that said the child could be indentured until the age of eighteen. While some families treated the train riders with love and respect, oral histories collected over the decades show that many foster families regarded the children as chattel.

The legal aspects of these arrangements foreshadowed those of the closed adoptions of the next century. The children, often too young to know their surviving family's addresses, were sent to new homes with no means of remaining in touch, or of ever finding their parents or relatives. Over time, a growing number of child welfare advocates became concerned about the haphazard placement and abuse of the Orphan Train children.

But they were also troubled by a new development emerging in the early twentieth century: a rise in urban prostitution and out-of-wedlock births. Evangelical reformers, largely female and intent on abolishing prostitution, approached pregnant women in brothels with offers of redemption in "maternity homes" far from the docks and barracks. There, the reformers promised, the women would be cared for during their pregnancies—and, with the proper tutelage, recover from their "fallen" status.

Maternity homes sprang up nationwide, offering shelter to all unwed pregnant women. Many, such as those founded by the Salvation Army, were based on fundamentalist Christian ideology, and were intent on keeping together the small family unit of mother and child.

But where evangelicals saw the possibility of salvation, others sensed an economic opportunity. A new brand of entrepreneurs created homes that took in the newborns and promised to rear them in exchange for a hefty fee, allowing their mothers to return to prostitution or factory work. Many of these institutions, called baby farms, appeared in US cities in the late nineteenth century.

Their squalid conditions attracted the scrutiny of Progressive Era leaders, who from 1890 to World War I were determined to expose and reform the problems caused by the rampant corruption, urbanization, immigration, and industrialization of the Gilded Age. In 1914, George Walker, a doctor, published an investigation of baby farms in Baltimore called *The Traffic in Babies*. Walker wrote that owners there had promised the mothers that they would care for their infants until their mothers could reclaim them. But in truth, they had no intention of ever raising the children. Instead, they fed them sloppily prepared milk in bottles with dirty nipples. Unpasteurized milk, which commonly carried typhus and tuberculosis bacteria, was dangerous for healthy adults. It was deadly for infants, who lacked the natural immunity breast milk provides. The vast majority of the infants in baby farms died soon after they arrived—Walker reported a death rate as high as 96 percent.

Walker put it bluntly: "It would be far more humane to kill these babies by striking them on the head with a hammer than to place them in institutions where four-fifths of them succumb within a few weeks to the effects of malnutrition or infectious diseases," he wrote.

Newspapers ran details from similar investigations around the country, showing images of starving babies and scores of tiny skeletons that had been heaped in mass graves. The muckraking coverage sparked outrage and calls for reform, marking a dramatic shift in Americans' views toward helpless, parentless infants. At least one jurisdiction passed a law demanding that mothers and babies remain together for at least six months.

The baby-farm revelations coincided with changes in the country's views on child-rearing, at least among the upper classes. In part, this was because the domestic lives of those with disposable incomes had been transformed by mechanical advances that reduced the labor of caring for a family. Washing machines had replaced scrubbing boards; vacuum cleaners could suck up tiny crumbs brooms could never make vanish; toasters browned the remarkable sliced bread now available from corner bakeries. These improvements not only freed up wealthier women; they also liberated American children. With much of the burden of household chores lifted, they had suddenly gained a childhood. In one decade, the focus of youth had shifted from the virtues of work to the advantages of play. Mass-produced teddy bears, Raggedy Ann dolls, Crayola crayons, and train sets—all introduced in the early twentieth century—had become essential elements for a youngster's development. For the first time, a child's emotional needs outweighed his or her value to the family as a farmhand or wage earner. The experience of raising children—the term "parenting" would be coined a few generations later—evolved from one of economic necessity to one of providing emotional benefits.

Among upper- and middle-class women of the era, motherhood became a reward unto itself. Indeed, many women aligned with the Progressive movement believed they were uniquely suited to solve social problems involving women and children, including infant mortality, public housing, and child labor and safety. They called such aims the politics of "maternalism," and its advocates began creating new arenas for themselves in local, state, and national governments before they even had the right to vote.

The grisly stories about the baby farms in the early 1910s provided powerful evidence of the need to regulate the new industry of nurturing strangers' infants—but with some important caveats. Many Progressive reformers were influenced by the eugenics movement, which believed in improving society by encouraging only the most competent, attractive, and healthiest people to procreate. They were disturbed by the nation's fast-growing immigrant population, which had vastly different customs and beliefs from the white, Anglo-Saxon Protestants at the seat of power. More established, wealthier Americans had better access to hygiene and advances in medicine, and were producing smaller families. This horrified the eugenicists, who projected that the "better Americans" would soon be outnumbered by untrustworthy, "feeble-minded" immigrants. The declining birth rate among Anglo-Saxons so alarmed President Theodore Roosevelt, he warned they were risking "race suicide"—and the nation's future.

Meanwhile, children in the nation's cities were routinely orphaned or abandoned by parents who were unable to care for them. The government, which had largely ignored children until this period, became increasingly concerned with their plight. In Washington, the Taft administration established the US Children's Bureau in 1912 to oversee child welfare; the private Child Welfare League of America followed a few years later. While a handful of states had passed laws regarding adoption in the mid-nineteenth century, a 1917 law in Minnesota marked a turning point. In contrast to the arbitrary, on-the-spot placements of the Orphan Trains, lawmakers passed legislation requiring the state to investigate whether a proposed adoptive home was suitable for a child. It also called for the sealing of adoption records, but allowed them to remain open to the adopted person, birth parents, and adoptive parents.

In New York, some prominent women who were inspired by the good intentions of maternalism developed a direct approach to helping the city's needy children. They included Louise Waterman Wise, the wife of the distinguished rabbi Stephen Wise; Alice Chapin, who was married to a respected pediatrician; and the educator and suffragist Clara Spence. In the years preceding World War I, they were among the first in the country to create specialized adoption agencies that took orphans, abandoned children, and infants born out of wedlock and placed them with wealthier families—often, their friends. At the Free Synagogue Child Adoption Committee, the Alice Chapin Nursery, and the Spence Alumni Society, these social leaders pioneered a new idea: with proper "mother love," children from any background could thrive, regardless of their backgrounds.

The approach came to be called "sentimental adoption," and it marked a clear reversal in the notion of what made a family. (On the subject of illegitimacy among the more privileged, the record is largely silent, presumably because more discreet measures were taken.)

These women demonstrated the model through personal involvement: Wise, alarmed at the lack of institutional support for orphaned or abandoned Jewish children, sought to find them proper Jewish homes. Chapin, who was childless, fostered many neglected children in her home. Spence, along with the female partner with whom she lived openly, adopted four children.

New York codified what the three agencies were already doing by passing a religious-matching law in 1921, and all the leaders continued to place homeless children with friends in their social circles. Soon the idea of molding a foundling or poor orphan into a productive citizen appealed to many wealthy families.

While many maternity homes had been funded by charities, some catering to the daughters of the wealthy charged their parents enough to finance the organization. Over time, the new adoption agencies came to rely on donations as well as fees collected from adoptive parents. It was the opposite of the baby farms. Instead of billing poor mothers for the care of their children, the adoption agencies collected one-time fees from couples who took on the responsibility of raising them into adulthood. (Greed in the adoption process would emerge a few years later.)

The growing popularity of adoption agencies coincided with the rise of a newly minted workforce: professional social workers. In the late nineteenth century, universities began to offer degrees in social work for people who were committed to solving the problems of urban America. The ranks of this new profession were predominantly women, who replaced the religious volunteers of a generation before. The needs of the growing immigrant class, widows, and orphans far surpassed what naive do-gooders could address, and cities saw a role for a more professional stable of helpers.

Adoption agencies recruited young social workers to help find homes for youngsters. By the early 1920s, the agencies had begun to approach adoption as a scientific puzzle as they sought to match babies to families. Many Americans still clung to the fear that children born to poor mothers might be "feeble-minded," but adoption officials had begun testing the children with newly introduced IQ tests that foreshadowed Karelitz's studies decades later. This systematized process helped give Americans more confidence in accepting strangers' children, and was the first step toward the institutional structure Margaret would later confront.

Among the nation's elite, adoption quietly became fashionable as a form of both family-building and altruism. As the country sank into the Depression, adoption became a prevalent—and hopeful—motif in popular culture. It ranged from the fictional Little Orphan Annie, the innocent cartoon vagabond adopted by the wealthy Mr. and Mrs. Warbucks, to the very real adoptions by prominent Americans. By the late 1930s, some of the country's biggest celebrities, including actress Joan Crawford, entertainers Bob Hope, George Burns, and Gracie Allen, and the Nobel literary laureate Pearl S. Buck, were adoptive parents. They openly discussed the way they created their families in magazine and newspaper interviews, often mentioning The Cradle, the Illinois agency many of them had used. (It soon developed a reputation for providing babies to stars in Hollywood and New York.)

Perversely, while scores of unknown unwed women were shamed for having their babies, rich, famous ones were celebrated for adopting them. In a strange twist of social mores, the traditional women's magazine *Ladies' Home Journal* published a 1937 essay by the divorced author

Laura Hobson. In "I Just Adopted a Baby!" Hobson described her busy, fulfilled life as a single working mother in Manhattan. A few years later, the unmarried Hobson, who went on to write the novel *Gentleman's Agreement*, would conceive, and bear, a second son. To avoid the disgrace of an unmarried pregnancy, she pretended she'd adopted him too.

And then there was Joan Crawford. California's prohibition against single women adopting didn't stop the divorced Crawford, who drove to Nevada to legalize the adoption of her oldest child, Christina, in 1939. In public, the actress was effusively affectionate toward Christina, as well as the boy and twin girls she subsequently adopted. She invited reporters and photographers to document everything from bedtime to Brownie meetings, often appearing with Christina in matching mother-daughter pinafores that looked more suited to Dorothy in Kansas than to glamorous Crawford in her Brentwood home. They didn't just seem like costumes: they were exactly that, only worn when cameras were around. But the goofy getups weren't the half of it. In *Mommie Dearest*, her tell-all book after Crawford's death, Christina—whom the actress originally named Joan Crawford Jr.—wrote that the big, beaming family was nothing more than a Hollywood publicity stunt. After some box-office failures, and a well-earned reputation for belligerence, Crawford's career had been in tatters. The actress, whom Christina described as a tyrant with a vodka problem, hoped her portrayal as a mother might boost her image to studios and fans alike.

CRAWFORD HAD REASON TO blur the truth about her family. Rather than work through The Cradle or other established agencies, Crawford engaged the services of private baby brokers. Notably, she obtained the twins through Georgia Tann, a Memphis social worker with a reputation as a baby peddler to the stars. Tann's client list included other actors, including June Allyson and Dick Powell, as well as high-ranking businesspeople and government officials.

Tann started out in 1924, finding adoptive Memphis couples for the babies of unwed Tennessee mothers. At the time, the adoption fee in the state, where most residents were of British, Irish, and Scottish origin, was seven dollars. But as adoption became more popular in the 1930s, Tann realized that the desire of distant, wealthy clients who wanted the same blond, blue-eyed children she was placing in Memphis homes could make her rich.

Nobody asked questions about how she acquired the babies and began transporting them across state lines. Nobody really wanted to know. Even with the lax laws of the time, Tann's actions were flagrantly fraudulent, and were shielded by her insistence on the importance of closed adoptions. Tann would eventually be exposed, but her favored legal arrangement—the sealing of original birth certificates—would become the standard practice of every mainstream adoption agency in America.

For years until her death in 1950, Tann operated from the Tennessee Children's Home Society, in a stately home in Memphis she used as a front for her lucrative black market business. Through her connections in Memphis, she was able to move the stolen babies through the courts to other states as easily as if they were mere mail-order widgets. Yet outwardly, she was a compassionate defender of poor children in need of "good homes," earning respect from even the White House. Eleanor Roosevelt sought her advice about child welfare, and Harry Truman invited her to his inauguration.

Tann was ruthless in her pursuit of thousands of babies she would ultimately steal, and then sell, to wealthy customers like Crawford. Her methods were anything but subtle. She took the babies of mothers who were institutionalized in psychiatric hospitals. She persuaded indigent unwed mothers still foggy from anesthesia to sign documents, not explaining that they were adoption papers. She visited poor women with sick children, promising to take them to the doctor. She stole them instead, telling the mothers their kids had died. She became so brazen, she even snatched toddlers from nursery schools.

Then Tann would dress the children and market them from the parlor of her mansion. She wasn't the first to advertise children in catalogs—The Willows in Kansas City had also promoted cherubic babies in its promotional materials. But Tann took the advertising of children to a new level.

She enticed reporter friends to write gushing articles about her for the local paper, accompanied by photos of her prettiest babies. Their captions read "Could YOU Use a Christmas Baby?" and "Yours for the Asking!" The stories, timed weeks before the holidays, made the youngsters sound like game-show grand prizes, not human beings. Word of her work traveled widely—and fast.

She became a millionaire from an elaborate scheme in which she charged adoptive parents in California or New York as much as $5,000—equivalent to $90,000 today. She claimed the money was spent on background checks, paperwork, and expensive airplane tickets for the courier who would bring the baby from Tennessee.

The adoptive parents collected their babies in the lobbies of elegant hotels as casually as one might sign for a FedEx package, never suspecting that the nurse who had traveled to their faraway state was transporting as many as six other babies she would deliver to six other couples. A shrewd businesswoman, Tann charged everyone the same outrageous sums for the services she was offering, even though she never carried out the background checks, and only one nurse was making a single trip. This made the shipments of multiple children highly profitable.

Her clients had the means not to flinch at the cost—and they wielded powers at the highest levels. Abe Fortas, a future Supreme Court justice, appealed to Tann's lawyer, Abe Waldauer, to find a baby for his sister. Both men came from the small Memphis Jewish community, and Waldauer, who was active in many national organizations, became a conduit to Jewish families seeking babies to adopt without the red tape of adoption agencies. Unlike the rigorous selection process at Louise Wise, Tann and Waldauer's operation was on a much more relaxed (and openly commercial) level. As Tann's reputation grew in the 1940s, Waldauer received hundreds of requests from Jewish families throughout the country. Some sought special features—green eyes, for example, or a baby with both English-Jewish and German-Jewish backgrounds. To one customer he deemed overly demanding, he archly wrote that "babies are different from dry goods."

Indeed, if clients wanted Jewish babies, Tann was happy to oblige—regardless of whether they'd been born that way. Following state laws, like New York's, that demanded babies be of the same faith as their adoptive parents, Tann passed off dozens of babies as having been born to Jewish mothers. It's not as if anyone would ever know, since Tann was a steadfast proponent—and promulgator—of a new approach to adoptions that kept birth certificates, and the identities of the parents, hidden from public view. The new system Tann promoted, which started taking root in the 1930s, worked this way. When a child was born to a single mother and then adopted by a new family, courts would seal the child's original birth certificate and issue a new document that listed the adoptive parents as if they were the original mother and father. Just as with Stephen's adoption decades later, the falsified record, the argument went, would erase the perceived taint of illegitimacy from the adoptee, and protect the adoptive parents from the fear that birth parents might one day attempt to disrupt the happiness of the newly created family. This approach also made adoption a transaction in which the adoptee might never know the mother who bore them, the father who begat them—or for that matter, their identity at all.

The existing legal framework for adoption had provided transparency, particularly in the cases of widowed parents. Pushed by Tann (and many others), state after state adopted the new system. Publicly, the explanation for the new laws seemed compassionate. Sealing original birth certificates would protect children in their new, better life. Tann didn't have to go far to convince lawmakers in New York State: one report indicates that she provided at least one of Governor Herbert Lehman's three adopted children. (It is possible that Waldauer and Lehman were casual acquaintances; they served together on the board of American Friends of the Hebrew University.) In 1936, Lehman signed the first of a suite of laws that required the sealing of original birth certificates for adopted people. Eventually, similar laws were passed throughout the country.

With original birth certificates locked away in state archives, it was difficult if not impossible for mothers to find the sons and daughters Tann had abducted. The new laws had understandable appeal to adoptive parents. The amended documents allowed them, in essence, to rewrite their family's history as they wished it could have happened.

The laws served Tann's business model, allowing her to operate with impunity. But in early 1950, several adoptive parents reported her scheme to Tennessee governor Gordon Browning, and state officials moved to examine her crimes. Tann never suffered any ill effects. She died of cancer in September 1950. Three months later, the state closed her orphanage.

News of Tann's treachery made national headlines, and in 1955, the progressive Tennessee senator Estes Kefauver, an advocate for consumer protection, launched a US Senate investigation into abusive adoptive practices. After days of hearings that exposed kidnapping and the black market baby trade, Kefauver proposed a bill to prohibit the commercial sale of babies. At the time, thirty-four of the forty-eight states had no laws of any kind banning the sale of babies. The bill did not pass.

It didn't take long for adoption agencies to play to adoptive parents' fears that the private route to parenthood was the most perilous. Around the country, agencies told prospective clients that only by paying fees and submitting to a screening process—one that had filtered out all but the "right" kind of girls—could aspiring parents feel confident they would get the "right" kind of baby.

A Louise Wise brochure warned of the "dangerous risks" posed by adopting through a doctor, lawyer, hospital, or friend: "Court records abound in cases where the natural mother changed her mind and demanded the return of a child . . . [and] there are many instances where an unsuspecting couple found they had acquired a baby with a severe but previously unrecognized mental or physical defect. These risks are virtually eliminated in dealing with an authorized agency, for no babies are placed until they have been legally surrendered to the agency and the child's physical and mental condition is accurately reported to the adoptive parents."

Throughout the 1950s and '60s, Louise Wise Services and other New York agencies discussed making a film that would emphasize the importance and "safety" of adopting through agencies. The zeitgeist of the period was that positive outcomes were likely, if not certain, provided one stuck with professionals who were well versed in the art of matching children to the right parents. The agencies wanted the film to echo, if not outdo, a 1951 movie called *Close to My Heart*. In this sappy picture, Gene Tierney and Ray Milland star as Midge and Brad Sheridan, an infertile couple in Los Angeles determined to adopt a baby. Midge learns about a foundling called Danny whom other couples have rejected because of his uncertain parentage. Brad is wary of the child's possible flaws, telling Midge, "We don't want any off-brand babies."

Midge perseveres, bringing Brad to Danny's "intelligence" test at an adoption agency. A white-coated adoption worker places the chubby nine-month-old in a high chair and hands him a series of objects. "If only he passes," Midge whispers. Danny touches blocks, removes a cube from a cup, and smiles into a mirror. Anxious-sounding violins give way to a heavenly harp, and the blond baby's face is suffused with light. "He passed with flying colors," the adoption worker exclaims. "A baby is the only living thing without a past," the agency director says, "only a future."

10.

The Right Future

By the time Margaret got pregnant in 1961, Tann was dead, Louise Wise was running on all cylinders, and the baby boom was in full swing. The United States, it was clear, had a glittering new future—one that was full of children. If you couldn't have one, there was only one way to get one: from young women in trouble. Adoption offered the women a safeguard from their disgrace. But the transfer process to the families was as hazy as the stories about storks delivering babies on doorsteps. The women who carried the babies remained utterly out of sight—and mostly out of mind.

The new trend in closed adoptions promoted by the agencies was also consistent with the prevailing view of women who became pregnant out of wedlock—that they had morally transgressed and needed to be punished by losing contact with their sons and daughters forever. The principles of eugenics—still embraced by doctors trained in the 1920s and '30s—offered a scientific underpinning for this argument. Many believed that unmarried women who became pregnant before marriage had a moral flaw that made them unfit to raise children: they could not control their sexual impulses.

These beliefs remained surprisingly mainstream into the 1950s. Framed by Freudian theories on female desire, the largely male medical profession, and society as a whole, viewed women who'd become pregnant out of wedlock as deeply neurotic social deviants. Surrendering a child for adoption was seen as the only prudent course, for the women, their children, and society. This theory was entirely at odds with the basics of human biology and, more important, how young men and women were conducting their lives.

It's IMPOSSIBLE TO EXAGGERATE the scope of the changes wrought, and driven by, the baby boom, as wave after wave of children vastly reshaped the country's culture, economy, and demographics. Although they had access only to basic forms of birth control—condoms and the diaphragm— married women who came of age in the 1930s had an average of 2.4 children. By the 1950s, the average woman bore 3.2 children. For fertile couples, having children was easier and safer than it had ever been. Post- war medical advances significantly reduced infant and maternal mortal- ity, diminishing the fear many women had of dying in childbirth. The social pressures generated by all this change were immense. As Betty Friedan would note in her treatise on postwar housewives, the only "real" way a woman could know fulfillment was to give birth to a child.

During the baby boom, society was re-embracing the historical no- tion of the United States as a land of endless fecundity (within the bounds of marital legitimacy). Couples who remained childless became the objects of scrutiny or pity, if not suspicion. The national sacrifice needed to combat the Depression and the Nazis gave way to a focus on personal fulfillment and happiness, which were best found in tidy new subdivisions from Long Island to Los Angeles. For the growing number of middle-class whites who bought into this idea of the American dream, children were the symbols of an idyllic lifestyle. Whether they were trained experts like pediatrician Benjamin Spock or amateurs like the advice columnists Ann Landers and Abigail Van Buren, these au- thorities offered guidance to parents on how to space the births of their children and dress and discipline them.

The government played its role in the pro-family chorus, offering low-interest loans for college education and credits on mortgages and taxes. It seemed the real victory on the battlefields of Europe and the Pacific was the chance to get married, buy a home, have kids, and move to the suburbs. It is important to note that those government subsidies, and the freedom to leave cities, were almost entirely limited to white veterans.

Many of those who couldn't have children—this new manifest destiny for whites—saw themselves as second-class citizens. A 1963 article in the journal *Fertility and Sterility*, based on in-depth interviews with "barren" couples, captured those sentiments. Men said they felt "inadequate," "re-signed," and "feeling like I had failed my wife." Women responded far more emotionally: "I'm absolutely heartsick," wrote one. Others described feeling "desolate," "bitter," "despondent," "inferior," "hopeless," "like a flop as a wife and a woman." While infertility affects both genders equally, women were often blamed for a couple's "sterility." Infertility treatments were rudimentary at best. Surgery to repair blocked fallopian tubes, for example, was risky and often resulted in more scarring inside the delicate tissue. In 1953, doctors helped a woman achieve a successful pregnancy using frozen sperm. But artificial insemination, pioneered in the late nineteenth century, was still uncommon in the 1950s and deeply controversial: some religious leaders and divorce judges considered it adultery. Assisted reproduction reached another turning point in 1967, when the Food and Drug Administration approved the fertility drug clomiphene citrate, or Clomid. Adoption, for many people who could not reproduce, was the most reliable route to parenthood.

Single motherhood, so commonplace today, was all but unimaginable in the 1950s and early 1960s. It inevitably was accompanied by ostracism, poverty, and unrelenting shame. For young men, a hasty marriage and instant fatherhood were seen as complicating, if not foreclosing, chances for higher education and advancement. The GI Bill had made college affordable, allowing more people to strive toward a white-collar lifestyle and paycheck. Between 1947 and 1967, the number of young American men graduating from college, while still small, nearly doubled. As it did for George and Margaret, an unexpected pregnancy threatened that dream. Not only did middle-class white parents like the Erles and the Katzes support the decision to place a child for adoption, they typically arranged it— and turned to outside agencies that could outsource the entire "problem."

In black families in which unwed women became pregnant, mothers and children faced a very different future. For a good part of the twentieth century, many adoption agencies declined to serve African American birth parents and their babies. Their story is deserving of its own detailed examination. While the rates of unwed pregnancies in the postwar years were higher among black women than white women, demand for white babies was far higher. Yet in contrast to white middle-class families, many black families, regardless of their socioeconomic status, refused to allow the children of their unwed daughters to be adopted by strangers. In 1965, the rate of black unwed motherhood was about 20 percent higher than that of whites—and to many, this constituted a serious national crisis.

The attitude toward pregnant, unmarried women like Margaret and the pressure on them to relinquish their babies for adoption by more suitable parents was as overwhelming as it was hypocritical. It is not a stretch to say that the millions of unmarried white women caught up in an increasingly commercialized system of adoption were like products propelled to market by the conveyor belt of a relentlessly efficient factory. They were castigated as immoral, but their children were highly valued products. Carol Schaefer, who surrendered a son in 1966, puts it this way: "Let's not mince words. For a generation of Americans, we were broodmares."

THERE IS ONE ELEMENT missing from the mythical win-win model that gave babies to the infertile and a second chance to the miscreant mothers. A research subject that did not get a lot of attention was the question of how hiding a pregnancy, giving birth alone, and then relinquishing an infant might reverberate through the life of a young woman. Instead, social scientists, overwhelmingly male and overwhelmingly steeped in Freudian theory, devoted a considerable amount of energy to shaming and demonizing young women who'd become pregnant out of wedlock. In his 1957 doctoral dissertation on unwed mothers, Edmund Pollock of New York University declared that they were "dominant, aggressive, narcissistic and bitterly hostile." It would have been hard for Pollock to more completely pathologize his thirty-five subjects, who were unaware they were being studied as part of a research project. He wrote that in becoming pregnant, the women were trying to punish a rejecting parent, and that they suffered from penis envy so profound that it could only be expressed by having a child. He theorized that the women were acting out of an "infantile incestuous fantasy of having a baby with their father."

Other findings were equally damning. One psychiatrist said unwed mothers had been "stripped of the greatest human gift: rational thought." Two Harvard psychiatrists stated flatly that every unmarried mother "is to some degree a psychiatric problem." Another NYU scholar, sociologist Wyatt C. Jones, studied the social "deviancy" of both white and black single mothers. He laid the blame on everyone involved in this social aberration, but mostly, of course, on the women. Not surprisingly, he declared them more "paranoid, avoidant, anxious and depressive" than a control sample of college girls whose concerns were more limited to their term papers.

Social scientists also pathologized the girls' families. A journal article about separate group therapy sessions for the parents of Lakeview girls, and the girls themselves, was clear about the treatment's aims: to make the parents and the girls aware of a "psychic problem forced on the family by a physical symptom—the girl's obvious pregnancy." Through the therapeutic guidance of the Lakeview social workers, many of the families realized that their daughters "might be acting out sexually some of [the parents'] own suppressed desires." Only occasionally did social scientists give thought to unmarried fathers. One found they had a "neurotic need" to prove their virility.

Nowhere did the researchers entertain the possibility that both partners might enjoy sex—or that the pregnancies, like Margaret's and so many scores of others, had been accidental.

THERE WAS NEVER ANY QUESTION about who, in fact, held the most power in the adoption process: those in the middle. Some were not shy about expressing the pleasures they derived from their omnipotence. "Every time we place a child for adoption, we feel like we're playing God," a New York State child welfare official said in 1960, "with all the hazards of playing God."

The agencies played God far more often than they publicly acknowledged. In several instances, Louise Wise Services deliberately omitted revealing that the babies it was placing had been born in psychiatric hospitals to women who were severely mentally ill. During the 1950s, some doctors theorized that the cold behavior of mothers could cause mental illness in their children. The concept was soon discredited, and it is unclear whether Wise officials embraced this belief. But how much to reveal about the mothers—some of whom were not ill, and had been committed against their will by angry parents—was a topic of frequent discussion. The agency decided to keep such information to itself, even though Viola Bernard acknowledged that excluding information about a mother's background made some people uneasy.

"There has been and is discomfort about suppressing information," she announced at a 1964 staff meeting. "Would we relieve the discomfort by sharing information and letting parents decide? Would this stir up anxiety needlessly? Do we know that our misgivings are their misgivings?"

Louise Wise and other agencies opted for deception—and not only about mental illness. As late as the 1960s, some adoption officials told mothers their babies had died.

Other times, agencies offered young women elaborate, intricately constructed fantasies about the lives their babies would have. When sixteen-year-old Delores Swigert was at the Salvation Army White Shield maternity home in Portland in 1968, she told her social worker that she hoped her baby would grow up with music, and one day attend an elite college. Swigert's violinist father had completed high school; her mother, only eighth grade.

Swigert had an induced, violent labor that was timed for the convenience of the home's visiting obstetrician. As with Margaret and so many other unwed mothers, girls at the Salvation Army home were not allowed to see their babies after they'd delivered. But as Swigert recovered from the difficult birth, she grew angry, and declared that she was going to take her son and walk out. Her threats seemed so real that the Salvation Army sergeants were afraid she might pull it off, so for the next five days, they quietly brought her son to her room for a few hours, making her promise not to tell the other girls.

In the meantime, one of the sergeants fabricated a story about a waiting adoptive family that appealed to every aspirational detail Swigert had expressed for her son. The sergeant described a blue-eyed Latino adoptive father who combined the looks of Swigert's boyfriend and her mother, who was of Apache descent. The man, she said, was a professor at a renowned university who had played football—a suggestion that he would instinctively know how to raise a fine American boy. The sergeant also said that the adoptive mother had a degree in music; that the couple had a daughter, and had long hoped for a son. Best of all, they lived in a magnificent home with a circular driveway. Swigert, whose parents had divorced when she was young, had grown up poor in a rural Missouri town. Could this family offer her son an Ivy League education? Swigert asked. Of course, the sergeant replied. The life promised to her son seemed irresistible, and something she, as a single teenager, was doubtful she could provide. She signed the papers, and for decades told herself that she had "done the right thing." She often drove by elegant homes in Portland and imagined that her son lived there.

Delores, who went on to become a fashion model, a licensed clinical social worker, and an adoption-rights activist under her first married name, Delores Teller, gave birth to three more children. She reunited with her firstborn when he was twenty-eight, and learned that nothing she had been told was true. Her son's adoptive parents were school-teachers who lived in a modest home in a fishing and lumber-mill town on the Oregon coast. His adoptive mother had a severe drinking prob-lem, divorced her husband when her son was five, and relocated to Pitts-burgh. He had been raised by his adoptive father, who abused him.

Jane Edwards, who gave birth to a daughter as a single woman in San Francisco in 1966, was explicit when her caseworker mentioned the possi-bility of placing her baby with a Mormon family in Idaho. Edwards, an ag-nostic college graduate from Alaska, knew a lot about the Church of Jesus Christ of Latter-day Saints. While she held no personal animus toward its members, she was unsettled by what she viewed as the faith's cultlike as-pects, and the subservient role it ascribed to women. Under no circum-stances, Edwards told her caseworker, was her daughter to be placed with a Mormon family. The social worker said she couldn't guarantee Edwards's request, but nevertheless prepared a statement spelling out her wishes. Ed-wards signed the document; it gave her a modicum of comfort.

Edwards's experiences as a young woman subsumed by the adoption system ignited her own feminist activism, and she became an attorney devoted to women's rights. She married, moved to Portland, and had three more daughters. In 1997, Edwards's firstborn, Rebecca, located her by using the limited information provided by the adoption agency. Ed-wards was thrilled and scared—but was also shocked to learn that her daughter's adoptive parents were conservative Mormons from Idaho who

had reared Rebecca to believe, among other things, that feminism under-
mined families. And while the files to which Rebecca had gained access
had allowed her to find Edwards, they had not included her signed statement about religion. The early years of their reunion were rocky, as mother
and daughter had differing views about the role of women in society. Edwards had long challenged the patriarchal system that separated her from
Rebecca in the first place; Rebecca, meanwhile, had grown up accepting
it. Their initial arguments, now smoothed, were a double blow.

A Bronx woman also suffered a series of devastating betrayals when
she became pregnant in 1959 by her African American boyfriend. When
her Jewish parents discovered the pregnancy, they sent her to Lakeview
with a plan to commit her to a psychiatric hospital after she gave birth, a
tactic sometimes used among parents of single mothers at the time. The
woman delivered her son in November at age sixteen. Meanwhile, a case
filed by her parents had moved through the courts, and under wayward
minor laws, she was declared guilty of "willful intercourse, which resulted
in the birth of a child." This, her court papers said, made her a danger to
herself and others. She was remanded back to Lakeview for two months
of observation, and a judge awarded Louise Wise custody of her son. In
her third appearance at the family court in January 1960, the Bronx
woman was brought before Justine Wise Polier, the judge who was also
the president of Louise Wise Services. (Few, it seems, objected to the
obvious conflict of interest of a family court judge who made rulings on
the clients her agency served.) Wise Polier ordered the woman to undergo psychiatric treatment as an outpatient, and put her on probation.
Meanwhile, the woman asked—consistently, frequently—about her
son's whereabouts and well-being. Social workers told her that he was
"in care," which the Bronx woman initially believed was a single foster
home.

By the time her baby was eighteen months old, the Bronx woman
had persuaded adoption officials into allowing her to see him about
a half dozen times at the Louise Wise offices. The woman knew

intuitively that something was wrong with her son. He had an increasing lack of affect, and made little eye contact with her and the social worker who supervised her visits. When she demanded to know more about his caretakers, social workers told the Bronx woman he was being moved frequently. Why was he being moved frequently? she asked. "That's what we do," the social worker said. In May of 1961, the Bronx woman was four months away from legal adulthood and had made clear that she intended to regain custody of her son. Her probation officer told her that she had the authority to extend her case until she was twenty-one years old. "You will never get that child," she told her.

She sought help from her boyfriend's family, but Louise Wise officials were resistant to any option aside from the Bronx woman's signing papers. During one visit to see him in May of 1961, the social worker led her to a room in which her son was crying and screaming, repeating the name "Barbara." The Bronx woman was horrified, and understood immediately that his continued lack of a home—and love—had contributed to his mental state. She signed surrender papers that day. Shortly after, she asked her Louise Wise social worker if she could see her son. The caseworker told her that he had already been adopted by a professional couple.

In fact, the Bronx woman's son had passed through several foster homes and at least one facility before he was two and was not legally adopted until two months past his third birthday. In 1996, she learned from an acquaintance with strong research skills that, when he was twenty, her son had overdosed on heroin in New York City the day after Christmas. Her social worker had been correct about one thing: Her son's adoptive parents were, in fact, professionals. His adoptive father was an executive in an actors' union. His adoptive mother was an executive at the city's Bureau of Child Welfare.

Perhaps adoption workers felt such duplicity was necessary to soften the blow of what they fundamentally understood: that surrendering a child was painful and deeply traumatizing for the vast majority of

mothers. In her 1954 book describing her forty years as Lakeview's director, Sara Edlin acknowledged that the thousands of young women who
had come under her care left the home scarred by the experience of
losing a child. "It is a sad and tragic conclusion to a sad story when a girl
in search of love and security is propelled into unwed motherhood," she
wrote. "In the majority of cases, she has had to go through pregnancy
and childbirth, only to be compelled by circumstances to give up the
child and return to the outside world empty-handed and burdened with
remorse."

She went on: "I have been led to consider adoption as the solution in
the average case, yet I cannot but feel that it is at best, a compromise.
Theoretically and practically, it is necessary. And yet, whenever I see a
girl lift her child out of its crib, and hold it for the last time before it is
taken away, I feel the human pain of it."

By Margaret's ten-week stay in 1961, the attitude of Lakeview administrators had hardened. No one except the cook showed her any
kindness at all.

11.

Childless Mother

The months after Margaret signed the papers passed by in a haze. She thought about Stephen constantly, praying every morning and night that he was safe in some warm, sunny country with the diplomat and his wife. Maybe he was in Spain, or Italy. Maybe he was in Israel, a baby pioneer. Even so, she couldn't help but wonder about any black-haired babies she saw on the street. Sometimes on the subway, or walking down the street, she'd find herself staring at a little boy who caught her eye. Did that one have a dimpled chin? Did this one have George's ears? She studied photographs of George as a baby, engraving his childhood face into her mind. Stephen resembled him at three and five months; maybe he looked like him as time went on too. So she envisioned George's face on a little boy who, like so many others, had a haircut like little John F. Kennedy Jr.: long bangs, swept to the side. Sometimes her searching made her feel like a teenage spy.

In early 1963, Margaret moved back into her family's apartment to save money. Stephen, like other family secrets, remained one, and no one ever discussed him. She and Gertrude engaged in their own personal cold war, avoiding each other as much as possible in the small apartment. Margaret was looking ahead, thinking about when she and George could get married.

For her birthday in June, George, sensing her longing, surprised her with a beagle puppy he got from a pet shop. Margaret called her Taffy. In a photograph, she stands on the street outside a neighborhood church, cradling the tiny dog's head with one hand against her chest, and her rump with another. Her dark brown eyes look soberly and tenderly into the camera, the midsummer afternoon light casting long shadows.

Margaret on her nineteenth birthday, with a beagle puppy George got her after her second childless Mother's Day

Taffy was adorable, and Margaret was happy for the distraction—as well as for having an object for her abundant affection. When she died a few weeks later—she had not been properly vaccinated—Margaret cried for days. She longed for another dog, but George convinced her to wait. So they solidified their plan to elope. One afternoon in late August, they met in the Diamond District to pick out wedding rings, matching thick gold filigreed bands.

In early September 1963, Margaret, nineteen, and George, twenty, bought their bus tickets to South Carolina. Margaret had found a motel that was down the street from the courthouse, and made a reservation for two nights after frantically shoving half a roll of dimes into a pay phone.

With both their parents monitoring their comings and goings, Margaret began hatching a cover story about a long-weekend visit to a nearby city. Since Washington, DC, had become a magnet for young people and was on the route to South Carolina, she decided that it would make a good alibi. The glamorous, youthful Kennedys were in the White House, inspiring many young Americans to join the government. Margaret, who shared with Josef a growing sense of outrage as the country's civil rights crisis worsened, had watched rapt as the television news brought images of hundreds of thousands of peaceful protesters who had recently joined Martin Luther King Jr. in his March on Washington.

So, she reasoned, her visiting the capital would not seem out of the ordinary, and she announced that she was visiting there with some friends. George told his parents the same story. They planned to meet up in Norfolk, Virginia, where Margaret had a friend stationed in the navy.

She gazed out the window as the bus passed through unknown territory: Delaware, Maryland, and Washington. She caught sight of the Capitol dome, gleaming white in the distance, and tried to contain her excitement. This was the closest she'd been to regaining Stephen.

The next morning, she met her friend for breakfast, and then left to greet George's overnight bus at the station. He carried only his gym bag. Margaret had just a few clothes as well, but it would be their honeymoon, of sorts, so she had splurged on a knee-length white nightgown with a matching chiffon peignoir and white slip-on mules with kitten heels and fur pom-poms. At home, she had kept the ensemble in its bag, hidden under heavy sweaters.

On the morning of September 12, they boarded the bus to South Carolina. They arrived in the early afternoon, stepping out in air so dense it felt like they were walking through a curtain of hot fog, and took a taxi to their motel. As Margaret got out of the cab, she turned the pearl from the ring George had given her toward her palm, and the couple nervously checked in as George and Margaret Katz. Then they walked to the courthouse with their birth certificates to apply for their marriage license.

Margaret and George had an early supper in a local diner. George watched a young African American boy struggle with a broken pinball machine. He got up to help him, joking with the boy and trying to help him fix the internal lever.

Almost immediately, a policeman who was sitting at the counter walked menacingly up to George. He adjusted his felt hat and put his hand on his gun.

"Boy," he bellowed. "What are you doing?"

"I'm helping this kid with the pinball machine," George answered, bewildered.

"You some kind of a Yankee?" the policeman demanded.

"Matter of fact, I am," George said, standing at his full height.

"Whites and coloreds might mix where you're from, but not in these parts," he commanded. "You sit yourself down or I'll arrest you."

George quickly returned to his booth. Margaret's hands were shaking. The boy looked down, and returned to his mother's table. As Margaret got up to wash her hands, she saw a sign on the bathroom door that said "White Ladies Only." She shivered. It hardly felt like an auspicious start to the first night they would ever spend together.

They returned to the motel, and Margaret stepped into the bathroom to take a shower. She fluffed her hair, which had gotten wavy in the stifling heat, and freshened her makeup. She donned her white lace negligee like a new bride, and with all the same qualms. Did she look sexy? Did she even know what sexy was? What if she didn't please George? The thought of her own pleasure never crossed her mind.

She opened the door a crack, and stepped out into the humid motel room. George gazed at his bride-to-be with adoring eyes. He smiled sweetly, his dimples showing, and took her hands. It was over in a moment.

The next morning, Friday the thirteenth, they returned to the brick county building that housed the justice of the peace's chambers. When their names were called, they entered nervously to see a female judge, her platinum hair teased high, in a black robe with a frilly white collar. She sat beneath a massive wooden cross and a huge picture of Jesus with long blond hair and blue eyes.

"What if God punishes us for this?" Margaret whispered to George. "Will this marriage even be valid in his eyes?" He clasped her hand.

"Just go along with what she says and we'll make it right under God when we get home," he whispered back.

"In Jesus's name, I now pronounce you man and wife," the judge said. Margaret tried not to wince at the words. George slipped Margaret's gold band onto her ring finger, and she slipped George's onto his.

In Judaism, a wedding is only lawful after a series of rituals take place, and Margaret could not imagine anything further from it than the blond judge and Jesus. But the next morning, she woke first, cuddled in George's arms. She felt happy—but also so sad, and scared. They were married now, but could their parents make them annul their vows?

Excited with their new status—but so nervous about their cover-up stories—they took separate trains from the bus terminal back uptown. When they each arrived at their respective apartments on Saturday night, they distributed the mementos they'd purchased at a roadside stand. No one asked questions about their trip—and no one seemed to care.

The next week, the Erle family prepared to attend the bar mitzvah of a cousin. Margaret, chatting amiably with her younger brother, Allen, by then seventeen and a student at one of New York's most prestigious high schools, the Bronx High School of Science, was snapping the magnet Margaret had given him on and off the refrigerator. "Can I tell you a secret?" she asked her brother. "Sure," he said, looking up with wide eyes. He, of course, had known about his sister's pregnancy but had never spoken to her about it.

"George and I eloped last week," she said.

"Oh," he said. Then, puzzled, he asked: "Where?"

"South Carolina," she told him. "But don't tell anyone."

At the bar mitzvah, she sat near a cousin who had come from out of town. Her secret, after years of keeping them, was too hard to contain. So she told her cousin too. Her cousin squeezed her hand and said, "I'm happy for you."

But the couple, now legal husband and wife, still slept alone in their childhood beds.

TEN DAYS AFTER THE WEDDING, and two days after the bar mitzvah, on September 23, 1963, a social worker who was handling Stephen Mark Erle's case recommended finalizing adoption with the Rosenbergs. Ephraim, who led his congregation in song at the Sons of Israel, a large synagogue in the Bronx, had decided to rename the couple's new baby David Aryeh, after two brothers who'd been slaughtered, along with his parents, by the Nazis. David represented both the past and the future.

A day later, George called the Katz family's rabbi to inquire if he would marry them in a traditional Jewish wedding. "Come by this afternoon at five thirty," his secretary said. Margaret and George dressed formally for the visit, doing their best to look mature and respectable. They were nervous as they entered his office, aware that the rabbi knew of Fritz's objections to Margaret. "Why aren't your parents here?" he demanded of George, who, after all, was still a minor. "Because I'm a grown man, and I want Margaret to be my wife," he said solemnly. He sat up straight in his chair, towering over the broad, bearded man. Now it was his turn to say what Margaret had repeated to every person of authority: "We love each other, and we want to get married."

The rabbi pressed his fingertips together, then pointed them first toward George, then toward Margaret, and back to George.

"What's the rush, George?" he asked, his eyes narrowing. "You're not twenty-one."

"We're ready to marry," George said. "We've loved each other for three years, and it's time."

The rabbi narrowed his eyes again.

"Have you had *sex*?" he demanded.

"No," they replied in unison.

"I see," he said. "We'll have to look at the calendar."

No sooner had the couple left the rabbi's office than the rabbi called Fritz to tell him about the visit. When George arrived home, Fritz rushed to the door, the veins in his forehead popping. "With that one still?" he cried. "The *Erle* girl?"

"Yes," George said, standing tall. "We're in love."

"Love?" Fritz cried. "What do you know about love?"

Though he was shorter and slighter than his son, Fritz swung his fist, landing it squarely on George's nose. The force of the blow made a loud crack, and blood gushed down George's face onto his shirt. George pinched his nostrils to try to stanch the flow, then straightened himself to his full height. He brought his face close to Fritz's.

"More," George told his father, "than you."

Lizzie, running from the kitchen, implored her husband to stop.

"She's white and Jewish, Fritz," she pleaded. "What more do you want?"

GERTRUDE WAS SCARCELY MORE PLEASED. When George arrived to ask Josef for Margaret's hand in marriage, her face turned to shale. But Josef smiled when he heard the news. "Mazel tov," he whispered into Margaret's ear as he embraced her, and to George's face as he shook his hand. The rabbi set the date for November 10, a scant six weeks away.

For her wedding dress, Margaret picked out as conservative a pattern as possible, along with a thick white brocade fabric. When she visited the Spanish seamstress who would sew the dress, Margaret was so self-conscious about her stretch marks she didn't even want a stranger knowing the truth. She hid them in a minimizer bra, a slip, and a girdle. "You're so young—just a *nena!*" the woman declared as she wrapped the tape measure around her breasts, her waist, her hips. "Why do you need all this underwear?" Margaret just smiled. At the final fitting, she gasped when she saw herself in the dressing room mirror. Finally, she would be a good girl—at least to people who didn't know.

The couple found a one-bedroom apartment they could afford off the Grand Concourse in the Bronx and put down a security deposit. They took extra care to get a building that allowed dogs. And although Margaret believed Stephen had left the country, her eyes still scanned the subway, the street, and buses for coffee-eyed little boys.

Everyone was on their best behavior the cool Sunday afternoon of November 10, 1963, when, in Jewish custom, George and Margaret signed the *ketubah*, the wedding contract, in the rabbi's chambers. Fritz's business partner and George's best friend, Hank Edelman, were the witnesses. In Orthodox observance, only males can perform this function.

George's parents walked toward the rabbi and stepped to the side of the *chuppah*, the wedding canopy. A moment later, Margaret, her face covered by a friend's tulle veil, walked toward them with Gertrude and Josef. As is Jewish custom, Margaret circled George seven times. There are many interpretations of this tradition, but Margaret had always believed that the act symbolized the seven-day process in which God created the world. Already, she thought as she moved slowly around her groom, they had created their own private world—and another human. Now, she thought as she looked up at George through her veil, they were legitimate.

As she took her place under the chuppah, the rabbi led the ceremony. George's best man handed George the wedding bands they had already worn. George trembled as he placed Margaret's gold band on her finger, but belted out his vows. Margaret placed George's ring on his finger, and repeated hers in a loud, clear voice. When it was over, George smashed a wineglass wrapped in a napkin as family and friends shouted, "Mazel tov!"

At the reception, their families and high school friends filed through the buffet line and toasted the couple with wine and cocktails. Everything looked perfect: Margaret in her virginal white dress and white gloves, clutching a bouquet of white roses, with vases full of white chrysanthemums arranged on all the tables. Even the cake her father had baked was white: vanilla inside, with vanilla frosting and white roses on the outside.

Margaret and George Katz after their synagogue
wedding, November 1963

After dinner, the couple danced the hora. George's friends hoisted the couple up on chairs, and they laughed as they bobbed above the crowd, each grasping a corner of a white napkin between them. The ritual symbolizes the difficulties married couples are destined to face, but that they remain bound together. Already, young Margaret and George had weathered so much, but as George carried her across the threshold of their new home, Margaret looked into his eyes and kissed him. She had never felt so much happiness—and so much sadness—at once.

ON THE CHILLY MORNING of November 26, 1963, sixteen days after the Katzes got married, Ephraim and Esther Rosenberg put twenty-three-month-old David in a stroller, and strode from their small Bronx apartment building to the Bronx County Courthouse, where they signed the papers finalizing David's adoption. The couple were thrilled to have their new son, but the mood at the courthouse was somber: it was the day after the heartbreaking televised funeral of John F. Kennedy, and the nation was numb with grief.

But the addition to the family was cause for celebration. When a baby is born, families naturally think of everyone who came before. The sacrifice of David's birth mother crossed Esther's mind. She tried not to think of her—she was his mother now. Still, she sent out a silent prayer of thanks, and held her new son close.

Hours later, Esther called her sister in Israel to tell her the adoption was official. "Mazel tov," Yafa said. Esther held the phone up to David's ear so he could hear the voice of his aunt, half a world away.

On December 16, New York State officials issued a second, amended birth certificate listing the Rosenbergs as David's mother and father. Stephen Erle's original certificate was sealed, visible to only family court officials.

Esther and Ephraim adored their baby son. After the trauma of wartime, after all the years of trying, after all the years of dashed hopes—now they could call themselves parents. All the love they had; all the love they'd willed into starting a family; all the love they'd ever have for the future— finally it had a vessel. Esther was especially delighted to be able to share the joy she took in her faith on Shabbat and holidays.

Just a few blocks from the Rosenbergs, Margaret began to fully set up house, although it was difficult to be excited about their new start. As she watched endless news of the assassination's aftermath, Margaret found herself sobbing—for the country, for the Kennedys, and mostly, perhaps, for herself.

Her mind wandered to Stephen every day, but she discussed her thoughts with no one. She took the subway to her job at the department store headquarters, and George went off to work as a collections man. At night, he continued to take classes at Bronx Community College. Fritz grumbled every chance he could about his son's lost scholarship— and the fact that George rejected his offer to work in the family business. The couple shrugged off his comments.

Thinking that she and George might save some money first before having another child, Margaret halfheartedly scheduled an appointment with Dr. Grunstein. She walked into his office again, this time as Mrs. Katz, and sat down in the waiting room. The same nurse from before called her to the examining room, acting as if she'd never seen her. She ushered her into the doctor's office and pointed to a wooden chair. Margaret sat nervously, her legs shivering inside her nylons, as she waited for him to enter.

When the door opened, Dr. Grunstein smiled widely. He held her chart in his left hand and reached out his right to shake hers. "Why hello, Mrs. Katz," he said loudly. "What can I do for you?"

"I'm here for some . . . birth control," she stammered.

"Of course," he said. "Let's get you fitted for a diaphragm."

Margaret breathed a sigh of relief. No lectures, no shame, no harassment. Then the nurse glanced down at her chart, and led her down the hall to the exam room where she had been with Gertrude. The woman's eyes narrowed, and she pointed to the cotton gown on top of the examining table.

"You know what to do," she muttered.

Margaret felt the old wave of humiliation rush through her, but purposely passed her ringed left hand in front of the nurse's face as she placed her purse on a hook. Would she ever, she wondered, escape shame? She only listened halfheartedly as Dr. Grunstein explained how to insert the diaphragm and cream. She brought it home and tucked it in the drawer of her nightstand. It stayed there, inside its plastic case. She'd gone through the motions to get contraception, but in reality, both she and George wanted another baby as soon as possible.

For many months, Margaret continued to let herself believe it was just a matter of time before she and George could get their son back from the diplomats and that the family they'd already started could begin anew. Had his young brain recorded her face during their two brief visits? What was he eating? How tall was he? Would he by now sleep in a real bed? And mostly: Was he happy? Did the diplomats love him? Sometimes her thoughts were so absorbing she didn't hear the news she was listening to as she made dinner. A few times, she didn't even remember walking home from the subway to her apartment in the late winter slush. She just suddenly found herself in the apartment lobby, her mind far away.

One day, a few months into her new married life, she realized that she had missed a period. She put it in the back of her mind—she had worked so hard to ignore the signs of the first pregnancy, she couldn't really remember how she had felt. But her breasts were heavy again, and one morning she felt so nauseated she could hardly stand the smell of percolating coffee. She waited another month, and then called Dr. Grunstein's office. The secretary scheduled an appointment for six weeks later—it was customary, at the time, to confirm pregnancies only after the biggest danger of miscarriage had passed, at twelve weeks. By mid-spring, Margaret had no doubts, and Dr. Grunstein confirmed her condition. This time, when the couple called their parents with the news, they congratulated them.

Margaret was elated—and terrified. Dark fears popped up when she least expected them: What if something happened to this pregnancy? What if something was wrong with the baby, as punishment for having sex before marriage? She tried to push the thoughts away, singing the same German lullabies she had for Stephen. But this time, she did nothing to conceal her growing belly. She began wearing maternity clothes—tent tops with skirts and leggings with a built-in panel—even while she could still fit into her regular ones, and made a point of cradling her stomach whenever she sat down on the subway.

One late spring day a few weeks after Margaret began wearing her new wardrobe, her boss summoned her to his office. Although her main job was in accounting, from noon to one every day she filled in for the attractive blond receptionist who sat at the front desk. Her boss had specifically selected Margaret as the fill-in, he told her, because she was an equally pretty brunette. For eighteen months, the two women had alternated their lunch shifts, with Margaret answering phones and greeting visitors for an hour every afternoon.

Once in his smoky office, her heart began to pound. "What is it?" she asked. She hadn't been invited to sit.

"Are you pregnant?" he asked, drawing on a cigarette.

"Yes," she said.

"I'm afraid we're going to have to ask you to leave," he said. "We can't have you out front there looking like that."

Then he added, "Or anywhere."

He looked down, and crushed out his cigarette into the half-full ashtray. "You're a married woman expecting a baby," he said. "Pregnant women should be at home." He nodded his head toward the door, motioning for her to leave.

She had expected to stop working in her last trimester. Now she kicked herself for wanting to broadcast her condition.

Angry and demoralized, she filed for unemployment benefits and spent weeks trudging around all five boroughs—once again, trying to conceal her six-month belly. Some potential employers asked her outright, and she couldn't lie. She made follow-up calls after her initial interviews, but no one returned them. In 1964, all this—including getting fired for being pregnant—was legal.

One late June morning as she readied herself for another discouraging day, the radio announcer interrupted his broadcast with a breaking news alert. Three young civil rights activists—James Chaney, a black man from Mississippi, along with Andrew Goodman and Michael Schwerner, two white Jewish men from New York City—had vanished while attempting to register African Americans in Mississippi to vote. Remembering South Carolina, Margaret doubted that their disappearance was an accident. "Oh my God," she said aloud, turning to George as he shaved.

"Margaret," George said, putting his razor down, "all this bad news, all this disappointment—it can't be good for you. Please stop looking for work."

"But we need the money," she said.

"There are only some things we can control," he said. "We'll find a way to make ends meet."

With her job search suspended, she found herself obsessed with the details of what was called the Freedom Summer case, and the search for the activists. It was conducted by the FBI, four hundred US sailors, and state and local authorities. (Some good that would do, she thought.) One night in August, as she sat knitting a yellow baby blanket while watching the evening news, she exclaimed out loud when Walter Cronkite announced the discovery of the men's bullet-ridden, buried bodies. They had been abducted and shot by the police and local members of the Ku Klux Klan.

George stood up and walked over to the television. He spread his arms in front of it as if to shield Margaret from any more loss, and switched the channel to a Harry Belafonte concert.

"Please," he said, in a rare allusion to their lost son, "I just want everything to be OK this time."

SIX WEEKS LATER, on the morning of October 9, 1964, Margaret went into labor for the second time. This time, though, George was with her until orderlies wheeled her into her midtown hospital's maternity ward. He blew her a kiss goodbye as she disappeared behind the swinging double doors with a sign that read "Hospital Personnel Only: No Admittance."

If Margaret thought giving birth was going to be easier for a married woman than it had been for an unmarried one, she was sorely mistaken. Childbirth at midcentury had morphed from a natural process at home into one that had become exceedingly medicalized and obstetrically violent. By 1960, nearly all American women gave birth to their babies in hospitals. And while that development had significantly reduced both maternal and infant mortality, it also introduced a host of interventions. (Some referred to the practices as "knock 'em out, drag 'em out.") Few had little to do with modern science, or the medical well-being of mothers and babies. Margaret's marital status had certainly fueled hospital staff cruelty during Stephen's birth on Staten Island, but harsh treatment, in fact, extended to women in delivery rooms everywhere. Women were shaved, a practice left over from the turn of the century, when some mothers had been infected with pubic lice, and they were given enemas because of the mistaken belief that intestinal bacteria could infect the baby. Their hands and feet were also restrained, since the narcotics that anesthetized women often agitated them so much they sometimes struck out in anger, or writhed so violently they risked falling off the delivery-room table. The drugs were so sedating that women were unable to use their internal muscles to birth their babies and placentas. Obstetricians would make incisions, called episiotomies, at the base of the vagina and delivery-room nurses were instructed to apply "fundal pressure," using their own weight on the top of the abdomen to force the baby out of the birth canal. Doctors routinely used forceps to extract the baby, and later reached into the uterus to remove the afterbirth. They finished the process by suturing the vagina, sometimes adding what they called the "husband's stitch" to return the vagina to its pre-childbirth tightness.

At least this time, the nurses were kind to Margaret. Her labor was proceeding quickly, and a nurse put a cold cloth on her head as she clenched her teeth during the lengthening contractions. Another suggested that it was time for the anesthesiologist, expecting Margaret to follow most women's path, but she had insisted on remaining alert through the entire birth. "It's time for twilight sleep, Mrs. Katz," she announced. Margaret panicked—what if something happened to her baby while she was under?

"No!" she shouted. "I want to be awake!" The nurses looked askance at her. Determined, Margaret decided to keep whatever discomfort she was feeling to herself. "I'm fine," she said, even as the pains intensified. Three hours later, Margaret, awake, gave birth to a healthy daughter. Dr. Grunstein held her up for her to see. "You have a beautiful baby girl," he whispered as the nurses weighed and cleaned her. "Please give her to me," she called out, fear rising in her throat. Dr. Grunstein patted her hand.

"Everything's fine," he reassured her. A nurse handed the baby to her.

As promised, Dr. Grunstein marked on her daughter's birth certificate that Margaret was a first-time mother.

And this time, she was treated like one. All four grandparents, Allen, and George's sister Elaine came to the hospital often. Her room overflowed with giant bouquets of flowers and gifts: pink dresses; a pink blanket with satin trim; pink baby pajamas. In that era, new mothers were urged to rest, not walk, after birth, and Margaret was wheeled to the nursery to go see her daughter as often as she wanted. Nurses brought her baby in so she could breastfeed her, which she insisted on doing even though doctors and food companies had convinced women that the science behind infant formula was nutritionally superior to breast milk (as it turned out, it was not). The only tension was between Margaret and Fritz, who insisted they name the new baby girl after Lizzie's mother, Olga. Margaret refused, instead wanting to honor her own grandmother Elisa. She prevailed, naming her Lisa Jayne.

Margaret was overjoyed, but old memories kept haunting her. Once, she woke in the night fearful that Lisa might have been stolen. She bolted up in bed and buzzed the nurse. "I have to see my baby!" she declared. "I need to see her now!" The nurse assured her that all was well, but Margaret insisted. "Please," she said, "take me to the nursery—now."

Once there, Margaret asked if she could bring her back to the room to breastfeed her. She clutched a sleeping Lisa to her shoulder, her cheek touching her baby's. "I'd be more comfortable," she said sweetly.

"But Mrs. Katz," the nurse said, "you'll wake your roommate. And you need to sleep." Margaret demurred. What if her request would somehow give away her secret?

When it was time for Margaret and Lisa to leave the hospital, five days later, Margaret relished bathing her, diapering her, and slipping her tiny arms and legs into a dress-and-pants set and the yellow sweater and hat she had knitted for her. On a bright fall afternoon, she glanced down at her sleeping infant's face in happy disbelief. She and George stepped into the back seat of a taxi for the ride home. Margaret held Lisa tightly in her arms.

Lizzie and Gertrude waited to greet them in the parking lot of their apartment building, and as they stepped out of the cab, Lizzie excitedly snapped a photo. George held his pink-swaddled newborn in his giant hands and grinned dazzlingly into his mother's lens. Margaret, her makeup applied perfectly, her hair done up in a French twist, stood to his side, smiling ever so warily—and knowingly—at Gertrude.

George and Margaret as they returned from
the hospital after Lisa's 1964 birth

As she nursed Lisa, Margaret marveled at her baby's healthy pink skin, her darkening brown eyes—and at her own second chance. Several times a day, she'd kiss each digit, rub her belly, and coo to her endlessly. When she cried, she picked her up and offered her breast, or held her, stroking her back until she calmed down. Neighborhood mothers warned Margaret that she was "spoiling" her, but Margaret dismissed their admonitions. She loved her daughter, and she also realized that the tiny girl had legitimized her as a mother. She was born eleven months after the Katzes' synagogue wedding—people could count on their fingers if they wanted—and Margaret could hold her head high. She and George had a baby, a one-bedroom apartment, and even a sweet miniature poodle, Suzette. They were a respectable couple, doing just what everyone else was doing.

Still, though, when she readied herself for sleep at night, her mind drifted to the little boy she'd carried and delivered, but barely touched. Sometimes she thought back to the day she signed the papers, dreaming that she could go back in time, and walk out of that building with George and their son. As she boiled carrots and peas to make homemade baby food for Lisa, she wondered what Stephen was eating, and where.

But as Lisa began to crawl, to talk, and eventually to toddle, it began to sink in that their little boy might not return to them anytime soon—or maybe not ever. She'd murmur quiet prayers for his health and safety, but those could only take her worries so far. Occasionally, she screwed up the courage to call Louise Wise to inquire about Stephen's well-being.

All calls, in those days, were listed on paper phone bills, and she didn't want George to know that their son was still so present in her mind. So every few months she'd stop at a phone booth and dial the agency's number.

"My name is Margaret Erle Katz, and I gave birth to a son named Stephen Mark Erle on December 17, 1961," she'd say. "I'm calling to see how he is."

The answer was always the same. "Don't call here," a receptionist would tell her.

Margaret comforted herself with the idea that, in Stephen, she had brought an angel into the world, a child with every opportunity to grow up and accomplish great things. For all her praying, for all her resolve, Margaret was slowly confronting a sad truth—one that she may have suspected all along: Maybe the separation was simply God's will. Maybe it was time to accept it.

When the weather was good, Margaret would tuck Suzette into Lisa's pram and roll them both to Joyce Kilmer Park, outside the Bronx County Courthouse. She'd watch toddlers scamper on the grass—she'd never stopped staring at little boys with black hair—and make small talk with other mothers.

She could not know that she sometimes walked right past the Rosenbergs' apartment—or that Esther Rosenberg took little David to the same green expanse almost every afternoon.

12

Breathing Exercises

Margaret delighted in being a housewife and mother, making recipes she clipped from women's magazines, and baking cookies from her red Betty Crocker cookbook. George loved being a father, and Lisa rushed to the door every night as soon as she heard his key in the lock. On nice weekends, they walked for an hour from their now-crowded apartment in the Bronx—Lisa shared their bedroom, and Suzette had had three puppies—across the Alexander Hamilton Bridge to go visit their parents in Manhattan. One day, Fritz announced that he had pulled strings to find them a spacious two-bedroom apartment near him and Lizzie. No one was more surprised than Margaret that he wanted to have them close by, and in late 1965 they moved in. Their new life seemed like a dream, except for the recurring nightmare Margaret had of Stephen, who called out to her from a staircase in a dark alleyway, screaming that he needed help. Always she'd wake in a panic just as she neared her little boy's desperate voice. She'd sit upright, gasping for breath. "What is it, Margaret?" George would ask, trying to calm her. By this point, it wasn't worth talking about. There was nothing to say, and nothing they could do.

In the spring of 1967, Margaret discovered she was pregnant again. This time, she did not ignore her symptoms. She called Dr. Grunstein to make an appointment as soon as she knew she'd be three months along, and fairly danced out of his office when he once again confirmed what she already knew. Her pregnancy passed uneventfully, but still her mind raced with worries. She'd gotten lucky with Lisa, but what if God decided to rebuke her now? She prayed each night—and whenever the anxiety would arise—for her family's and Stephen's safety. But the nightmares returned, with Stephen calling for help from a frightful, foggy alley. And she still could never reach him.

That summer, she and George rented a modest bungalow in the Queens beach town of Far Rockaway. Like many other city families, they sought seaside refuge from the stifling summer heat, and George commuted from their rental home each morning and night. Alone during the day with Lisa, Margaret would play in the sand, stroll on the boardwalk, and splash in the surf as she chatted with other mothers. Sometimes she approached mothers of dark-haired little boys who looked like they might be Stephen's age. Even though she believed he was in a different country, she couldn't help herself. (What if the diplomat's wife had family in New York, and returned with Stephen for the summer?) She always found a way to insert birth dates into the conversation. "And when was your son born?" she'd ask. She'd make up stories: "My cousin has a son about that age. He was born on December 17." Sometimes she feared she looked to them like she was prying—or just plain nuts.

At night, she watched television reports of tens of thousands of hippies her age who converged on San Francisco for what would come to be known as the Summer of Love. Inspired by the beatnik poet Allen Ginsberg and the Harvard psychologist Timothy Leary, the hippies were drawn to the prospect of communal living, enlightenment through hallucinogens, and casual sex. The idea of free love was a cornerstone of youth culture, and by now, a whole generation of her peers had access to the birth control pill. As she put Lisa to sleep at night, she wondered especially about the young women. Their choices—and lives—were a world away from hers: the high chair on whose tray she put carefully cut-up vegetables and roast chicken; her maternity swimming suit; her evening walks with George. At twenty-three, Margaret Katz was a proper wife and mother.

Some of the young women she spoke to every day were appalled by the images beaming from Haight-Ashbury—men with flowers in their long hair; braless women smoking joints. But to Margaret, their search for meaning merely seemed curious. On the outside, at least, Margaret had everything she wanted. That lifestyle didn't tempt her in the slightest, but she didn't condemn it either.

One evening near the end of summer, Margaret, George, and Lisa took a stroll along the boardwalk. Lisa was toddling between their outstretched hands as they passed the arcade. With its goldfish in tiny bowls, pink and blue teddy bears, shining lights, and loud, tinny music, it beckoned like a casino for children—and the parents who wanted to try their luck for them.

"Daddy!" Lisa cried, looking up at George. "Can we go?" she asked.

"Sure!" George said, scooping her up in his arms. He kissed her neck. "Let's see what we can win!"

Margaret felt a wave of panic rise in her throat as she remembered the time the couple had gone to the same arcade during her weeks of semi-denial at their friend Mark's house. Hearing the carnival workers holler, and seeing the coils of tickets unfurl, she flashed back to the clandestine toaster and blender George won when they were still in high school. She balked now, glancing down at her unhidden, third-time pregnant belly, then at her daughter and husband. Their eyes gleamed with excitement. Maybe she could replace unsettling memories with happy ones like George had. Why couldn't she? She smiled as they passed the fortune-teller and walked into the arcade. Metal balls clanked in pinball machines, and sirens whistled to announce winners. Lisa clapped her hands in delight.

The family stepped up first to a wooden table for a game of Fascination. Time after time, George aimed a rubber ball at the board's tiny slots. He hit them so effortlessly, Margaret's anxiety gave way to pride.

"What do you want, baby girl?" he asked, holding Lisa up, again and again, to look at the offerings. This time, practicality was the last thing on the young couple's mind. Margaret watched as Lisa first chose a giant pink teddy bear. Then she selected a fat yellow tiger. Next, George tried his hand shooting baskets. He won at that, too, and Lisa picked a Betsy Wetsy—a plastic doll with thick synthetic blond hair plugged into her scalp, and heavily lidded, lashed blue eyes that closed when you laid her down. What really drew little girls was the tiny water bottle they could tip into a small hole into the doll's mouth. She would wet the diapers that came along handily in an accompanying diaper bag.

Margaret, exhilarated and exhausted, watched as Lisa delighted at the thought of playing mother.

"What else do you want?" George asked his little daughter, dimples flashing.

"George," Margaret said. "Enough. How are we going to carry all this stuff? Where are we going to put it?"

"We'll find room," he said.

Before the night was over, they tied their winnings—still more stuffed animals, one more doll—to the shiny red tricycle Lisa was at least a year away from riding, and went back to the bungalow.

Six years earlier, Margaret had clumsily perched George's winnings on the pregnant belly she so feared and did not acknowledge. Now she paraded it, her sweet little girl, and her husband's talents, all the way down the boardwalk. They were just normal parents.

BACK IN NEW YORK CITY, Margaret became friendly with a new mother and feminist activist who had just moved upstairs. She'd recently given birth using a new "natural" method named after the French obstetrician Fernand Lamaze, who'd observed Soviet women using breathing exercises to relax themselves during childbirth as an alternative to medical interventions. It became popular in France during the beginning of the

Cold War in the 1950s, and spread to the United States as American feminists began to reclaim the birth process away from the aggressive surgical approach that had become so commonplace.

The neighbor, a first-time mother, delightedly told other young women of her empowering experience. Some of the women scoffed. Who needed instructions for something the body did on its own? one asked. Another dismissed the idea. The doctors knew what they were doing—why not let them do their jobs? But the method had imminent appeal to Margaret, and for her third delivery, she was eager to try it. She asked the neighbor to teach her the techniques, and she practiced them diligently, envisioning a swift, uncomplicated childbirth.

Late in the afternoon on Saturday, October 28, Margaret felt her first labor pains. She felt more than prepared—and capable—as she and George rushed to the hospital once Lizzie arrived to take care of Lisa. In the delivery room, she calmly told the nurses that she had mastered the Lamaze method, and to keep the anesthesiologist at bay. Feminism was budding at that moment in New York City, and an older nurse rolled her eyes at what seemed like a foolish new concept. Margaret's fears—that someone would take her baby; that somehow her secret would be exposed—weren't even subconscious. Despite everything she and George had done to make sure their lives were legitimate, worries nevertheless flooded her. Paradoxically, the joy she felt with this new life also touched off her grief.

A few hours later, Margaret gave birth to a healthy baby boy she and George named Mark Wayne. For his bris on November 5, friends and family members came from as far as Michigan, North Carolina, and Florida, pouring into the Katzes' apartment. Fritz and Lizzie had ordered a huge spread of bagels, expertly sliced lox, capers, tomatoes, and several golden whole whitefish on giant platters. There was bottle after bottle of kosher wine and schnapps. When they added the dessert trays to assorted card tables, they dipped in the center from their weight.

Margaret was thrilled with her two beautiful babies, but the morning of the ceremony, she could not help but recall her mother's harsh words about Stephen's bris on the cold December day six years earlier as they left Lakeview for their apartment. Now Gertrude was beaming—and Margaret, despite her joy, also felt resentment Was she betraying Stephen, she wondered, with these festivities? Just as quickly, she reminded herself, Margaret, you had no choice.

As the ceremony was about to begin, she realized she couldn't watch and led Lisa down the hall to the children's room as she braced herself to hear her baby's cry. Instead, she only heard the crowd erupt into the words "Mazel tov!" Lizzie, smiling, brought Mark to Margaret to nurse. As she put him to her breast, she tried to push away thoughts of Stephen. How was it, she wondered, that a simple piece of paper—her wedding contract—had allowed her to go from being shunned to being celebrated? Nothing else about her had changed.

A few weeks later, she took Mark and Lisa out for a walk, and they both fell asleep in the stroller. She passed a phone booth and ducked inside, watching her babies as she dropped a dime into the coin slot and dialed Louise Wise's number—by now, she'd memorized it. She blurted out that she and George were married, and that their firstborn son now had two siblings.

This time, the receptionist was especially insulting. "He's not your son, and there is no Stephen Mark Erle," she snapped. "Don't call here ever again." Then the line went dead. Margaret, stunned, looked at the smudged gray telephone in her hand. She put it quietly back into its cradle and took her handkerchief out of her purse. She had a story ready in case any of the neighbors saw her crying: she'd tell them she'd gotten something caught in her eye.

Stephen might have other parents now, but it was impossible not to think of him as her son. And as she watched her little boy grow, she couldn't help but compare Mark's photos to the images she had of Stephen, frozen in time as an infant. Was he loved? Did he have siblings? Where was he? she wondered. At night, after everyone was asleep, and before her nightmares interrupted, she envisioned her love reaching out from her heart to his, and hoped it was received.

THE LOVE DID NOT have far to travel: David Rosenberg lived a short bus ride away. He had started kindergarten at a yeshiva near the synagogue where Ephraim's majestic voice drew worshippers from across the borough. He was learning Hebrew in school, and picked up his parents' Yiddish at home. Esther and Ephraim lavished him with love.

Sleep did not come easily to David, and at night he would clutch the light blue blanket with satin trim Esther had wrapped him in as a baby. If he awoke in a panic, as he sometimes did, Esther coaxed him back to sleep with Yiddish lullabies, and indulged him, until he was in kindergarten, with a bottle of warm milk. Ephraim earned a modest salary as a cantor, which was supplemented by Esther's work in the garment industry. In addition to her talents as a hatmaker, Esther was a gifted saleswoman, and worked in clothing stores on the Lower East Side. She could size you up in a single glance and help you choose the most flattering clothing for your figure.

Esther was a slim woman with ivory skin, dark blue eyes, and thick black hair she wore in an elegant bob she styled to one side. She favored tasteful knit suits and dresses she adorned with silk scarves, and loved to cook. She made cabbage rolls and a delicious chicken soup she loaded with carrots and light, airy matzo balls. She was especially skillful as a baker, and early Friday morning in preparation for Shabbat, she baked a flaky strudel and a yeasty golden challah so beautiful, hardly anyone wanted to break them apart at sundown. But it wasn't only her culinary skills that drew friends and admirers. Her childhood friends in Bucharest used to say that Esther's temperament was so sweet, her skin was coated with honey. She, too, had lost family in the Holocaust—a brother was killed trying to leave Romania for Israel—but she liked to dwell on the present, not the past.

Ephraim, a reserved man with a broad, friendly face, a dimpled chin, and thinning black hair, had a strong handshake and a giant heart. Above all, he was modest, despite his proficiency in English, Hungarian, Hebrew, Romanian, Russian, and Yiddish, and prodigious talents as a scholar. In some ways, he discovered them by accident. At the beginning of the war, he had been expelled from the Romanian army because he was Jewish. He was left jobless, rootless, and scared as the war raged. His parents had been deported to Auschwitz. Ephraim, heartbroken, looked to his faith for solace. When he channeled his grief into song, the young man's voice not only stood out: it was so sublime, the rabbi who first overheard it thought it was the voice of a famous singer on the radio. He offered him a job on the spot. Ephraim quickly mastered the liturgical music. He never discussed his loss—his parents and two brothers were eventually killed by the Nazis—but when he sang, his voice was so full of emotion it gave his congregation goose bumps. His connection with the divine had the same effect on him: during the High Holidays, it was not uncommon to see the great *hazzan* with tears streaming down his face.

With Esther at work in Manhattan, it was Ephraim who walked from the synagogue to pick up David after school, and the two had developed a ritual of their own. After a snack and sweet tea or juice, Ephraim tutored his son in all aspects of Jewish learning, from the Torah to the ancient melodies of their faith. He also taught him to play the piano. Davidel, as Esther called him, was growing tall, and was a diligent student with a quick wit. His musical talent was striking, even as a little boy. He, too, had a voice that rose above the crowd, and like Ephraim, had the gift of perfect pitch. He was physically hearty, with an equally strong temperament. He was eager to please his parents, and they were just as eager to please him. The family of three settled into a cozy routine.

Ephraim and Esther told David early on about his adoption. When he was little, they told him that his mother wasn't able to care for him, and that God had planned for them to find each other. David accepted this as fact, and the family rarely discussed it. People in their Orthodox universe didn't much talk about David's adoption. But occasionally, friends would marvel about the miracle of it all: this esteemed couple had surely rescued the little boy from uncertain circumstances. But the reality felt quite different to Esther and Ephraim. They felt like their little boy—so full of hope and promise—had rescued them.

Sometimes strangers pointed out that while David had dark hair like his parents, his skin tone was darker. "Is he yours?" a woman once asked on the subway. Esther held her son near and didn't deign to answer. In their traditional community, birth control was discouraged—children were a gift from God, and each was to be welcomed. Adoption, despite its prevalence, was rare in Orthodox circles, and occasionally, women she knew told her she was "wonderful," and that David was "lucky." Esther usually smiled, and said nothing.

But one time, an acquaintance volunteered that her sister "had had to adopt."

"It's brave," she told Esther.

"Brave?" Esther asked, irritably. "I'm his mother."

"You know what I mean," the woman went on. "Adopting a stranger's child."

"Brave?" Esther asked again, incredulous. "Brave to love?" She said nothing more to the woman. She didn't have to.

THE SUMMER OF 1967, Esther traveled with David, as she did every year, to see Yafa's family in Israel. They arrived in the heady months after the Six-Day War, in which the Jewish state had defeated its Arab foes in a stunning military victory. Esther tucked David's blue blanket into his suitcase. He needed it. Who did it hurt?

Yafa, seven years Esther's junior, had had her first child, Shlomo, at eighteen. Young Shlomo, then just barely twenty, had served as a paratrooper in the army, and little David looked up to him. Just as David woke up one morning in Yafa's apartment, Mirage fighter jets were streaking across the sky. Frightened, he came to the table with his blue blanket. Esther stirred anxiously in her seat. She looked at her sister, her strapping nephew, and her son.

Yafa, standing at her sink, poured milk into a small glass and put it on the table in front of David. "Davidel," she said. "You're a big boy now."

And then, tousling his hair, she said: "It's time to throw away that blanket. It's for babies." She stood at his side, her hand outstretched. David clutched the blanket tightly, wadding it up under the table. Yafa reached her hand closer. Then she asked: "Don't you want to be big and strong, like an Israeli boy?"

David's face grew solemn. He looked at his mother, his aunt, and his grown-up cousin. He looked at the blanket, and then his lap, and then into his aunt's big blue eyes.

"Won't you give me the blanket?" Yafa asked again, wriggling her fingers playfully.

David's face turned solemn. He handed her his blanket, and she threw it in the trash.

THE NEXT YEAR, Ephraim was offered a job at a larger synagogue in Toronto. He was approached during the bleak, restless weeks after the assassinations of Martin Luther King Jr. and Robert F. Kennedy. Riots had erupted nationwide, including in nearby Harlem. New York was obsessed with its own frightening murders, and Esther, like much of the city, was on edge. In early July, several high-profile homicides, including the gunning down of three men in the Bronx, and the shooting deaths of a twenty-four-year-old woman and an eighty-year-old man by a Bulgarian neo-Nazi, had the city spooked. Had they survived the war in Europe, Esther wondered, only to fear they could again be hunted in a city full of Jews?

The decision to move was easy. While Esther was close to the Herstics, her cousins in New York, Toronto seemed a better place—less cramped, more civilized—to raise young David. Precociously intelligent, he had also

shot up half a head taller than his classmates, and was extremely rambunc-
tious. His cousins sometimes called him a *vontz*, Yiddish for "troublemaker."
One Sunday, the two families met at Fort Tryon Park in Upper Manhattan,
the same hilly park where Margaret and George had come in high school to
make out. Something caught David's eye—a butterfly? a bird?—and for a
second, he wandered off. The Rosenbergs and the Herstics had been deep
in conversation, and for a split second, no one had been watching him. Suddenly Esther sprang to her feet. David was nowhere in sight. The park was
full of other families who had come to enjoy a peaceful afternoon.

The adults launched a panicked search with the two Herstic boys,
Mitch and Bryan, each branching off in different directions. Esther
stayed put in case David wandered back. When they finally found him,
Esther told her cousins she didn't know whether to kiss him, punish him,
or both. They suggested that the boy needed a good *"patsch* in the *tu-
chis"*—a good spanking—but Esther and Ephraim could never quite
bring themselves to do such a thing. They cherished him too much to
ever bring him pain.

On the rare occasions they discussed David's adoption, they had always explained that they had found each other. "I may not have carried
you, but God chose you for us," Esther told him. Other friends had been
born; he had been chosen. What was it about him that made his birth
mother *not* choose him? David kept the question to himself.

Their small apartment in the Bronx was cramped, and Esther knew
her son needed an outlet for his boundless energy. Sometimes he acted
out in ways she and Ephraim didn't understand. She didn't feel safe letting him play kickball or baseball with other little boys in the area, and
Toronto seemed to offer more opportunity—and structure.

THE NEIGHBORHOOD IN TORONTO near the new synagogue had many
advantages over the one in New York. It had more shops, restaurants,
and businesses, as well as a large park. Esther would be able to find a

job close enough to walk to work. That way, both she and Ephraim
could keep an eye on David.

They enrolled him in the Eitz Chaim yeshiva, which Ephraim had
chosen. He knew David would receive a rigorous Jewish education and
would learn both *Yirat HaShem* and *Ahavat HaShem*—to fear God and
to love God. David became instantly popular with a close-knit group of
boys with whom he openly discussed his adoption. He retained his impishness, and was highly competitive. Before morning services, the teachers served the boys from trays of pink popcorn, soda pop, and doughnuts,
and he wolfed down the sugary treats.

On bike rides after school to the nearby Viewmount Park, he popped
more, and higher, wheelies—and got closer to the towering maples—
than any other boy. He beat everyone at the new game, Ants in the
Pants. David also told his buddies that he could withstand extreme pain.
He dared them to pull his thick black hair as hard as they could—he
claimed to have no nerve endings in his scalp.

Esther, David, and Ephraim Rosenberg in Toronto in the late 1960s

Not long after arriving in Toronto, he discovered the most Canadian of pastimes: hockey. The aggressive game was foreign to the Rosenbergs, but for that matter, so was North America. David took to it instantly. He was gifted on the ice, and his quick reflexes made him a natural goalie. He excelled at other sports, too, and was such a good athlete, everybody always wanted David—whom classmates had nicknamed Rosy to distinguish him from the many other Davids in his school—on their teams. He was smart and fun to be around. He also had a temper: In sixth grade, David and some friends spent two days building a snow fort during their lunch recess. On the third day, some boys from an older class came to destroy the fort. David picked up a piece of wood and began hitting the ringleader so hard, he broke several of his ribs. Eitz Chaim officials suspended him for a week. Esther and Ephraim, at a loss over how to help him, sent him to a psychiatrist. They had sessions for six months, and worked on ways for David to manage his anger.

ACROSS THE BORDER, David's brother, Mark Katz, seemed to possess the same uncontainable energy and curiosity. Mark was a happy-go-lucky child like Lisa, but Mark's vigor sometimes exhausted Margaret—despite the ample help she had from Lizzie, Gertrude, and Josef. Still, she felt fulfilled, seeking to become the mother she wished she'd had. She raised her children with love, patience, and encouragement, not the seething rage she had endured. To everyone else, she and George had the perfect family, a girl and a boy spaced three ideal years apart. If people only knew, she thought, when strangers commented that she could "quit." In fact, she wanted an even larger family.

Their friends, mainly ones they'd had since high school, were also the children of German-speaking refugees. Many were like-minded progressives who had grown up attending the Stern Summer Camp, set in New York's Shawangunk Mountains. George had been a counselor at the barebones facility, and once Margaret had gone to visit. It wasn't much to look at. It had a swimming pool with a slimy bottom, and a bare, weedy baseball diamond. But it had a magical hold on its alumni, in part because it offered a break from the twin threads of their lives: their parents' unspoken tragedies, and the pressure they put on their children to achieve. To those who had lost so many forebears in the war, campers became extended family.

When it closed in 1965, plans among its alumni to buy and recreate the place as an American-style kibbutz became an obsession. At a meeting one evening in the Katzes' home, their friends discussed plans to all get out of the city and start a loose sort of commune of their own. They could build a large social hall and a school, and they'd help share chores—cooking, gardening, cleaning, child-rearing duties. Margaret, her hands full with two babies, embraced the idea, but George, who was more socially conservative, wanted no part of it.

So she began to focus on what she could do in New York. Her early years of motherhood coincided with difficult ones for the country, and their brief time in Dillon had underscored the urgency of the civil rights struggle. The political assassinations had left Margaret in a state of stunned apprehension, but her conscience would not let her rest alone in the apartment. She put Mark in a pram, let Lisa stand on its platform in back, and joined girlfriends from her apartment building in peace marches, weekend after weekend.

Partly, she was moved by her own sense of outrage and hopelessness. Partly, she was moved by her twenty-four-year-old sense of righteousness, as she and friends of all backgrounds helped one another drag their strollers down subway stairs to meet in Central Park. She saw the hippies, heard the loud Beatles music, and smelled the marijuana smoke wafting from apartment buildings. Something was changing, she felt— and not just in America. She felt something shift in her too.

As THE CHILDREN GREW, the family started to feel crowded in their two-bedroom apartment, and they had now saved enough to make a down payment on a house in the suburbs. Like Esther and Ephraim, Margaret and George wanted space and quiet. They looked in New Jersey, at first in close-in towns that were too expensive, and finally in the southern part of the state outside Princeton. One of George's colleagues had moved to a small town created on socialist principles in 1937 to help resettle Jewish garment workers on farmland as part of Franklin D. Roosevelt's New Deal. Surrounded by acres of cornfields, dotted with red barns and silos, the new town was a world away from New York City.

The town, renamed Roosevelt after FDR's death, did not retain its status as a federally funded utopia for long. But newspaper ads touting its fresh air, good schools, and easy commute into Manhattan continued to draw a trickle of Jewish New Yorkers into the 1960s and '70s. Margaret and George were among them, and in August 1972, they moved into a modern bi-level house on a street called Farm Lane with four bedrooms and giant windows overlooking a thick grove of maples, elms, and oaks. George went to work in the city every day, and Margaret busied herself with adjusting to suburban life.

The years passed, and Margaret immersed herself in Roosevelt's fabric. She volunteered to be class mother, again and again, pitching in at the library and chaperoning field trips. She helped make costumes for Purim and Halloween. She carpooled. She made sure the kids got their shots.

Some of their friends smoked pot, and there were also rumors of spouse-swapping. Margaret felt as opposed to this sort of experimentation as George had about moving to a commune. But who was she to judge? It was none of her business what other people did, and when gossip bubbled up, she changed the subject.

She thought the town was idyllic. To some extent, it was. Nobody even bothered to lock their cars or doors.

A FEW YEARS AFTER they had settled, she conceived again. So many women on her street were pregnant at the same time, her local obstetrician joked that it should be renamed "Fertility Lane." She had an uneventful pregnancy, and during labor, she again used the Lamaze techniques, breathing through each contraction. By then, the feminist movement had made many gains in childbirth, and Margaret was surprised to see a delivery-room table that lacked restraints and let her sit upright. "Are you sure you don't want any pain relief, Mrs. Katz?" a nurse asked her, without judgment. Margaret declined. Soon after, a beautiful daughter they named Cheri Rose arrived. Margaret and George knew their family was now complete—or at least as much as it could be.

Their lives were busy, and full. One of them was always serving on the board of the synagogue, or the school board, or both. George coached the children in all their favorite sports, from softball to Little League and soccer. He also had season tickets to see his beloved Rangers. Sometimes Margaret left the kids with neighbors to join him for weekday games, and occasionally they'd drive into the city to see a play. Their parents came to watch the children; their siblings came to visit. Fritz and Lizzie had even moved to New Jersey to be closer to them and George's sister Elaine.

As their four parents aged, it was Margaret who saw to their well-being. She cooked, cleaned, and drove them to doctors' appointments, often shuttling from softball games in southern New Jersey to her parents' hospitals in Manhattan. Fritz was diagnosed with prostate cancer; Lizzie, with breast cancer. Gertrude's breast cancer returned.

Concerned about the illness that laced through the family tree, Margaret called Louise Wise to inform social workers after every worrisome diagnosis. She was now the one who monitored the phone bill, so she wasn't afraid of calling anymore. Writing seemed far riskier: someone from the agency might send a letter back to the house, and her secret at Roosevelt's tiny local post office would be unmasked.

In the mid-1970s, she started with Fritz's news, then Lizzie's news, then Gertrude's. Careful always to call when no one else was in the house, she'd report, spitting out the words quickly: "This is Margaret

Erle Katz, and I gave birth to a son named Stephen Mark Erle on December 17, 1961. I don't want to interfere with his life, but please let my son's family know that his grandfather has prostate cancer."

And then: "Please tell my son's family that his paternal grandmother has breast cancer."

And again: "Please inform the family of my son, Stephen Mark Erle, born December 17, 1961, that his maternal grandmother's breast cancer has returned."

Then George, only in his late thirties, began to suffer from a series of health problems too. He had put on weight over the years, and he began to complain of a sore knee. It was red and inflamed, and ached almost constantly. His doctor drained fluid from it a few times, only for the swelling to recur. Finally, he was diagnosed with gout, a painful and complex form of arthritis that can be hereditary. Because many of his relatives had perished in the Holocaust, no one knew if it ran in the family. But Margaret called anyway.

"Please tell the family of Stephen Mark Erle that his biological father has gout."

A few years later, George began coughing almost nonstop. He'd been an athlete with strong lungs his whole life and had never smoked. But he was wheezing and short of breath no matter what he did, and his lymph nodes were swollen. Doctors were skeptical that it could be cancer but checked his lungs with an endoscopic camera called a bronchoscope. It showed nothing, but the condition worsened. He'd always been full of energy, but suddenly was drained.

After several months of coughing around the clock, he was admitted to the hospital for a biopsy. Doctors found inflammatory cells called granulomas, signs of an autoimmune disorder called sarcoidosis. The condition could be a reaction to a substance—unlikely, since George worked in a clean office—or hereditary.

Again, Margaret called Louise Wise. "Please tell my son's family that his father has an autoimmune disease called sarcoidosis."

Not long after, George was diagnosed with diabetes. She called Louise Wise the very next day.

Always, the social worker on the other end said: "I'll be sure to put this in his file." But no one ever notified David or Esther Rosenberg of any of Margaret's medical updates.

When Gertrude's breast cancer spread, and Josef's emphysema worsened, Margaret insisted that they move into the Katzes' spacious ground floor so she could better look after them.

Margaret always knew to buy more groceries, and make more food, than for just the seven people who lived in her house. The Katz home was so inviting, neighborhood children were always pulling up extra chairs at the dinner table and staying for sleepovers. Sometimes they arrived late at night after they'd had fights with their parents.

The woman once deemed unfit to be a mother had become one, in fact, for everybody.

ALTHOUGH MARGARET HAD BEEN interested in government since she was a girl, her political activities in Roosevelt were limited to local boards. She and George had a traditional marriage, and Margaret was responsible for almost all of the domestic chores. That was their agreement, and despite her flirtation with the commune idea, she and George respected each other's roles. But privately she began to question the ways in which women were treated unfairly in the larger world. She watched Gloria Steinem, Betty Friedan, Eleanor Smeal, and others appeal on national television for the ratification of the Equal Rights Amendment, and recalled her unceremonious firing for the offense of being pregnant. She listened intently as they, and so many others, pressed the case for far-reaching changes in the status of women. The feminist movement demanded equality under the law and rights to reproductive freedom. As the issue of abortion—once only a word to be whispered—became front-page news, Margaret followed with interest. While she considered pregnancies a gift from God, she believed that women should have the right to make the decision to end them. And in 1973, as the Supreme Court legalized abortion nationwide, she paused to think of how that would shift the futures of girls who were in trouble.

Despite all her responsibilities, Margaret still thought daily about Stephen. She continued to be plagued by fears about his welfare. What, God forbid, if he were on the street? She had no one except George with whom to discuss her feelings, but her husband, loving as he was, was practical: Look ahead, not back, he told her. Sometimes, though, she wondered if his compulsion to gobble down boxes of day-old doughnuts he bought at the bakery outlet was driven by a sadness he never spoke about. His unspoken belief, Margaret understood, was this: What good does it do to discuss what we can't change? Their lost son only ever hovered above their conversations when they'd make occasional trips to the horse track, or sometimes drive down the shore to Atlantic City. When George asked Margaret which horses she wanted to bet on, she'd always give the same answer: one and seven, for Stephen's birthday. When he'd ask her what she wanted for a lucky number at the craps table, she'd answer seventeen. On the rare occasion when that number won, she took it as a sign that Stephen, somewhere, was all right.

On the morning of Stephen's thirteenth birthday, Margaret awoke with a heavy heart. Would he be called to the Torah for his bar mitzvah that coming Saturday, to be counted, in Jewish tradition, as one responsible for upholding the commandments? she wondered. Would he be surrounded by his family? Had Hebrew school been easy for him?

She checked the portion of the Torah he'd be called to read that day, if her hunch was correct. The Torah portion, or parashah, which is read week by week in synagogue, would be Vayigash. It includes the story of Joseph's brothers, struck by famine in the land of Canaan, as they travel to Egypt for provisions. There they meet Joseph, whom they had sold into slavery years before. Joseph, now a powerful man, recognizes his brothers, but does not identify himself. Eventually the brothers show remorse for their earlier behavior. Joseph reveals who he is, and forgives his brothers for selling him into slavery. Joseph saves his family from starvation, and they rejoice in being together.

IN FACT, David Rosenberg had been studying that very passage of the Bible for months. And on the morning of December 21, 1974, three thousand congregants and guests gathered in Toronto at Beth Sholom, the elegant synagogue where Ephraim was cantor. David, nearly as tall as Esther, wore a white tuxedo with a black velvet lapel and a large black bow tie; Ephraim wore a black tuxedo with a large black bow tie to match his son's. Esther wore a stylish floor-length yellow brocade dress and a matching jacket. They smiled as they flanked their son, radiating joy. The Herstics came from New York for the day.

David, skillfully trained by Ephraim, had a celestial voice of his own. He was called to read the Torah with his Hebrew name, David Aryeh ben Ephraim—David, son of Ephraim. As he sang the words from Genesis in the ancient melodies, the women in the family opened their purses for their handkerchiefs to dab their eyes. David, triumphant, sang like a young master and smiled as he finished the parashah. He then chanted his haftarah, a separate passage of stories with its own set of melodies. When he was finished, the congregation shouted, "Mazel tov." He looked up at his father and beamed. Ephraim, standing next to him, put one hand on David's yarmulke so as not to knock it off, and kissed his son's cheek.

Bar mitzvahs, in deeply patriarchal Orthodox Judaism, are charged with tribalism.

A boy reads the Torah chanted by his ancestors for generations, hoping to please his elders and impress the community with the precision required of the honor; a parent wants to take pride. These were roles into which David, Ephraim, and Esther naturally stepped. The joyousness of the occasion is often a moment for comparing a child to his elders. This is what happened too.

In the months leading up to David's bar mitzvah, he shot up in both height and attitude. David often came to the synagogue after school so his father could guide him through the prayers the younger Rosenberg would have to lead on the day of his bar mitzvah. Ephraim, who had a remarkable dry wit, used both humor and firmness as he worked with his son, both in chanting and in the lessons of the Torah. Mostly David accepted his father's advice. (As he worked on memorizing the portion, he belted it out at school so often, the other boys learned it too.) He revered Ephraim so much, he often played a recording of Ephraim's voice for his friends. But sometimes when David was frustrated, he lashed out. "You're not my real father," he would mutter to Ephraim. "I don't know whose son I am."

No amount of Ephraim's reassurance could shake the thought. David may have had a beautiful voice like his father, but he didn't act like him, or Esther. And he didn't look like them. He got so tan in the summertime, people asked him if he was Italian. What if he was? And why did Esther and Ephraim's history have to be his history? At yeshiva, David saw all the boys who looked like their fathers and mothers, had their blue eyes, their lanky builds, their curly hair.

David's fleeting curiosity about his appearance was not unusual among adolescent adoptees, who commonly notice the likenesses that run in biological families. These observations can underscore their sense of loneliness. The psychologist Erik Erikson said that adolescents' essential task is to develop a sense of identity. They rebel against, but also look to, their chief role models, their parents, as they ask questions about who they'll become. Among adoptees who lack access to their personal history, this process is complicated by the knowledge that no matter how they are loved, wanted, and wished for, they understand that a crucial part of themselves is lost. This can become a source of identity confusion, and some researchers say it results in shame, feelings of abandonment, embarrassment, and low self-esteem.

Perhaps sensing this, well-meaning friends would occasionally point out that David and Ephraim shared a cleft chin. Sometimes David smiled politely; occasionally, this small similarity made him feel good. But sometimes he acted as if he hadn't heard the comment. It was no more meaningful than the fact that they both had dark hair.

At the ceremonial lunch, or kiddush, after his bar mitzvah, women kissed him, and men shook his hand. "The apple doesn't fall far," one man said, unaware of David's past. "That voice!" Yafa was especially proud. "Now you are a man," she told David. This message is often delivered to boys from their elders on their bar mitzvahs, the day they metaphorically cross into manhood. In Judaism, to be a bar mitzvah (or bat mitzvah) is to have reached the age at which a person is held accountable for his or her actions.

But this mantle is not one thirteen-year-old boys are always ready to bear. And in any case, the evening of his bar mitzvah, David was acting like a kid. Friends and relatives poured into the Rosenbergs' apartment on the twentieth story of their Toronto building, where there was a table loaded with meats, salads, fish, and sweets. There were several loaves of challah, and bottles of kosher wine. With the adults in the living room, David summoned his cousins and friends to his bedroom at the back of the apartment, which overlooked a parking lot. He was the darling of the day, the star of his family. But maybe something wasn't sitting right with him that evening. Or maybe he was just being a *vontz*. "Watch this," he told the gathered cousins and friends. Then he picked up a hockey puck from his desk and held it in his large palm. He opened the window and hurled the puck outside into the freezing air.

It was the Saturday before Christmas. Shoppers were scurrying inside the building with gifts, and revelers were entering for parties. The youngsters gasped as they watched the puck descend, gain momentum, hit the icy ground, and then rebound back up. "That could have killed someone, or smashed a car," one boy said. The puck bounced a few more times, and finally scuttled to a stop.

The day, and the incident, braided the disparate strands of David's young life. He was flourishing in his Jewish education, guided by Esther and Ephraim's nurture, knowledge, and patience. But he had his own nature too: a remarkable voice, quick, deep passions, a powerful athleticism. And as he forged his own sense of himself, sometimes those forces seemed at war. The intense physical demands of hockey gave him an outlet for his energy. He had found another channel for it, too, in organizing a successful local production of Andrew Lloyd Webber's *Joseph and the Amazing Technicolor Dreamcoat*. His skills on the ice and on stage made him even more popular at school and in his youth group.

Increasingly, he began to challenge the authority of his parents, of his teachers, and of rules in general. If he didn't agree with yeshiva instructors, he'd shout, "That's just wrong." When their backs were turned, sometimes he shot rubber bands in their direction. During breaks, he made uncanny impressions of their old-country accents. One day, the principal caught David flouting the ban on classroom snacking and ordered him to stay home for the rest of the week. "I want to run the school for a change," he declared.

David had his reasons for acting out. Toronto may have been more peaceful than New York, but the school, and the insular Orthodox community it served, had its challenges. Some teachers took to humiliating the boys, threatening that they'd never amount to anything if they didn't memorize the whole Mishnah, Judaism's authoritative oral law. One railed against the dangers of secular life, reserving special warnings for the dangers posed by universities. The math teacher erupted in rages at a moment's notice, throwing pencil sharpeners at kids' heads. And another teacher was later arrested on a child sex-abuse charge, to which he pleaded guilty.

At the time, though, the boys kept these abuses to themselves. They certainly didn't mention them to their parents, many of whom, like Esther and Ephraim, had endured enough for several lifetimes. The children of parents who've survived severe trauma often trivialize their own problems, imagining that their elders' experiences outweigh any of their own distress. And besides, how could David complain? Esther and Ephraim told him he was their golden boy, their chosen one. He loved them fiercely in return, and felt protective. How could he disappoint them?

But stress—maybe from school, maybe from his own ordinary adolescent angst—had begun to gnaw at him. He started to put on weight. Esther made lower-calorie foods, but David would just eat more of them. When David's friends congregated at the Rosenberg apartment for Esther's baked goods on Shabbat, Esther worried aloud—in front of him and his friends—about how to make him thinner. "Maybe a little less, Davidel," she'd say whenever he reached for seconds. He responded to her, but out of earshot he'd shrug off her comments and refill his plate. "I'm adopted," he'd tell his friends, as if it was an explanation.

Once or twice when he was a young teen, he asked questions about his birth mother. It seemed only natural: Judaism, after all, devotes great attention to creation stories. The Torah teaches that God created everything: light and dark, the heavens and the earth, Adam and Eve, all of nature, the Sabbath. The faith's greatest prophet, Moses, begins life escaping a death threat on Hebrew babies when his mother places him in a basket and floats him down the Nile. He is plucked from the reeds by Pharaoh's daughter, who adopts him as her son. And Judaism says its structure—the Ten Commandments—was written by God's finger on tablets of stone. Why wouldn't a boy be curious about his origins? But he also knew his mother was fiercely protective, and knew this was a sensitive topic. He was hesitant to broach the issue. How had he come into being, and why had his mother given him up?

Adoptees often show curiosity about their conception during adolescence, when their own sexuality is igniting. Just as commonly, adoptive parents can interpret such interest as a sign that they have failed in their role as parents, as if it might indicate that their child doesn't love them. This can fuel a difficult cycle: The adopted child's insecurity reinforces the mother's anxiety, and an anguished internal dialogue can bubble below the actual questions. The mother wonders, What more could I have done to make my child love me? Wasn't I good enough? Meanwhile, the adopted child thinks, Who was I before I was yours?

Esther told him what she knew, repeating what his documents had said: That his mother and father cared for him, but that keeping him would have interfered with their education. They came from kosher homes and wanted the best for him, caring enough for his Jewish future to ask that he be circumcised, Esther said. Whether it was in the papers, or whether it was added, Esther also told him that his birth parents wanted him reared in an Orthodox home. Surely this was comforting information to a boy in a religious household—and besides, Esther and Ephraim cherished David with all their hearts.

But the message communicated a dozen years earlier by Louise Wise—intimating that Margaret had a scientific future (maybe as a doctor!), perhaps meant to elevate David's pedigree—also conveyed to David that he had been an inconvenience. Because they often know hardly anything about the circumstances of their births, adoptees feel rejected by their biological families. Sometimes they feel sadness; sometimes they feel anger; sometimes, despite the great love around them, they feel inferior. What was so wrong with me when I was born? Many are afraid of being abandoned again. The Rosenbergs showered David with praise and love. After Esther answered his questions—it was clear they had made her uncomfortable—he said very little to his parents about the topic again.

When he acted out, Esther was loath to chastise him. This is common among adoptive parents: many who have unresolved feelings about infertility may unconsciously fear losing the child's love—or the child leaving them for his biological parents. Still, when she complained about his mouthiness or his physical outbursts to Yafa, Yafa said she should have been enforcing more discipline all along. She, too, said that David deserved a good spanking. Now it was too late, Esther told Yafa. David was so big and athletic, she said, if she struck him, she'd break her hand on his backside.

13.

Agency

While Margaret and George did not speak openly about their lost baby, others during the politically vibrant 1970s were beginning to challenge adoption's secrecy. Many adopted people and their birth mothers had begun to discuss out loud, in public, the issue of closed files and adoptee rights, and to reform the laws that kept mothers and their sons and daughters apart—especially in New York.

The highest-profile group, the Adoptees' Liberty Movement Association, or ALMA, viewed the access to original birth certificates as a fundamental civil and human right. Founded in New York in 1971, ALMA was led by Florence Fisher, an adopted woman who helped develop a registry that both adopted people and birth parents could sign into, indicating they wanted to find their mother or child—regardless of who had signed what papers when. If both parties registered with the organization, ALMA volunteers could help reunite them.

Florence had had a difficult upbringing with her adoptive parents in Brooklyn. Florence was fine-boned and small of stature, and her sturdy Russian Jewish parents, Rose and Harry Ladden, made her sleep in a crib until she was ten years old. She was a willful child, making up for her size with exuberance as a singer and dancer. Her vivacious, talkative nature annoyed her grandmother so much, she referred to her as the *momser*, Yiddish for "bastard." Florence could always sense that she wasn't like her strict, taciturn parents. She didn't look like them, and she didn't

talk like them. They didn't like the same things. The differences were impossible to miss—and she began to think they were linked to a big secret.

When she was seven, Rose asked Florence to find her a handkerchief, and Florence dutifully went to her mother's dresser. In a drawer
tucked beneath stockings and ironed handkerchiefs, Fisher noticed a
formal-looking document, a photostat. She withdrew it and read it with
puzzlement. It was an adoption certificate that listed her parents' names,
and the name of the girl they'd adopted, Anna Fisher.

When Florence returned to the kitchen with her mother's handkerchief, she asked her about it. At first her mother said the paper belonged
to someone else in the family, and when Florence questioned her further, her mother slapped her. Later, Rose burned the certificate. But the
name on it, Anna Fisher, had been seared into Florence's consciousness.

This was in the middle of the Depression, and formal adoption was
still uncommon, so she didn't know what to make of it all. From time to
time, Florence wondered about the paper, and if it could explain her
parents' abusive, erratic behavior toward her. Her mother vacillated between emotional distance and hysterical possessiveness, threatening
suicide whenever Florence made new playmates. "You love your friends
more than you love your mother!" she'd scream, locking herself in the
bathroom with a razor until Florence promised never to love anyone
else. Her father was physically violent, beating the tiny girl with a belt
for the slightest infraction. From the time she first found the document,
she couldn't stop thinking about its mysterious provenance and dramatic disappearance, especially since her parents had made it clear that
the subject was taboo.

At the end of her life, Rose had electroconvulsive therapy, which regulated her moods for the first time. For a brief period before her death in
1950, she and Florence developed a warm relationship. Florence was
bereft: at twenty-one, she had finally gained a mother, only to lose her.
When relatives began dividing Rose's jewelry, she felt more alone than
ever. No one advocated for Florence, her own daughter, in the negotia-

tions, and Florence realized that Rose's kin never accepted her as family. Florence confronted a cousin about the document she'd seen as a child, and she confessed the truth. Florence had been adopted as a baby.

Then a wife and mother, Florence began a twenty-year search to find her true identity, just as the postwar adoptions were in full swing. Public opinion about adoption, and the rights of adopted people to know their origins, had hewed toward complete secrecy. But Florence longed to know—*had* to know—more about her origins. So after Rose's death, she wrote to New York City for a copy of her birth certificate. Not letting on that she knew she was adopted, she used the name Anna Fisher in the correspondence. To her surprise, the ruse worked, and the clerk sent it. It listed her birth date and parents' names, Florence Cohen and Frederick Fisher.

She pursued all leads to find them. She combed through phone books. She pored over birth and death records. She spoke to lawyers and funeral directors. She charmed rabbis, judges, and court clerks— almost all of whom rebuffed her, and told her that she should never have received her original birth certificate in the first place. She also found the doctor who delivered her. At first, he told Fisher her own original identity was none of her business.

"This isn't any concern of yours," he said. He was ruthless when she pressed ahead with questions. "Can't you understand, you're illegitimate." But Florence refused to be turned away, demanding details. Finally, he acknowledged that both her adoptive and birth mothers had been his patients—one who sought his help for infertility, the other for prenatal care. He had organized the adoption himself in a "gray-market deal."

Eventually, Florence located her birth mother. She called Florence Cohen, pretending to be a distant relative, and the two arranged to meet. Although Florence Fisher had the documents to prove that Florence Cohen was her biological mother, Cohen initially denied it. Finally, she admitted that she was, but said that such a discovery would destroy the relationships she had with her husband and two other children. The two Florences had an awkward relationship; Cohen spoke by phone with Fisher only when no one else was around.

Florence Fisher learned that her mother had become pregnant as a teenager by a young sweetheart, and quickly married. The older Florence's mother objected to the union, and threatened to send her to juvenile hall if she didn't surrender the child for adoption and annul the marriage as soon as she delivered the baby. Like Margaret Erle, she had also been a minor. In addition, the doctor who brokered the adoption—the same one who told Florence Fisher her own identity was none of her business—had made sexual advances toward her. Terrified of him, and of her fearsome mother, she relinquished her baby daughter to the doctor, and the young couple parted ways forever.

Soon afterward, Florence found her father, Frederick Fisher, by then a stuntman in Los Angeles. A muscular man with blue-gray eyes just like her own son, he welcomed her instantly, and with great joy. At their first meeting, he introduced Florence to everyone in the Hollywood restaurant as his daughter. Trying to make up for lost time, he took his middle-aged daughter on a trip to Disneyland.

Florence published a groundbreaking memoir in 1973, *The Search for Anna Fisher*. It made waves nationwide. Fisher, an attractive woman with bright brown eyes, impeccable style, and a bouffant of red hair, appeared on talk shows throughout the country, in popular magazines, and in major newspapers. She challenged the fundamental orthodoxy of adoption, which held that married parents could offer a better life than unmarried ones, by openly discussing her difficult, abusive childhood. She said repeatedly that adopted people should not be made to feel like "ingrates" for wanting to know their biological identities. Working with lawyers and legislators, she helped draft a bill to open New York's records. She placed ads in New York newspapers about her new organization, listing the group's name and post office box.

She faced the emotionally charged subject head-on: society still saw adoption as a benevolent gesture for which adoptees should feel unquestioning appreciation, she said—and this wasn't always the case. While everyone has a history and kin, Florence said, adoptees are asked to forget about them, living a contrived identity in a contrived reality. Every adoptee, she insisted, has the right to pursue the truth of his own life.

While Fisher received plenty of hate mail, she also helped start a national revolution. Virtually overnight, ALMA mushroomed to thousands of members, attracting mostly female adoptees and birth mothers. The grassroots group compiled a registry of mothers, fathers, sons, and daughter who were looking for one another. Eventually it spread to other states. Members were relentless in lobbying their legislators. In New York, the group filed a class action lawsuit that challenged the constitutionality of the closed adoption records. It argued that knowing one's original identity was a constitutional right.

Fisher was piercingly clear in her aims: Adult adoptees should demand open access to their original birth certificates and to the records of their adoptions. The legal strategy of the case emphasized the rights of adopted people to due process and equal protection under the law, and used moving testimony by adopted people that focused on the legacy of adoption secrecy, the stigma of illegitimacy, and the long-term emotional trauma brought about by the inability of adoptees to discover their original identities. Birth mothers, likewise, spoke about the weight of their loss, and the trauma of not knowing what had happened to their children. The lawsuit was dismissed, but Fisher, other advocates, and their attorney were undeterred.

Among the lawsuit's main opponents were large adoption agencies and many adoptive parents, who claimed that any search for original birth certificates was an invasion of privacy for both adoptees and birth parents. One organization called the Adoptive Parents Committee quickly grew to a thousand members. It claimed that happy adoptees would have their lives disrupted if they were contacted by their birth parents without warning, and that birth parents, likewise, would resent being reminded of their painful pasts.

But Fisher had come to believe that the happiness of an adoptive home was beside the point: adoptees, she argued, deserved to know their origins if they wanted. Objections to her argument were often hostile, and opponents were frequently cruel. Some adoptive parents called Fisher and other ALMA members "neurotic and maladjusted."

Several other voices gave momentum to the emerging adoption-rights movement of the late 1970s as well. New York adoptee Betty Jean Lifton published two memoirs that examined the emotional impact of adoption in *Twice Born: Memoirs of an Adopted Daughter* and *Lost and Found: The Adoption Experience*. In Southern California, a trio of mental health professionals who had worked in the adoption field published a seminal book that also examined the aftereffects of closed birth records. In *The Adoption Triangle*, Arthur Sorosky, a psychiatrist, and Annette Baran and Reuben Pannor, both social workers, advocated for changes in adoption practice. And Jean Paton, a Michigan-born adoptee and social worker who had first written about the adoption experience in the 1950s, argued that the tendency for society to consider adult adoptees as children obscured and diminished their lifelong struggle for identity. Together, adoption-rights advocates founded the American Adoption Congress in 1978 as a national organization committed to adoption reform. At its first conference a year later, Paton, reclaiming the word so often levied at her and other adoptees, distributed buttons that read "Bastards Are Beautiful."

Birth mothers also began to demand change. In Massachusetts in the mid-1970s, Lee Campbell, who'd surrendered a son as a young woman, had attended some adoptee-support meetings and believed women like her needed their own platform. In 1976 she founded a group called Concerned United Birthparents. The organization helped popularize the term "birth parents" as a replacement for "natural mother" and "natural father," or the longstanding "real" mother and father. Campbell and other birth mothers appeared on the daytime talk show hosted by Phil Donahue, who occasionally featured tearful reunions between birth mothers and their long-lost sons and daughters. The episodes, listed in newspapers and previewed in television commercials, attracted record audiences. In 1979 journalist Lorraine Dusky wrote the memoir *Birthmark*. It detailed the wrenching surrender of her daughter, conceived during an affair with a married colleague, in 1966, and Dusky's wish to reunite with her. Its publication landed her in newspapers and magazines, and on national television shows. Birth mothers and adoptees championed her, but many adoptive parents attacked her. "You're our worse nightmare," one told her.

It wasn't just the shame that was dissolving. The fortified legal walls shielding secret adoptions were beginning to crumble too.

ONE MORNING IN THE LATE 1970s, while Margaret was taking Gertrude to the doctor—she was always taking someone to the doctor—she picked up a weathered copy of *People* magazine in the waiting room and thumbed through the pages. She saw a headline that made her heart beat fast: "An Adopted Woman Who Finally Found Her Real Parents Helps Others Search for Theirs," and she felt her face flush. She was so afraid someone might see her reading it that she hid the issue inside another magazine.

The story, in a question-and-answer format, described Florence Fisher's story, and the fears many adopted people have of being considered ungrateful. Margaret was stunned, and her mind raced with possibilities. What if the teenage Stephen wondered about her? As she read on, one question, and Fisher's answer, stuck with her: "Do most natural parents want to be found?"

Yes, Fisher replied—in all the six hundred cases she'd helped with in the four years since ALMA's founding, only three women wished not to be found—and one was her own mother. "I've watched hundreds of families reunite, and nearly all are hysterical with joy. They're desperate to be found."

Margaret scanned the other questions, but kept returning to that response. She almost couldn't believe her eyes: there was an organization for people just like her and Stephen, and its headquarters was in New York City.

She snapped the magazine shut as Gertrude's name was called. She felt so lightheaded when she stood up to go with her to the examining room, she thought she might faint.

For a few days after she read the article, she thought constantly of Florence Fisher—and of Stephen. Could she actually find him now?

She considered checking out Fisher's book from a library in a nearby town, but quickly dismissed the idea. It had a distinctive yellow cover. She could certainly conceal it inside a different book jacket, but if she checked it out, what would the librarian think? What if someone she knew saw her? Or someone in her family found it?

And then she banished the idea of searching for her son. He was still a minor, and she didn't want to disturb him. The people at Louise Wise had seen to it that he went to a couple who were superior to her and George. Sometimes she grew angry that the system had broken apart the family she and George had made to create a new one, but always, she shifted her thinking. He has a better life, Margaret, she told herself. It was God's will.

That summer, just as the summers before, she would think of Stephen as she watched her children play on the deep green grass of her backyard in Roosevelt. Sometimes she envisioned her firstborn there, playing catch with his little brother. Throwing a football back and forth with George. Playing hide-and-seek with Lisa.

She would feel tears well, or dread surge, and stop herself. First, she'd try the exercise she'd learned years before on the boardwalk with George and Lisa when her mind rushed back to her hidden pregnancy, and she'd try to plant herself in the present: in her nice kitchen, in a happy marriage with beautiful, healthy children. Then she'd say a prayer of thanks, and ask God to look after her phantom son. She'd direct her mind to his happy life with his sophisticated parents who had introduced him to countries, to languages, and to ideas from around the globe. This, she willed herself to think of, over and over.

And yet, despite all the years that had passed, despite the respectability she'd gained as Margaret Katz, despite the decorum with which she lived her life, she remembered the malicious nurses in the hospital. The hissing on the Staten Island bus. She thought of the sad glances of the Lakeview girls who had understood, long before she had accepted it, what was about to befall them.

And then she'd hear the judgments, and the warnings, the threats, the insults.

"You *Hure*."

"You're just a teenager. What have you got to offer him?"

"You're damaged goods."

"Don't let anyone know your name."

"We can put you in juvenile hall."

"With that one still?"

And then she'd think of a nearby couple who had adopted three children from a New Jersey agency. Sometimes, fleetingly, she wondered about their birth mothers. But just as expertly as she did when she thought about Stephen, she'd tell herself: Those kids are happy! They have had good lives. Their parents were doting. Those kids were well-adjusted; they were good students. Adoption worked out just fine. Didn't it?

It was obvious to Margaret that her neighbors loved their sons and daughter, and didn't need a biological connection to cherish them. Margaret recoiled when she heard what one woman said to her neighbor when she was pushing her two boys in a stroller: "You treat them just like your own, don't you?"

"They *are* my children," Margaret's neighbor replied icily.

Surely, Stephen had a mother who loved him just as much as her neighbor loved her kids, and she tried to put it out of her mind. Besides, she had so many demands on her. All the parents were getting sicker. The kids got strep throat. Ear infections. They had concerts and baseball games; plays and softball practice. There were PTA meetings, synagogue meetings. The yard needed landscaping.

Margaret was a dutiful housewife in the country who made her fried chicken from scratch—no Shake 'n Bake for her. She pounded her veal cutlets for the schnitzel George loved. She made chocolate chocolate-chip cake and fudge marble cookies. She browned George's rice the way Lizzie always had. Even what passed as junk food was homemade: when the kids wanted French fries, she peeled her own potatoes and fried them herself. The older two had Hebrew school. Lisa took art classes. Mark had Little League. The days were full.

But Margaret, like others in Roosevelt, embraced progressive ideas. After Cheri was born, Margaret became involved in the local La Leche League, the support group for mothers who nursed. She knew that breastfeeding was a protectant from the breast cancer that ran through her family tree, and she had nursed each child for a year even though formula had been more in fashion for those who could afford it. One day, she saw a notice for donations of excess breast milk for nearby preemies whose mothers weren't yet producing enough. Margaret called to offer hers, and health workers came to pick it up. When they did, her mind turned to the days in the hospital when she tucked her lactation suppressants into the side of her cheek. After Stephen, Margaret took agency over her body, giving birth to and breastfeeding her infants exactly as she'd wished. Now her nurturing could extend even to babies she'd never lay eyes on.

Margaret took command as a mother, raising her children with guidance, gentle boundaries, and acceptance. She set rules: the children helped with chores and had regular bedtimes, but she was also patient, trying never to raise her voice. And while she had a traditional female role in her household, she taught the kids to believe men and women were equal. In fact, when Cheri wanted to play softball, there weren't enough girls in the small town to comprise a team. Margaret and George saw to it that she joined the boys' baseball team.

The only thing Margaret couldn't take control of was her shame.

As much as Margaret sought to ignore the topic of adoption, it continued to bubble to the surface. One day, during a quiet moment, she picked up a newspaper and saw a headline that read "Parents Want Proposal Defeated." The article addressed the concerns of adoptive parents, who were trying to block the passage of a bill to allow New Jersey adoptees access to their original birth certificates. In the brief piece, a woman who represented the group Concerned Adoptive Parents said such a bill represented an "intrusion into the sanctity of the home and personal lives," and was a "betrayal" that would benefit no one.

How, exactly, was the legislation a "betrayal"? Margaret wondered. She certainly wouldn't feel that way if Stephen found her and got in touch. Didn't Stephen have the right to learn more about himself? And didn't she have the right to learn what had happened to him, her own flesh and blood?

Focus, Margaret, she told herself. Focus. Look at your beautiful family. She envisioned Stephen at the Louvre; at the Colosseum; praying at Jerusalem's Western Wall—and above all, with the loving parents who were raising him. She turned the page.

When Gertrude died of metastatic cancer in 1978—Margaret cared for her till the end—she felt a complex range of emotions: sadness, guilt, and a feeling that a weight had lifted. The secret remained, but with Gertrude gone, the force of its hurt had begun to diminish ever so slightly. After the funeral and shiva, Margaret turned her attention to Josef. Ill with emphysema, he fell into a deep depression. When he wasn't silent, he'd have angry outbursts. "Let me die," he'd say when doctors tried to drain his lungs. As she often did, Margaret winced with remorse as she remembered how she'd shamed her parents with the pregnancy. Was it somehow, after all these years, worsening his anguish? She tried to put her invisible son out of her mind.

But one day in early 1980, she looked down at the classifieds section of a New York newspaper that was sitting on the kitchen countertop. She saw a notice for an ALMA meeting the following week at a large Protestant church in midtown Manhattan. She took it as a sign that she couldn't wait to find Stephen a moment longer.

On the appointed evening, after an early dinner, she told George she had to attend a school meeting in another town. "It will go very late," she told him. She dressed in her best slacks and jacket, raced in her wood-paneled station wagon to a parking lot at Princeton Junction, and took a train into the city. She took the subway uptown, exiting a few blocks from the church. She anxiously glanced to see if anyone she knew was behind her as she double-checked the address, and scanned the street again as she stepped gingerly up the steps of the red sandstone church. She walked upstairs to the second floor, where she heard voices floating from the social hall. A woman in the doorway noticed her standing there.

"You're here for the ALMA meeting?" she asked. Margaret nodded, too shy to speak.

"Come on in," the woman said.

More than a dozen people stood near a table in the meeting room, drinking coffee and eating cocktail nuts. Most of them were women. Margaret, anxious, glanced around the room. She didn't recognize a single face, but she sat on a metal folding chair in the back just in case.

Then a woman about Margaret's age stood up before a lectern. "Can everyone hear me?" she asked in a clear, calm voice. She wore overalls and had creamy, pale skin and thick chestnut hair in a braid that dangled over one shoulder. When she smiled, deep dimples punctured both cheeks. She introduced herself as Pam Hasegawa.

She was born, she said, in New York City in 1943, the year before Margaret, and adopted at birth by a Manhattan couple. She was their only child. She had never touched a blood relative until she delivered her firstborn, Sergei, a boy she and her Japanese-born husband named after the composer Rachmaninoff.

She spoke about the profound need for adoptees to have access to their original birth certificates, and how state laws in all but Kansas and Alaska prevented them from doing so. She spoke kindly about her gentle adoptive father, but did not shy away from her lonely childhood, and the difficulties she'd had with her late mother. Her mother had been mentally ill, and was often institutionalized during severe mood swings in which she lost touch with reality. Pam was candid: when her adoptive mother died when she was twelve, she felt a burden fade.

At the same time, though, her relief seemed to fuel even more frequent fantasies about finding her birth mother. Pam said she envisioned her as a kind, steady presence who liked classical music as much as she did.

Her mission, and ALMA's—Pam was also helping to lead legislative efforts in New Jersey—was to learn the most basic of truths: who she was, and where she came from. She smiled sadly as she ended her brief talk. "I know many of you will understand me when I say this much: whenever I see people with dimples, or wavy brown hair that's the same color as mine, it's really hard not to stare," she said. "You always wonder: Are you my mother? My sister? My brother? My father?"

By then, Margaret was rapt. She hadn't spoken a word about her missing son in years. She'd spent seventeen years looking for him in crowds, wondering if boys with dimpled chins might be him, then reminding herself that it couldn't possibly be him—Stephen, after all, lived abroad. Margaret had been riveted by Florence Fisher's story, but she'd wanted to believe her rocky childhood had been the exception. Adoptees were supposed to have better lives. Better parents. A new start.

Now she was hearing about the experience of another adoptee, in person, whose experiences echoed both Fisher's and her own. Did Stephen think she had rejected him, or was a "bad girl"? What if he was angry at her and never wanted to meet her? Worse, what if he was sick? Or, like Pam, felt unloved? As Pam's words sank in, Margaret tried not to cry. Maybe Stephen missed her, too, and was looking for her. Maybe he had questions about his heritage. What if his adoptive parents were dead, and he had nobody?

Pam—a lost daughter—had kept her composure, so Margaret—a lost mother—resolved that she could too. Margaret, of course, had met many other pregnant girls at Lakeview. But the national scope of adoption had never dawned on her. Pam's passionate discourse spelled it out: What had happened to mothers like Margaret and to the children from whom they were separated was a profound, cruel wrong with corrupt roots. Together, they could help set things right.

As Margaret listened, she began to understand, for the first time, the enormity of what she had endured. Pam, who had become a close friend of Florence Fisher's, described the experience as a massive injustice. It wasn't just Margaret, George, and Stephen who suffered from the silence, secrecy, and judgments surrounding adoption, it was in fact millions of others. Hasegawa, citing figures widely circulating at the time, said that in 1980 there were more than 5 million living adoptees. And despite the claims of adoption workers, adopted people were not tabula rasa, and adoption was not a discrete event: it affected everyone involved, for generations. According to Pam, few people in the United States could claim that adoption didn't touch them. By adding birth and adoptive parents, plus siblings, half siblings, and eight grandparents, she said, adoptee-rights advocates estimated that approximately a third of Americans had a link to adoption in their direct immediate families.

After the talk, Margaret mustered the courage to introduce herself and ask what she could do to find Stephen. She had no desire to register with ALMA; what would postal workers think if they saw a letter from the organization? Worse, what if the kids found it? Pam suggested they sit down, and as they faced each other at a plastic folding table, Pam explained the steps Margaret could take to search for her son. Luckily, Pam said, Stephen had been born in New York City. Pam explained that in New York City, the birth of every child is recorded in an index with a number that also appears on his birth certificate; at the time, the indexes were stored in giant ledgers at the main branch of the New York Public Library.

For New York City adoptees, the same number issued on the city index appeared on four records: in the index with their birth names, on their original birth certificates, in the birth index with the adoptive name, and on the amended birth certificate. Pam told Margaret to search through the ledgers to find Stephen's number in the birth index. It would appear with Stephen's name, his birth date, and a code noting that he had been born on Staten Island. Once Margaret found Stephen's index number, Pam explained, she could use it to match him with his adoptive name.

Margaret left the meeting feeling almost giddy. Now she had a map.

But every time she thought of making the trip to the library, some urgent matter arose. Josef was increasingly ill, and with three small children, it seemed too risky to sneak into Manhattan for the day.

Then, in April of 1981, Josef died.

She loved her father, but as she cleared out his clothes after the shiva, she also realized that now she had more freedom than ever to begin her search. The children were all in school, and while the tasks of cooking, cleaning, and carpooling were almost entirely hers, she finally had time to herself. After nearly two decades, her yearning to find her son had only intensified. She could go into New York City without having to worry or explain herself—at least not too much.

One day in late spring, she planned her trip with great care. She told

George she needed to buy some sheets on sale at Macy's near Herald Square, and made a show out of clipping some coupons from the local newspaper. Once George left for work, and the children for school, she dressed in a skirt and blouse, packed herself a turkey sandwich, and drove to the station. She got off the bus at Port Authority, striding past the very same gate where she caught the bus to elope. Nearly eighteen years had passed since that moment, and Margaret took it as a sign. In Judaism, eighteen is the symbol for the letter *Chai*, and the number and its multiples are symbols of luck.

She walked the three long blocks east to the majestic library, past the marble lions and up the worn steps to the entrance. She knew the place well, of course—she had also come to the library to study bus schedules and the state rules for marriage. Now she was coming to try to find her son.

The librarian in charge of the birth indexes demanded her driver's license. Margaret sensed that the man knew why she was searching the records, and her heart fluttered at what she felt was a disapproving glance. She made sure to display her left, wedding-ringed hand when reaching for the first giant brown ledger of 1961 births. The man issued a warning, already posted in several places. "No purses, no bags, no pens, pencils, or paper allowed," he bellowed.

She almost didn't know where to start. Pam had explained that the births were listed alphabetically by surname, but when Margaret took down the first ledger of surnames from *A* to *K* to find Erle, she was so overcome by nerves she couldn't focus. She returned the ledger, her search yielding nothing. She checked her watch every few minutes, terrified she'd be late to pick up the linens, terrified she'd miss the bus back to Roosevelt. Terrified someone would find her out.

Finally, she left empty-handed—and dejected. She rushed eight blocks south to Macy's and bought the first set of sheets she put her hands on.

On her return to Roosevelt, she caught sight of her reflection in the window. She was about to turn thirty-six. Her hair was long and wavy. Her eyelashes were long, her almond eyes were rimmed with liner, and her face still looked youthful. Or did it? In the bright afternoon light, she noticed the faintest of crow's-feet and a small crease between her eyebrows.

A few weeks later, Margaret told George she had to visit a sick friend in Manhattan. She got off the bus, raced toward the library, and confidently asked for the ledger containing the *E*'s. This time, she found the listing immediately. It was proof of her son's birth—and her as his mother—in black and white. As Pam had promised, Stephen's name, the date and location of his arrival, and the last four digits of his city birth record number were all there. When she saw the listing—she committed the numbers to memory—her heart leapt. Now all she had to do was find the matching number in the index next to his adoptive name.

SHE DEVISED NEW EXCUSES to go into the city. George didn't ask questions, and by now, her trips to the library were almost routine. Margaret was on a mission as she returned to the room of ledgers. She had Stephen's birth date and the four-digit ending as clues, but had little else to go on as she sought the index entry of his new name. The indexes were arranged alphabetically by year, and Margaret assumed that Stephen had been adopted shortly after she had signed the surrender papers in May of 1962. Hour after hour, trip after exhausting trip, she combed through seven months of 1962 ledgers looking for the numeric match that would reveal her son's adoptive name.

She tried to push away haunting thoughts, remembering those months after Stephen's birth when she lived at the YWCA, so desperate to get him back. She thought of the weeks she'd spent in this very building, scouring bus routes in her naive belief that eloping would keep her new family together. She thought of the tiny images of Stephen as a somber three-month-old, and of his giggling the last time she saw him. What did he look like now? Surely he was in college: Did he live at home with his parents and commute to school, or did he live on a campus? What did he like to eat? Did he like sports, like his father and Mark? Was he artistic, like Lisa? Did he like Billy Joel? Did he like show tunes and jazz, like her? Did he have a knack for singing and performing, like Cheri? Already the little girl had a powerful voice that belied her small body. With perfect pitch, she'd already begun singing complex lyrics into a toy microphone.

One day, not long after Thanksgiving, Margaret stepped out of the bus terminal, greeted by canned Christmas music, bright lights, and Santas ringing Salvation Army bells. It was cold and rainy, and she wore galoshes and a rain bonnet to cover her hair. She had been searching for six months, combing through hundreds of columns for the matching digits, with her eye especially on common Jewish surnames. She raked through names from Ackerman to Cohen, from Franken to Mossberg, from Pasternak to Wasserman.

When she was down to the letters between *W* and Z, she gave herself a pep talk. Maybe he'd been adopted by some Weissmans. Or someone whose last name started with Z. But when her eyes finally made it through the Zwerdlings, she wanted to cry. All those books, all those names: Had she missed one? Could she have? Should she start again? And then she told herself no. She had been so careful. She had used an index card to guide her descent through each page so she wouldn't skip a line, so her eyes wouldn't play tricks if she was tired. She'd read each 1962 book twice, scanning for the four-digit match that would give her her son's new name. It never dawned on her that the adoption had happened nearly two years after he was born. His name would not be anywhere she was looking.

On that dreary day, when she got up to return the final ledger to the librarian, she felt some hope flee. Maybe he'd been adopted in Israel. Or Italy. Maybe it just wasn't meant to be.

She stifled tears as she shuffled back through the crowds to Port Authority, and forced herself to think about what she did have: a husband and three children she cherished. She climbed aboard the bus feeling despondent. But then something strange happened: she got angry—an emotion she hadn't felt, not really, since the days in the hospital when she demanded to see her son. She thought of Florence Fisher and the failed legislation. She thought of Pam, and the crowd of others at the church. She thought of the futility of her search at the library. Why was this so hard? And wasn't there something more she could do?

Margaret did what she usually did with her mind and hands, and made herself busy. Hanukkah was approaching, so that evening on her way home from the station, she stopped at the store to buy the potatoes and onions she would make into pancakes and freeze for the first night of the holiday later that month. She was quiet that night as she made dinner; she was quiet as she helped the kids with their homework. George watched hockey on television, and after she kissed Lisa, Mark, and Cheri good night, she retreated to her bathroom and drew herself a hot bath. She poured in a cup of Epsom salts and stepped in as the water lapped around her, muffling her sobs.

She woke up the next morning, made breakfast for everyone, and set about grating the vegetables and frying the latkes. She made stack after stack—enough for her family, enough for the neighbor kids, and enough to give her time to think as the smell of the oniony oil permeated her kitchen. Instead of focusing on her first, fruitless search, she thought of a new way to find Stephen. Her mind was a jumble. She knew this much: her son would be twenty in a few weeks, a legal adult in New York. The Twenty-Sixth Amendment, passed in 1971 during the Vietnam War, had lowered the minimum voting age to eighteen in all states; in New York it had become the age of majority for both men and women. What was stopping her from going directly to Louise Wise? After her dozens of calls about the family's medical issues, certainly they had a decent file on him; maybe they even knew where he was. She pushed aside her memories of the time she'd been there, arriving through the hidden entrance and then waiting, pregnant and terrified, as Gertrude and a social worker plotted her and her baby's future. But now she was someone different: Mrs. Margaret Katz. She would enter through the front steps and leave her contact information. Now the staff would treat her with respect. Surely, she believed, they would help her. Things were different now: a woman had just been appointed to the Supreme Court.

She dialed Louise Wise's number; she hadn't forgotten it from the clandestine calls from phone booths. This time, she made up a name and a story about how she and her husband were interested in adopting a child. She wanted to come in, she said, and needed to know their office hours. For the first time ever, the woman who answered the phone at Louise Wise Services was kind.

"Nine to five, Mrs. Meyer," she told Margaret.

"Thank you very much," Margaret responded.

"We hope to be seeing you soon, Mrs. Meyer," the receptionist said. "Please call to schedule an appointment when you are ready."

As she wrapped the latkes in tinfoil, she glanced at her kitchen calendar. She would visit the agency's elegant brownstone on East Ninety-Fourth Street on December 18, a Friday, twenty years and a day after she'd given birth to Stephen. He was a grown man now, and had the right to know his origins if he wished—to know she'd never stopped thinking about him. Never stopped wondering. Never stopped loving him. Maybe he would even want to meet. She'd seen tearful reunions of mothers who'd lost their children to adoption on television. Maybe, she thought, Stephen would want the same. She imagined embracing him; she imagined George embracing him; she imagined all four siblings embracing one another. Who would he most look like?

The morning of her journey, she announced to George nonchalantly that she had to buy Hanukkah gifts for the holiday's start two days later. He didn't flinch. If he suspected anything—and she believed he didn't— he never let on.

On that morning, a Friday, she saw everyone off and took a few bites of toast. She put on her best pantsuit and her long winter coat, and pulled on her brown leather gloves. It was cold, and she drove herself to the station with a single-minded purpose.

She brought a book to read on the forty-five-minute bus ride to Manhattan, but she was so excited, she couldn't concentrate. She tried praying. She tried breathing exercises. Her mind raced—what if there was a note from Stephen already waiting for her? The ride seemed to take forever, and Margaret checked her watch every few minutes as the bus chugged north in pre-Christmas traffic on the New Jersey Turnpike.

Finally, it pulled into Port Authority. Margaret pushed her way through the midmorning holiday crowds to the ladies' room. As she touched up her hair and freshened her makeup, she decided to splurge on a taxi. She looked pretty. Respectable. Ready to be received at Louise Wise.

When she stepped into the cab, her heart still fluttering, she again tried to visualize getting some brief news of her son. Maybe there'd be word about his wonderful childhood. She felt the same surge of hope she had felt as a teenager when the social workers reassured her about his bris. In her head, she practiced what she was going to tell the receptionist, making sure the words came out evenly.

As the cab traveled uptown and then across the park festooned with Christmas lights, Margaret again tried to calm her ragged breathing. When the driver inched toward the brownstone on East Ninety-Fourth Street, she felt buoyed with confidence. She hoped she'd return triumphantly to George that night with wonderful news of their son's whereabouts. Her mind flashed briefly to Florence Fisher's recalcitrant mother, so fearful of what her second family might think. Such worries could not have been further from Margaret's mind. Everybody who had been ashamed of her was dead. If the neighbors made a fuss, tough—they'd have to cope. Lisa, Mark, and Cheri would adore their big brother.

She'd even read some more recent stories about ALMA. There were lots of people out there looking for their parents. Surely her Jewish son, adopted by Jewish parents through a Jewish agency founded by the wife of one of America's most prominent rabbis, wanted to find her too. Despite how Gertrude and Fritz had acted, she reasoned, Jews, as a people, cared about family, above all else. Didn't they?

She looked up at the elegant building and the gleaming Palladian window she'd only glimpsed from the inside, walked up the front steps, and rang the buzzer with her gloved index finger. She heard a click and pushed open the door to the vestibule. She closed the heavy outside door behind her, stepped onto the black-and-white-tile floor, and pressed another bell.

"May I help you?" said a woman's voice.

"My name is Margaret Erle Katz," she said, making sure to keep her tone measured. "I'm here to leave contact information for my son. I gave birth to him on December 17, 1961."

There was no response. Margaret touched the buzzer again.

"Yes?" the same voice asked.

"His father and I are married, and he has three siblings. I've called many times with medical information." She paused. "I don't want to interfere with his life, but I'd like to leave my number and address for him," Margaret said.

There was no response.

Through the vestibule's glass panels, Margaret could see a woman in an office at the end of the hallway. The woman did not look up at her. Margaret rang the buzzer again.

She could hear a click, but this time, no voice. Margaret continued: "I'd like to leave contact information for our son, so that if he ever looks, he'll know how to find us. Can I please come talk to someone, so I can leave him our number?"

Her assurance began to flee; her indignation, to rise. All the years she'd called in secret; all those years fearing someone would expose her. All the years she'd wanted to write but didn't, afraid a return letter would reveal her secret.

She rang the bell a fourth time, aware, as she stood in the drafty space on marble tiles, just how cold it was outside. "Hello?" Margaret said again. "May I please come in?"

There was a pause. This time, the woman's voice was threatening, not aloof. "You'd better leave, or we'll call the police. You're trespassing."

It took a moment for the words to sink in. Then Margaret felt her knees buckle, and she crumpled to the floor. Curled into a fetal position, at first she was mute. When a cry finally emerged, it seemed disembodied, hanging in the air as if it had come from far away. Then she began to sob. Panic, rage, fear, and shame sprang from such a deep well, all she could do to gather her emotions was cross her arms and rock herself from side to side, as if trying to mother herself. Was Stephen dead, and they weren't telling her? Had he died of illness as a child? In a horrible accident as a teenager? Was that the reason she'd had those nightmares?

The voice called to her again. "If you don't leave now, we'll call the police."

Margaret forced herself to stand up and go.

As she turned to face the door, she shuddered uncontrollably. It was near-freezing outdoors. Her limbs were cold, but her body, under layers of clothing, began to perspire profusely. As resolved as she'd been as a teenager to claim her son as her own, this time, she felt the optimism she'd maintained for two decades drain through the soles of her black pumps.

As the family lit the candles on the last night of Hanukkah, the children played dreidel and opened small gifts. George and the children ate the gold-covered chocolate coins they'd piled up on the table, and as Margaret watched the nine little colored candles flicker in the hanukkiah before finally burning out, she knew the chances of ever meeting her son again were just as extinguished.

෴

FOR THE NEXT SEVERAL YEARS, Margaret resigned herself simply to praying for Stephen's well-being. When Lisa, and then Cheri, grew and began to date, the first question she asked about their boyfriends was not what they were like, or how they'd met. Instead, she interrogated her daughters about questions they found odd: "Where was he born? What do his parents do? When is his birthday?"

Life went on. The family took cruises to Bermuda, Mexico, and the Caribbean. They visited Key West and Walt Disney World.

They redid the kitchen wallpaper and added a bedroom. They celebrated birthdays and anniversaries, and they installed an in-ground pool.

Perhaps most telling of all, when George was diagnosed with a brain tumor, Margaret did not call Louise Wise Services.

14.

"You Are a Man"

In Toronto, David was maturing into a teenager who was equal parts hockey player, loyal Jewish son, and rascal. He was also developing a new passion: politics. In 1976, when he entered a new high school, a yeshiva called Or Chaim based on the principles of religious Zionism, he ran a friend's campaign for student government. He also horsed around. When the other boys chanted liturgical music during afternoon prayer service, David and his friend the political aspirant would belt out the lyrics to "Hotel California."

More and more, he and Esther clashed. David put on more weight; Esther, trying to fuel her son with homemade love, doubled down on preparing healthy food. She made borscht; she made eggplant salad; she made meatballs. Still, he filled up on doughnuts and Cokes after school. She responded with a concern that bordered on overpowering. "Davidel," she'd say, "why the junk food? You have stuffed cabbage!"

"It's none of your business what I eat!" he'd shout.

When she'd bring up his homework, or reports she'd heard of defiant behavior, he'd put his hand out like a policeman stopping traffic. "Teachers at Or Chaim!" he'd explode. "So what!" More than once, he stood to his full six-foot-two height and looked down at Esther. "What do I care? What do you care? I'm not even your son."

And his doubts about Judaism had bloomed from private thoughts to public acts. He started eating non-kosher food when he was on his own, and when he left his predominantly Jewish neighborhood, he put his kippah in his backpack—who needed the anti-Semitic comments it invited? Most pointedly, he wondered aloud about a God who could have allowed the Holocaust to happen.

When Esther, exasperated, fretted to Yafa about his teenage behavior, Yafa reminded her sister that David was not the first teenage boy to argue with his mother. Whenever Esther mentioned gentle approaches to smooth out her son's defiance, Yafa always had the same prescription: "That boy," she'd say, "needs the army."

David thought about the Israeli army, too, but not for the same reasons Yafa did. He had begun to take a keen interest in world news, and he followed developments in Israel especially closely. He'd read Ephraim's newspapers in the morning at breakfast, and again when he came home after school. Increasingly, he had begun to look up to Yafa's sons. For the Rosenbergs and their families (and millions of American Jews), support for Israel was both a belated response to the Nazis and an answer to age-old Jewish questions about identity in the Diaspora. For David, the battlefield bravery of his older cousins, both paratroopers, had made a deep impression. He loved his trips to the Jewish state and, after his bar mitzvah, had been excited to join his father in prayer at the Western Wall. And he was especially proud of his relatives there. He admired the boldness of the country, and of Israelis themselves. They—and it—represented another way of being Jewish: tough and self-confident. Theirs was a redefined narrative of determined might, and David liked it.

But David also deeply respected his elegant old-world father, a consummate gentleman who never spoke about his own accomplishments. At one point when David was in his father's study, he noticed a certificate of *semicha*, a record of Ephraim's ordination as a rabbi. (Rabbis function primarily as teachers, community leaders, and authorities on Jewish practice, while cantors focus on singing and prayer.) The *semicha* wasn't framed; it wasn't displayed. It was just on Ephraim's desk. David picked it up and studied it. "Why haven't you ever mentioned you were a rabbi?" he asked.

"Does it make me a better Jew?" Ephraim asked his son.

David at the Western Wall in Jerusalem, 1970s

NOT LONG AFTER DAVID entered high school, Ephraim's health took a sudden downturn. He didn't want to worry Esther by complaining about his chest pains; he knew she'd needle him to quit his lifelong cigarette habit, so he tried to conceal his shortness of breath. But secrets and

Esther were a terrible mix, and Ephraim's didn't last long. Soon it was obvious anyway: Ephraim's face grew pale, and it was increasingly difficult for him to sing. His doctor in Toronto diagnosed blocked arteries and said he needed an operation to repair them. The news was frightening—open-heart surgery was new, and risky, at the time, and Esther and Ephraim were clear with David about the severity of the condition. Yafa and her husband urged Ephraim to come to Israel for a second opinion. Scared and uncertain, the Rosenbergs planned a trip in late January 1978.

Since Ephraim and Esther planned to be gone for two months, they made arrangements for David to stay with Debbie and Laurence Cherniak, acquaintances from Or Chaim. They didn't want David to be alone, and it would be easy for him to go to and from Or Chaim with Laurence, the school's health and PE teacher.

In Israel, Ephraim and Esther met with a respected cardiac surgeon. He quickly agreed with the Canadian doctor, and told Ephraim he would need open-heart surgery as soon as possible. His diseased heart was pumping blood so weakly, only a fraction of it was oxygenated. The Israeli doctor could fit Ephraim into his surgical schedule the third week of February. But on the evening of February 16, Ephraim, resting at Yafa's apartment, collapsed with a massive heart attack. He died at the hospital several hours later. It was nighttime in Toronto, and Esther called the Cherniaks.

Early the next day, Laurence went to David's room, where he was packing for a weekend trip to visit camp friends in Montreal. "Good morning," David said.

"I'm so sorry," Laurence told him. "Your father has passed away." He left the boy alone so that he could collect himself and began making arrangements to get him to Israel as soon as possible.

The news was as shocking as it was devastating—Ephraim was still in middle age, and until recently had been leading his congregation in song, visiting his community's sick, teaching choral students. In Jewish tradition, the dead are buried as soon as possible. (Some believe that the soul's journey to heaven cannot begin until the body is buried.) Funerals are prohibited on Shabbat, and Ephraim's would be the following day before the sun set on Friday.

There was much to do in such a short time. David didn't even have a valid passport.

Laurence and David rushed to the Rosenbergs' apartment so David could pick up a copy of his identification and get the right clothes. On the wall, David saw the smiling photo of the family gathered for his bar mitzvah three years prior. He stood at his closet. He'd been to many funerals, although none for any parents he knew. Without thinking, he chose his synagogue clothes: a white shirt, some slacks, and a dark jacket. Then he and Laurence drove in silence to the family's lawyer, who arranged for David to get an expedited passport. If it was issued quickly, they'd just have enough time to make a flight to New York that afternoon. From there David would travel alone overnight to Israel.

Then they raced to the US consulate downtown. David stood in line for a new photo, his face solemn, his eyes bewildered. He sat next to Laurence as they waited. Someone called his name and handed him his new passport. On the drive to Pearson Airport, David held the booklet out the window so the ink would dry in the cold air.

NORMALLY WHEN DAVID LANDED in Tel Aviv, he couldn't wait to get off the plane. He loved to see his cousins, practice his Hebrew, and eat shawarma. His mind played images of his father. Ephraim always knew the right thing to say and do, and was so honored in Israel he'd been called to officiate at David Ben-Gurion's funeral, just a few years before. Gone? It seemed impossible.

When David landed, he was ushered out of the plane and whisked through customs. His cousin Shlomo was waiting to pick him up in his blue Volkswagen, and they sped to the cemetery.

The funeral was crowded with friends, family, and admirers who came to pay their respects to the great cantor. In Israel, civilian bodies are buried not in coffins but in simple shrouds, so that they might swiftly return to the dust from which the Torah says they came. The custom has another purpose too. When the mourners go to bury their departed, there is no buffer from the sound of the first shovelful of earth falling on their loved one's body. The finality of death is inescapable, and survivors must accept it.

At the cemetery, David stood beside Esther as they watched the rabbi dip his shovel into the fresh mound of red-brown soil. With the clay dirt of the cemetery, the thuds were deafening, and raw. The grief felt that way too. When it was her turn to come forward, Esther sobbed as she lifted the heavy earth onto the shovel, and watched as it descended over her husband. Jewish tradition holds that it is an honor to bury the dead. Some believe it is one of the purest acts of compassion. The dead do not know you are doing it, and can never reciprocate the kindness.

It was David's turn next. He stood straight and tall, his mouth in a solemn line.

DURING THE SEVEN DAYS of shiva, hundreds of people came to Yafa's apartment to pay their condolences. Esther was wearing a black dress she'd had to borrow. Who packs clothing for a funeral when you are traveling for hope? David knew hardly any of the mourners, but listened intently as they told him how Ephraim had consoled them during their darkest moments, helped celebrate their most joyous milestones. It dawned on him that these strangers had been the beneficiaries of Ephraim's greatness in real time. As a teenager, David had only just begun to appreciate it.

As the days passed, Esther cried from morning to night and could hardly choke down tea. Doctors gave her sedatives that put her into such a deep slumber that sometimes even the bright Mediterranean sun could not wake her. As David watched his mother dissolve in grief, he felt his doubts about his faith sharpen into anger at God. How could he have taken away such a great man? How could he let his mother suffer so much? David could not find an answer, and for the next thirty days, all he did was eat and sleep.

Jewish tradition has several stages in the mourning process—first the week of *shiva*; then a month, called *shloshim*; and finally a year, *shneim asar chodesh*—marked by rituals and restrictions that help the bereaved move through their grief. Esther turned to prayer, and wept. David, increasingly, lashed out. The passage of time didn't affect how much they missed Ephraim. It only seemed to underscore it.

Esther's siblings encouraged them to stay in Israel, but David wanted to finish high school in Canada. As a compromise, they bought an apartment two blocks from Yafa's so that Esther could eventually move there. In April, mother and son returned to Toronto. David had missed two months of school and had gained twenty-five pounds. The flight from Tel Aviv seemed endless, and they each dreaded the thought of entering the apartment. Despite his own profound losses, Ephraim had developed a remarkable ability to channel sorrow into humor, and to transform his tragedies so starkly that humble prayers from a Toronto synagogue—any synagogue—seemed like appeals to the Almighty on Mount Sinai itself. He at once provided steadiness for his spirited son and calm for his anxious wife. Each member of this tight-knit clan carried internal wounds, but togetherness had been a salve of stability for each of them, with Ephraim as its center.

Esther had her anguish: the war, repeated resettlement, decades of infertility. David, too, had his sorrows, even if he didn't fully acknowledge them—and now, the loss of the only father he'd ever known. Ephraim's death didn't feel so much a departure as an alarming desertion. Mother and son were equally heartbroken, but in their small apartment, their pain took different forms. Esther was inert but for her tears. In her traditional thirty-seven-year marriage, she had deferred to Ephraim in practical manners, particularly finances. She was fluent in so many ways—in the kitchen; as a mother; as a sister; as a friend in a half-dozen languages—but she had never so much as written a check. And now they had no income. Faced with these new tasks, alone for the first time in her life, she collapsed.

David's yeshiva training had instilled in him Ephraim's hope—both the fear and the love of God. Increasingly, those feelings gave way to even more rage than he'd felt in Israel as he had listened to strangers comfort him. He watched helplessly as Esther navigated her widowhood. To help out with finances, he got a job in a candy factory.

Mother and son became locked into a hostile cycle of despair. When Esther asked David to recite blessings, he bitterly declined. Yeshiva only seemed to make him angrier—every prescribed prayer reminded him of the same God who'd taken his father prematurely; every Torah chant, of his father's otherworldly voice. For David, Or Chaim was one long trigger. His grades plummeted, and he told Esther he wanted to quit. He was the first of his friends to lose an immediate family member, and most didn't know how to act around him. When one friend told him he knew how he felt, having just lost his grandfather, David scoffed. "You don't know how I feel," he said. "Nobody knows how I feel."

His only refuge was the ice. He was an excellent goalie, one of the best of his age in the city—and in Toronto, that was saying something.

After months of arguing, Esther finally allowed David to enroll at a nearby city high school, and things seemed to ease up for him. He befriended a swimmer named Ron Goldner, an Israeli student whose father was based in Toronto. Although he still had outbursts, his sense of impishness returned, and his mood lightened. His voice had matured into a beautiful tenor, and before long, he was singing in the school choir and at the Sweet Sixteen parties of his female friends.

David towered over most of his friends, and had a chest so broad, he started shopping at large-men's stores before he even had his driver's license. His appearance worked to his advantage: nobody ever asked for his ID. At sixteen, he loved going to a neighborhood pizza joint, where he sat alongside off-duty police officers and ordered beer. (When he finally turned nineteen, the legal drinking age, he turned to the cop who'd become his drinking buddy, and said, "It's my birthday—want to buy me a beer?" "Sure thing," the officer responded. "How old are you?" David grinned, and showed his license to the stunned cop.) Esther, meanwhile, remained unmoored in Toronto. She grieved for Ephraim, missed her sister, and fretted constantly about her son. David worried about Esther's well-being just as much as Esther worried about David's. David had school, friends, and hockey. Esther had David and a deep well of friends. But they were no match for her sorrow.

After high school, David enrolled in York University in Toronto. Esther, as planned, left for Israel to be near her sister. She moved into the apartment near Yafa's. David moved in with a group of friends, and poured himself into his chosen major, political science. His real outlets were his Jewish youth group and hockey, where he had honed his reputation as an aggressive goalie, and a testy one too. During an exhibition game, an opponent noticed the name on his jersey and began taunting him. "Fucking Jew," he muttered as he skated by. David whipped around. "The fuck did you say?" he said, and sped toward him. A few seconds later, David swung his stick at the player's leg. A loud crack reverberated throughout the stadium, and the man fell, crying out and clutching his broken ankle. Blood splattered over the ice. David skated away, unscathed.

The following summer, he attended an intensive camp hosted by the Rangers—George Katz's favorite sports team. He was so gifted, they offered him a spot as goalie. He declined. It was one thing to be a Jew who played hockey. It would be another entirely to be a Jewish hockey player—and besides, Esther hated the idea. All those years of yeshiva; the natural gift of his voice—there had to be another calling.

∽

SOON ENOUGH, there was.

In the winter of 1982, David was feeling a bit aimless and dropped out of school for an extended visit with his mother in Netanya. In June of that year, Israel invaded Lebanon in an attempt to force the Palestinian Liberation Organization out of the country, and David monitored every development, every battle, every gruesome casualty. His longstanding warmth toward Israel had blossomed into the central purpose in his life, the only thing that made sense. He saw the multifaceted conflict in the most tribal of terms. If Israel was under threat, he would say, it was his duty to protect it.

He completed making aliyah, the process of becoming an Israeli citizen, and a right accorded to anyone in the world with one Jewish grandparent. As is mandatory for most young Israelis, he signed up to join the Israel Defense Forces, or IDF. Enlisting had a deep meaning for David. He had no brothers or sisters that he knew about, and longed to belong to a larger group. Many adoptees are drawn to institutions organized around the idea of brotherhood, from the military to the police to firefighters and fraternities. For David, entering the IDF filled several voids. He'd lost Ephraim, and continued to wrestle with his faith as a Jew. But the Israeli army? That would be a family no one could ever take away. He wouldn't only be fighting for a country he loved. It was for Jewish existence itself.

But his weight was high. So was his blood pressure, and he had knee and ankle injuries from hockey. Although he was proficient in Hebrew, it was not his native language. That combination—as well as Esther's refusal to sign a letter granting her only child permission to join a combat unit—restricted him to a basic level of recruit training. Still, he improved his Hebrew in an immersion program called an *ulpan*, learned how to use an assault rifle to hit targets, and became skilled at first aid. As a native English speaker, he was assigned to serve as a spokesman for an IDF unit.

Although he was only in his early twenties, his health problems were escalating. Doctors told him that the pain he had in his feet was caused by gout, and linked his legendary thirst (which he had tried to quench with giant Cokes) to diabetes. It had been undiagnosed for years and was so severe by the time he was finally treated, he had briefly lost his eyesight. Yet for all the seriousness of his physical difficulties, he was more disappointed still that they (and Esther) prevented him from joining an elite combat unit. Military service, particularly on the battlefield, offers great prestige in Israel. Rank enhances political careers; many successful Israeli politicians have been war heroes. Still, David liked the camaraderie of the army and its larger mission.

David in the Israel Defense Forces, 1980s

~

HIS WORK AS A SPOKESMAN was hardly glamorous, but he liked the job and felt a sense of accomplishment. It was his personal life that felt incomplete. He told a friend in Toronto that while he didn't lack for female company, he was looking for "someone special." He was also reevaluating his relationship with Judaism. He had begun to get paying jobs as a freelance cantor, and studied weekly with a teacher who helped him fine-tune his holiday skills. But he was also questioning what it meant to live according to its many rules.

"There are times I miss the beautiful Shabbats I had when my father was alive, yet I also regret the many Friday nights I spent at home doing nothing when I should have been out having a wild 'n' crazy time," he told a friend, referencing a famous *Saturday Night Live* skit from the period. In fact, the only place he wore a kippah was at home—and that was just to placate Esther and her neighbors. "I learned and grew up with religion. I know what it is and why, so now I can decide for myself when and how to be as religious as I want. I'll go to shul on Shabbat, but what's so terrible about going to a party on a Friday night?

"I'm a better Jew than most, but I don't believe I should have to forgo a lot of the pleasures I have here," he said. Esther, meanwhile, had met, and married, an Australian émigré businessman named Yaacov. David loved his stepfather, and his stepfather loved him. David was especially grateful that he made Esther happy.

AFTER HIS STINT on active duty in the IDF, David enrolled at Hebrew University, a sprawling campus in the hills of Jerusalem. Still intent on becoming involved in Israeli politics, he decided to major in political science and international relations. One day in September of 1984, he rushed into a lecture hall in uniform, carrying the assault rifle required of reservists. Though they are ubiquitous in Israel, the army greens and heavy lace-up boots, however uncomfortable in humid, late-summer Jerusalem, were, to David, a matter of pride and a declaration of his identity. They were also, in part, a source of frustration: his uniform identified him as a man who'd had a desk job.

As he bounded down the stairs, he passed the Toronto swimmer Ron Goldner. Ron, who had just ended his own stint in the Israeli navy, recognized his friend David immediately. "Rosy!" he cried. "What the fuck are you doing here?"

"I made aliyah and I'm finishing the army," he explained.

"Do you have a roommate?" Ron asked.

"No," David replied.

"You do now," Ron said.

David called Esther in Netanya to tell her; she was overjoyed. Immediately she flew into action. She called Ron's mother in Tel Aviv to arrange a system of cooking for the boys. "God forbid they starve," Esther told Ron's mother. When they'd come home for Shabbat, the mothers loaded them with enough food to last a week: cheese blintzes, eggplant salads, zucchini salads, kugel, schnitzel, and meatballs. The food was always gone by Sunday.

For the rest of their university years, Ron and David roomed together, first in dorms and later in an apartment. While Ron leaned to the left politically, David tilted far to the right. The two agreed never to discuss politics. They also split tasks. Ron would handle all the weekly cooking and domestic chores; David would take care of academics and social life.

And that he did, first by always transforming their living space into an American-style fraternity. They had a full stereo system and an expensive large TV, and threw toga parties and all-night beer fests. David's attitude toward weekend amusement was unusual in Israel, where entering university students are older than in America or Canada, and often veterans of military battles.

Their accommodations were also the headquarters of a thriving business. David, who was a fast typist, had replaced his standard-issue desk chair with a big black office chair, where he typed other students' papers for a fee. He also had another, more lucrative gig. He had a file cabinet full of academic papers he'd both written and collected on every possible subject. He translated them into Hebrew and sold them to students who lacked the time for writing them themselves.

Esther and Yaacov moved to Australia for Yaacov's business. David made no secret of the fact that he was missing a father figure, and directed his longing to Ron's, a banker. Ron's father would take the men out for steak lunches and dinners; they always polished off several courses.

David also became an integral part of a political group called Gilad, which espoused views to the right of Israel's leading conservative party, the Likud. Many of its members were Sephardic Jews whose forebears had come to Israel from North Africa, or Mizrahi Jews whose ancestors had come from the Middle East. David was open about his adoption; based on his appearance, many in the group embraced him as someone whose birth parents were likely dark-skinned, Arabic-speaking people like them. He immersed himself in the group and earned a reputation as a devoted Zionist. Soon he was renting space in a local hotel room to help run all-night political campaigns, raising funds and registering voters for Gilad's representatives to dominate campus. The university was, in effect, a greenhouse for the country's political leaders, and David grasped quickly how the parliamentary system on campus could translate to the Knesset. What he may have lacked in battlefield bona fides, he made up for in devotion to Israeli politics.

The mid-1980s were tense years in Israel: the conflict in Lebanon ground on, with Israeli forces continuing to occupy the south of that country in what was becoming Israel's Vietnam. Many soldiers arrived on campus, sometimes only weeks removed from combat, and political debates were fueled by testosterone and existential fear for the Jewish state. Those on the left objected to the Israeli policies of occupation;

many allied themselves with the concerns of Israeli Arab students, protesting that they were being mistreated. Those on the right, like David, saw matters in an utterly different light. The polarization of politics was not always only verbal.

When left-wing students demonstrated on campus, some in Gilad were eager to dispatch David to take them on. He hadn't picked up a hockey stick in years, but his skill at the fisticuffs that Canadians hone on the ice had not diminished. For David, criticism of Israel's actions was tantamount to criticism of Judaism itself, and the slightest of disparagements could set him off. When David and his friends were within earshot, those conversations quickly escalated to shouting matches, and often ended in brawls.

David missed Esther, and the two spoke regularly. Often, he thought of Ephraim. He had been gone for years already, but David's longing for his father never quite diminished. When Ron's father suddenly died a few weeks before Passover during their second year, Ron was devastated. He returned to the university after the holiday, numb with sadness. As David observed him grow thinner, and a beard sprout on his face—Jews are encouraged not to focus on their appearance during the first thirty days after burial—he could see that Ron was trapped in grief. It struck David that he was not alone in such an early, wrenching loss.

One day in their room after classes, David sat down with him. "Look, I understand your dad just passed away," he said. "You're pissed and sad."

Ron looked up.

"But I've had enough of this doom and gloom of yours, and you'd better shape up."

Ron said nothing, his mouth in a straight line.

"You heard me," David told him. "Move it."

As much as David missed his own father, maybe, he thought, he could draw on his grief for Ephraim to help others—even if his form of comforting was brash. Time didn't necessarily heal. But it could ease the pain, if only a little.

DAVID'S OWN LIFE SEEMED to be filling up. Gilad operated like a tight-knit family. Nobody there questioned anybody's motives. His singing was becoming renowned, and offers for gigs—from synagogues, and for weddings and parties—were multiplying. It was fun just to be around him, in the car, or late at night on the campaign. You never knew what genre of music he was going to break into.

His adoption was no secret in Israel, and his male friends believed it was something he thought little about. While David acted tough around his male friends, he allowed himself to be more vulnerable around women. Sometimes, when he was with his female friends, he confided that he hoped to find his birth mother. He knew it would upset Esther, he told them, but it didn't keep him from wondering. He was in his early twenties now, pondering his Jewish future. In the land of his ancient forebears, he also had to wonder: What about his recent past?

Many of his friends were of Moroccan origin. "You're one of us," they assured him.

But deep down, David wondered. Was he? And how could he be sure?

15.

Going West

For the next few years, David devoted himself to Gilad. But as he reached his late twenties, he had slowly become disillusioned by the reality of the country's politics and his limitations as a non-native Israeli. He wasn't thrilled with either of his options: working in the Israeli foreign service or for members of the Knesset. But he was also tired of the political sparring. Maybe it was time to return to the States. He applied, halfheartedly, to American law schools.

Meanwhile, his voice was earning him attention and opening a possible career path. He realized what he really wanted: to sing. It was his passion, his gift, his legacy, and he was entering the peak decades of his vocal powers. So, in 1989, he began looking for US cantorial jobs. He received two offers: One was on Long Island, in a suburb crowded with synagogues. The other was from Rabbi Yonah Geller at Shaarie Torah, a synagogue in Portland, Oregon, that had been founded in the early 1900s. Unsure of what to do, he visited his cousin Mitch's father, Isaac, at his leather-goods store.

"David," Isaac said, "I'm going to tell you what to do: Go to Portland. Here in New York, you're going to be a little fish in a big pond. In Portland, you'll be a big fish in a little pond." He took Isaac's advice.

Moving to Portland was a culture shock for someone accustomed to the fast pace of life in modern Israel. It was even in evidence on the roads. Instead of racing to cut him off, drivers on the highway motioned him to go right ahead of them when he was trying to change lanes. Nobody needed numbers from a little red machine when they were at the deli—in fact, people often invited those who'd arrived after them to go first if they appeared to be in a hurry. People spoke slowly and quietly. Not even Toronto had been this placid.

For a young city, Portland had an impressively long Jewish history. (Coincidentally, Rabbi Stephen Wise had launched his career there in 1900, at a synagogue that was founded in the 1850s. And Louise Wise gave birth to the couple's two children, James Wise and Justine Wise, during the couple's six-year stay.) But the practice of Judaism there was less observant than David had experienced in Canada or Israel, and even prominent members of the city's most traditional synagogue sometimes ordered shrimp for lunch. David, who abided (mostly) by kosher rules, was jarred at first by their casual approach toward the rules of their faith. But as he settled in, he realized that these relaxed ways weren't right, and they weren't wrong. They were merely different.

In the sanctuary of the synagogue, David's pure tenor transfixed the congregation. At weddings and funerals, on holidays and every Shabbat morning, David's voice flowed from the present to the past; from the well to the sick; from the living to the departed. He felt especially close to Ephraim in these moments, and it showed. Members of his synagogue were hushed by his outsize gifts. Some said listening to him felt like being in heaven.

He quickly made friends, and let people know he was ready for a serious relationship. The rabbi's wife, Lisl Geller, had a woman she wanted David to meet—she would be a perfect match for the young cantor. Her name was Kim Danish, and her forebears had been among Shaarie Torah's founders. She had recently returned to Portland, home to her family for five generations, after years away for college and work on the East Coast, and study at a progressive yeshiva in Israel. David interviewed Kim for a weekend job to help rebuild the synagogue's Sunday school program. He hired her on the spot, and a few weeks later, asked her out on a date. Kim, an elegant brunette with an infectious contralto laugh, was intrigued. But David's ego gave her pause, and at first no romance developed. They worked together closely for two years, becoming each other's best friend. One day, they realized that they'd fallen in love.

In the meantime, Esther had been diagnosed with lung cancer. Her condition was serious, and she and Yaacov returned to Israel from Australia for treatment. Kim and David got engaged. Because Esther was too ill to travel to the States, they planned to quickly marry in Jerusalem. The April 1992 wedding was tinged with sadness; the joyous event was also a farewell. Esther loved Kim, and was relieved that she and David had found each other. Now, she told Yafa, she could die at rest.

When Esther passed away in early June, David and Kim flew back to Israel for her funeral, and stayed with Yafa during the shiva. They spent the week alternately crying, telling funny stories, and talking about politics.

David had Kim now. But sometimes he felt like a thirty-year-old orphan.

They didn't talk about it.

DAVID DEVELOPED AN INSTANT connection to the rabbi at Shaarie Torah, a learned and respected elder, and he embraced, and was embraced by, Kim's family. He loved their deep roots. His community grew: Ron Goldner and his family moved to Portland from Israel. And he connected with another transplant from the East Coast, Marshal Spector. Marshal, a divorce lawyer who had grown up in Maryland, was descended from a long line of cantors and had a strong background in liturgical chanting.

One Shabbat morning, David and Marshal were whispering quietly in the back of the synagogue. David showed Marshal a book he had on the lives of great European cantors, and noted a passage about a Pinchas Spector, teacher of Ephraim, in the Romanian city of Tshernovitz.

David pointed to the page. "Any relation?" he asked Marshal.

"Yeah," said Marshal. "He was my great-grandfather."

They were about as far away, in distance and character, as possible from the Eastern European world that had been home to their families. But there they were, two Jewish guys, singing the same ancient prayers that linked them.

David was settling in to Portland. He and Kim bought a large house in the Portland hills where they hosted Shabbat dinners and holidays, and they wanted to start a family. For the first time in his life, he began to think seriously about his biological history. With Ephraim and Esther gone, he did not feel it would be disloyal to their memories to finally search for his own blood relatives. He asked his cousin Mitch Herstic, a lawyer in New York, to help him learn more. Mitch made some inquiries at the Bronx courthouse where David was adopted. He informed David about a state registry that offered adoptees older than twenty-one the identities of their birth parents, but it required them to obtain the permission of their adoptive parents in order to request it. More important, it would only be useful if his birth mother had already submitted information about his birth. (Margaret, by then living in New Jersey, had never heard of such a registry, and had not.) The obstacles seemed daunting. David did not pursue it.

In 1994, Kim became pregnant. When Sam was born in January 1995, David held his son in his arms, a man transfixed. As it had been for Pam Hasegawa and so many scores of other adoptees, his infant son was the first blood relative he had known. He looked at his tiny son, kissed his forehead, held him to his chest. His wonder was boundless.

The next year, Kim became pregnant again, and gave birth to their second son on December 17—David's birthday. While he had always relished celebrating the day with friends and plenty of steak and single-malt Scotch, it also occasionally made him wonder vaguely about the circumstances of his own arrival. Now he had a completely joyful reason to cherish the day: his baby son Noah.

David threw himself into being a husband and father, and loved to spoil his wife and children with gifts. He'd see clothing on mannequins he thought Kim might like and buy it on the spot. He discovered eBay, and ordered little Sam's favorite toy idol, one after another. Kim, a calm woman with a frugal nature, wondered occasionally what all the boxes arriving on their porch might contain. But she never asked. One day, though, she stepped into the basement where David and Sam were playing floor hockey, little Noah trying to keep up. She saw a mountain of eBay boxes in a corner. There were two hundred of them—all containing Buzz Lightyear figurines.

"What are you doing?" she asked, furious. "Are you going to buy him a car when he's ten?"

David didn't flinch. "Yes," he said.

When Estee was born in 1999, he was equally overjoyed. Two sons and a daughter, each with his olive skin, his and Kim's flashing dark brown eyes. While Kim bought clothes for herself and the boys on sale at J. C. Penney, David took Estee to an upscale children's boutique where he got her fancy designer dresses and sparkly shoes. When Kim complained that he was spoiling her, David waved it off. "So what?" he said. "She deserves to feel like a princess."

The children went to a progressive Jewish day school, and he taught them the chants he had learned from Ephraim. On Shabbat, their home was filled with the aroma of chicken soup, brisket and potatoes, challah and vegetables; their table was crowded with friends. "It's good to be king," David would say. And then he would lead everyone in song.

DEVOUT AS HE WAS, David also considered hockey as essential to a balanced life. When the boys were two, he gave them skating lessons, and coached them in the fine art of his beloved sport. A conflict soon developed. Sam and later Noah grew so proficient in hockey that they made teams that traveled regionally, and attended summer camps in Canada. But games and tournaments took place on Saturday afternoons, and instead of observing Shabbat in quiet contemplation, as Jewish tradition holds, after synagogue David drove the boys to hockey. In contrast to Portland's more restrained audiences, he was all-out Canadian, all-out New York, screaming at the top of his lungs: "SKATE! Sammy, SKATE!" "Noah, stick on the ICE!" He got so worked up about referees' calls, once he even turned over a trash can. Other parents would stare in disbelief. The game officials did more than that, sometimes kicking David out of the arena.

He was unapologetic. "I wouldn't get mad if they were doing the right thing," he'd say.

He was a guy's guy, central in his group of friends. With Ron and other buddies, he'd head to a steakhouse that offered free seventy-two-ounce steaks if you could polish off the whole thing. (Ron once came close, finishing fifty-five ounces.) David was legendary for picking up the tab—for meals, for drinks, even for the sports jacket of a friend who didn't have one to wear to David's wedding. He was also a lavish tipper. He'd take his kids and Ron's girls, Romi and Shelly, to the arcades, distributing bags of quarters to each of them. He'd show them the art of pinball machines, of target games, of toy grabs. At the end of an afternoon, he'd load the car with stuffed animals. Wherever he went in Portland—restaurants, shops, the cleaner's—everybody knew him. "Hello, Mr. Rosenberg!" "Hi, David!"

As a teacher, he coached the children of friends how to chant Torah and haftarah, recording the tropes, the traditional Hebrew melodies, on cassettes. His reputation spread beyond just the synagogue: officials at the city's only major league sports team, the NBA's Portland Trail Blazers, asked him to sing the national anthem. He did, wearing a yarmulke emblazoned with the team's insignia.

The years passed, and David's health began to falter. He gained weight, his diabetes worsened, and his blood pressure and cholesterol skyrocketed. He had sleep apnea, and hardly got a night's rest. As a desperate measure, he went to a fat farm at Duke University. He lost weight along with everyone else, exercising and eating healthfully. But his cholesterol numbers and blood pressure didn't budge. A nurse told him, "Your numbers haven't changed, David. You just have shitty genes, and some people are going to have that." He told her: "Well, it's too bad you're not talking about the pants I'm wearing, but I understand." Occasionally fears about his genetic inheritance flickered in his thoughts. What else might be in store for him, healthwise? And what might he have passed on to the kids?

In 1996 David was diagnosed with thyroid cancer. His doctors told him it was imminently treatable and removed half of his thyroid. The cells, they said, were slow-growing, and only needed monitoring. He was in his late thirties.

Next came trouble breathing. He was winded at the slightest movement—especially going up the many stairs of his house in the Portland hills. Doctors diagnosed him with asthma. It was so severe it curbed his ability to sing. The weight, the diabetes, even the cancer—those he had taken in stride. But now he was practically silenced.

He became a part-time cantor with the voice he had left, and joined his brother-in-law in a less physically demanding enterprise, an upscale pizza restaurant. Within a few years, the business grew into an enormous success, with branches spreading throughout Portland. Eventually David stopped singing altogether.

In late 2006, David's kidneys stopped functioning. He could no longer work. After Thanksgiving of that year, he went on dialysis, a wearisome three-times-a-week process that flushes the body of toxins. When word got out that David would need a kidney to regain a semblance of normal life, many in the Jewish community stepped forward. Ron volunteered, but was diagnosed with prediabetes himself. This disqualified him as a candidate, and he worried aloud that he was letting his best friend down. David didn't see it that way. "Look at this as a blessing," he said. "Now you know, and you'll take better care of yourself. You'll be there for your kids."

Marshal also stepped forward. Against the odds, he was a perfect match.

I first met David in the dialysis center as he prepared for surgery in May of 2007. One day, as we were talking, he looked up from his BlackBerry and made an odd comment. He had been through heartache, of course, before: the loss of Ephraim at such a young age; his mother's death weeks after he married. It would have been tempting for him to ask, "Why me?" Instead, he gestured toward the others in the room, hooked to the deafening machines cleaning their blood. "You know what?" he asked me. "I had no idea people go through this—dialysis.

"It's draining, emotionally, physically, literally." He smiled at a nurse who headed his way. "And look at all these people, taking such good care. You take so much for granted in life."

He grappled with how to fully express his gratitude to Marshal, who was most certainly extending his life. "How do you thank a guy who offers to give you a kidney?" he asked. His face looked somber for a moment. But then he cracked jokes.

The operation went well, and in June, he was recovering from surgery at home. The Rosenbergs and other parents at Shaarie Torah sent their kids to a Jewish sleepaway camp, and their houses were quiet. Ron stopped in to see David, whose strength did not seem to be returning.

"Do you miss the kids?" Ron asked him.

David smiled. "I only miss the people who don't come back," he said.

As David struggled to manage his waning health, social forces were transforming the adoption system that had framed his life. The mid-twentieth-century practice, in which all-powerful agencies made behind-the-scenes matches for hopeful parents, was starting to become as anachronistic as video stores. Shifts in social norms vastly reduced the number of unplanned pregnancies, significantly decreasing the number of babies available for traditional closed adoptions. Schools began teaching sex education in the early 1970s. Birth control became more available to young people. The landmark *Roe v. Wade* decision in 1973 legalized abortion nationwide. Perhaps most important, single motherhood become more socially acceptable. These changes had an immediate, measurable impact. The number of babies surrendered for adoption in the United States dropped 26 percent in five years, from an estimated 175,000 nationally in 1970 to 129,000 in 1975. That year, mysteriously, the federal government stopped counting the number of adoptions, and never did so again. Private institutions and universities began gathering statistics on adoptions in the government's stead, but their figures remain incomplete.

Louise Wise Services was particularly buffeted by these changes. The state of New York was among the first to legalize abortion, in 1970, three years before *Roe*, prompting a sharp drop in the number of babies available for adoption. More than 100,000 women opted for abortion rather than childbirth in the ten months after New York passed its law. "The more sophisticated young women, both Black and white, are no longer coming to us," a Wise official lamented at a board meeting. The decline in babies was so precipitous, the agency was forced to sell the Lakeview maternity home in 1971. The number of parents looking to adopt was still high, even though the baby boom was over. To make up for the shortfall, Louise Wise redoubled its efforts, begun in the 1960s, to place children of color with its white clientele. The agency, along with many others nationwide, arranged adoptions of older children, black children, as well as Native American children, many of whom had been forcibly removed from their families and their tribal lands. Not surprisingly, African American and Native communities vehemently objected to this approach, saying it deprived the children of their cultural heritage.

Many adoption agencies turned to foreign countries in search of children who could be adopted. Until the 1970s, the adoption of infants from outside the United States was relatively unusual. A Baptist couple from Eugene, Oregon, pioneered the idea of adopting orphaned or abandoned babies, many of whom had been fathered by American servicemen, when they brought eight Korean children to the United States in 1955 through a special act of Congress. The Holts became a national sensation, and they founded an agency dedicated to settling overseas orphans from Korea and elsewhere with American evangelical families. Holt International had few requirements, demanding only that the adoptive parents be "saved," and be able to pay the child's airfare from Korea. News reports from the time emphasized how easily the Korean children "blended" into their white families, and how seamless such adoptions could be. Overseas adoption was cast as a humanitarian, altruistic gesture, a response to cataclysmic events in faraway countries. As the Vietnam War wound down in the 1970s, the United States brought two thousand Vietnamese children, many fathered by GIs, to the United States as part of what was called Operation Babylift. The Holt agency continued to arrange the adoption of thousands of Korean babies a year while expanding its operations to other countries, from Ethiopia to Uganda. Between 1955 and the early 2000s, Holt and other agencies in Korea facilitated the adoptions of an estimated 150,000 children by American families.

Global upheaval opened up new possibilities. As civil wars convulsed Guatemala, El Salvador, Nicaragua, and Honduras in the 1980s, Americans began adopting children said to have been orphaned by the fighting. And when Romania's Communist leader Nicolae Ceausescu was overthrown in 1989, journalists reported on the emaciated children who lay listlessly in rows of cribs in grim institutions. Tens of thousands of families from the United States, Canada, and across Europe rushed to adopt the neglected children. Following the collapse of the Soviet Union in 1991, the former USSR became a popular destination for prospective US parents. In the early 1990s, Americans also increasingly turned to China, which had enacted a strict one-child policy in 1979 as a means of curbing population growth. The authorities levied harsh penalties on families who exceeded their quota, and many relinquished daughters because of a cultural preference for sons. In the 1990s and early 2000s, Americans adopted more than 85,000 Chinese children, overwhelmingly girls.

Meanwhile, many agencies that handled domestic adoptions realized they could no longer justify their longtime policies of secrecy; this issue was described in the adoption community as the "sealed records controversy." Across the country, social workers encouraged prospective adoptive parents to read the spate of books written in the late 1970s about the experience of adoptees and birth mothers. The damaging effects of cutting adoptees off from their biological origins, and by severing birth mothers from their sons and daughters, were becoming impossible to ignore.

Among those deeply troubled by the traditional practice of closed adoptions was a young Michigan social worker named Jim Gritter. One day it dawned on Gritter that closed adoptions required women to place boundless faith in a system that had done nothing to earn it. "If a good friend asked to borrow my car to go get a gallon of milk, I'd probably relent but only after a thorough grilling: 'When will you be back? And what happened to *your* car?' We weren't asking these women to borrow their cars for an hour. We were asking them to entrust their babies—for eighteen years at a minimum—not to friends, but to total strangers."

Gritter didn't know it, but he was part of a national movement of people who were asking, Could there be another way? Gritter and his colleagues wondered, What if the hierarchy on which closed adoption was based were reversed, and adoptive families could become a resource for birth families? Could the families work together and replace the sense of shame and loss with a shared love for the child?

Their conversation was informed by a profound shift in the field of psychology. The Freudian view that single mothers were sexual deviants was being supplanted by a deeper understanding of the pivotal role of bonding in an infant's early life. By the 1970s, John Bowlby and other researchers had established the lifelong importance of the attachment formed between mothers and infants. In city after city, adoption officials began devising a new approach they called open adoption, which would allow birth mothers to retain some ties to their child. The idea began modestly, with the birth and adoptive parents exchanging letters anonymously. This led to more open correspondence, then picture exchanges, then first-name exchanges with the potential of ongoing contact between the two families. Ultimately it evolved into arrangements in which birth parents could help choose the families they wished to raise their child, and often stay in touch with their child throughout his childhood. Once women had more control over the process, the preeminent role of many agencies, along with their bogus testing methods, began to fade. Unlike the extensive "matching" period in which children had been tested, snapped with rubber bands, and scrutinized behind closed doors, children in open adoptions were placed almost immediately with the families their birth parents had chosen. The process was complex, and it still left birth parents with virtually no legal right to influence the course of their child's life. But it did give adoptees access to their medical history, their full circle of family, their heritage and ancestry.

Some of the new generation of social workers involved in open adoptions understood the pain on a deeply personal level. In her first years as a social worker for a public agency, Maxine Chalker, a Pennsylvania social worker and adoptee, helped many adoptees find their birth families. Their stories inspired her to search for her own biological family—and also to question how adoption was being practiced. "Why should a bunch of social workers sit around a table and pick the family to raise a woman's child?" she asked herself. "If a woman is going to place a child, she should have more of a say about where that child goes than anyone else." In 1984, she founded her own agency, Adoptions from the Heart, in her Philadelphia basement. As with open adoptions elsewhere, it began by showing birth mothers folders the adoptive parents had prepared about what they might be able to offer their baby. They often included stories about how the couples met, their level of education, their dedication to their families, and photos of their home. Researchers have documented the benefits of open adoptions, finding that children in such families experienced more life satisfaction than did adoptees in closed adoptions. Their birth mothers, likewise, reported less grief than birth mothers in closed adoptions.

BY THE 1990s, Louise Wise Services was faltering. This time, the blows came from its own practices, not the atmosphere surrounding it. For years, Louise Wise officials had pushed ethical boundaries, going beyond even what other agencies deemed appropriate by the loose standards of the period. It allowed physicians on its board, including Bernard and Karelitz, to conduct research on the very children they were professionally obligated to protect. It joined in the twin-and-triplet studies when other agencies declined to do so. The parents of the separated triplets had been unable to find a law firm willing to take a case against the agency in the 1980s. By the 1990s, the movement supporting the adoptees' rights was increasingly strong. More important, ideas about the supposed predominance of nurture over nature had shifted radically. Louise Wise had offered evidence of nature through sham tests that were meant to reveal a child's innate talents and personality in order to match him with appropriate new parents. The agency had promoted this "proof" at the same time as it lied about where the adoptees came from. In the meantime, scientists had come to understand that no amount of what Karelitz called "nutritive soil" could offset the decisive role genes played in everything from athletic ability to diabetes and mental illness. Angry clients of Louise Wise came to realize they had been misled about the histories of the children they had adopted, and they took their complaints to court, and to the media.

In one widely publicized case in 1991, Martin and Phyllis Juman, a Long Island couple who had adopted a son through the agency, filed a $50 million lawsuit for "wrongful adoption." When the Jumans were applying to become adoptive parents in 1964, a Louise Wise social worker told them that the birth mother of their prospective adoptee was a clever young college student and a gifted pianist who helped provide for her widowed mother. She had become pregnant during a brief affair, the agency said, after her fiancé had died of a heart attack.

Her child, renamed Michael Juman, had developed severe psychiatric problems as a young adult, veering between despondency and deep paranoia. In hopes of helping him, the Jumans sought information about his birth mother from Louise Wise. In 1985, Louise Wise sent a letter to the Jumans acknowledging that Michael's birth mother had a "history of episodic depressions, for which she was treated psychiatrically." The Jumans were not alarmed by this news; they understood it to mean that the birth mother had suffered from postpartum blues, understandable given the circumstances surrounding her son's birth.

Later, the Jumans learned Michael's birth name, Bruce Dayboch, and were able to locate some of his maternal relatives, who provided more information about his mother's medical condition. The news was shocking: Michael's mother, Florence Dayboch, had been lobotomized in 1944 after a diagnosis of catatonic schizophrenia, nineteen years before Michael's birth. His father was a fellow patient at the Brooklyn psychiatric hospital where they were both being treated.

With Michael's mental state spiraling—he, too, was diagnosed with schizophrenia, which is now understood to have a strong genetic component—the Jumans sued Louise Wise for misrepresenting Michael's genetic history. They were able to do this because of the passage of a 1983 New York law that required agencies to share with adoptive parents the non-identifying medical and psychiatric health of birth parents. The 1985 letter from Louise Wise had been a carefully crafted deception. His mother's mental condition was not episodic; it was nearly lifelong, emerging more than twenty years before Michael's birth. She was not a young, college-educated musician when she gave birth to him; she was a thirty-nine-year-old woman in a psychiatric ward.

Louise Wise's fictional portrayal of Margaret as a promising young scientist and George as a freckled college student was not, it turned out, an aberration. The agency had intentionally deceived countless other adoptive parents as well. Louise Wise Services had built its success on its deep roots in the Jewish community. But as was becoming clear, it had lied to the people who trusted it most.

The Jumans' suit was the first of its kind in New York, and focused on the agency's fraudulent portrayal of Florence Dayboch. Louise Wise sent the Jumans their son's records in 1996, five years after the suit was first filed, and two years after Michael died at twenty-nine from unknown causes. Doctors speculated that he died from a seizure or from a toxic buildup of his many psychotropic medications. It is also possible he took his own life.

From the Jumans' perspective, the Louise Wise records contained only one accurate statement: the couple had said they preferred to adopt a white Jewish child over a Native American one. Otherwise, the documents record a series of evasions. Because the Jumans had asked no questions about the birth mother's mental health, agency officials felt they were not obligated to disclose it. The Jumans were horrified: they had believed the moving tale about the capable, generous pianist, and had no reason to inquire about her psychological state. "Why would we question her mental health?" Marty Juman asked decades later. "They told us she was supporting her widowed mother and had won a college scholarship. We had no concern about her mental health whatsoever. Why would we? She was the perfect mother." The agency continued to justify its lying even after news about the case broke on television and in newspapers. As Barbara Miller, who had headed the agency's post-adoption services, told a reporter: "Once they say they're not concerned, you don't hit them over the head with it."

The Juman case didn't go as the family had hoped. A judge ruled that the statute of limitations for disclosing Michael's medical history had passed. Louise Wise Services offered the Jumans $800 in damages. The Jumans refused the money.

Attorneys for Louise Wise expanded their defense in a second case brought by an irate family. They filed an affidavit from a social worker who said the agency was simply following the practice of the time when it failed to tell parents about their adopted child's medical history. It was, she wrote, "the general opinion and belief of social workers and other professionals in the adoption field in the 1960s and into the early 1980s that nurture played a much greater role than nature in the development of a child"; that "mental illness would not be passed on if a child were placed in a loving environment." Besides, she added, disclosing such information about the health of the mother might "interfere with the bonding between adoptive parent and child and prove detrimental to the child, the parents and their relationship."

By the late 1990s, Louise Wise had ceased operations as an adoption agency, and was trying to survive on fees it collected for training and supporting foster care families and single mothers. Its financial support from public and private agencies was drying up. It had outlived its secretive business model.

MARGARET WAS UNAWARE of any of these developments in adoption or at Louise Wise. While she still thought about Stephen, still dreamed he was calling out for her, still prayed for him, she had long since put the agency out of her mind. Her final experience at the building had been so searing, she tried never to think of it again. When the memory resurfaced, she directed her mind to the productive lives of Lisa, Mark, and Cheri, all successfully launched.

She was also navigating dual milestones. In 1996 she had become a grandmother; Mark's wife, Judy, had given birth to Rachel. But George's health was failing as he increasingly suffered the complications of diabetes. A few years later, he had to stop working, and got on a waiting list for a new kidney. Margaret tried to buoy him with hope. George would smile wanly and reach out his hand to clasp hers as Margaret tended his home dialysis machine. Cheri, who was earning renown in Manhattan as an opera singer, came back to Roosevelt every weekend to help care for her father, and to give Margaret a break.

On Valentine's Day 2000, George was too weak to go out for dinner. Margaret made his favorite veal cutlets and bought him a sugar-free chocolate cake. He took a single bite and declared, "The bottom of my shoe is better than this." They laughed. "I like *your* cake," he told Margaret. After dinner, George settled in to watch ESPN, and Margaret went to sleep. Cheri called early the next morning to speak to her father, who had not risen at dawn like he usually did—sleeping in, he'd always said, was stealing hours from God. When Margaret went to wake him, she discovered he was dead. He was fifty-six years old.

MARGARET'S GRIEF WAS OVERWHELMING, and not only because she had buried her young husband. She had lost the one man she had ever loved, and her best friend of forty years. She had also lost her last tangible connection to Stephen. Although they had never discussed their son, his loss had remained a shared hidden wound. Aside from her brother, he was the only other person in her life who even knew Stephen existed.

After the funeral and the shiva, Margaret took on the monumental task of sorting George's things. When she went to look through her husband's wallet, she saw, in transparent plastic sleeves, the familiar small photos of their wedding; of the kids; of Rachel. Then, tucked deep inside a special compartment, she found the two tiny images George had taken of Stephen as an infant. All those decades, Margaret realized, George had carried his longing with him too—apart, and out of sight.

For more than a year after his death, Margaret was numb. The voids in her life were yawning. The house in Roosevelt was empty. Sometimes she left her bed only to let the dogs out. Finally, a friend convinced her to see a psychiatrist.

"You're depressed, Margaret," she said. "You shouldn't have to suffer like this."

Margaret was hesitant, but made an appointment anyway. After a few sessions, she screwed up the courage to confess that she was not only grieving for George. Her hands shaking, she told the doctor about Stephen's birth and the trauma of his forced adoption. Her worries tumbled out in torrents: What if Louise Wise had not passed on the medical information she had so dutifully reported? What if she died, and her children never knew about their brother? What should she do about her forty-year-old son? she asked.

The psychiatrist picked up the pad on his desk and began scribbling out a prescription. He tore off the small blue sheet and handed it to Margaret.

"There's nothing you can do," he told her. "Take the Zoloft, and forget about it."

Forget about it? It was exactly what the social workers had told her, and it was terrible advice. Margaret was devastated. Now she really had nobody with whom to discuss her concerns, not even the doctor whose job it was to help her. He kept suggesting that she increase the dosage of her antidepressant, but the medication only seemed to make her worse. It made her sweat; it made her sleepless. Her anxiety was intolerable. She went cold turkey on the pills, and on the psychiatrist too.

She had taken care of everyone all those years. Now she had to turn that attention to herself. With the support of her children and friends, she slowly dragged herself back into the world. She got involved with the synagogue and rejoiced at the birth of Lisa's daughter Gabrielle in 2001. In accordance with Jewish tradition, she was named in honor of her grandfather George.

As for the weighty burden, she turned to the only thing she could do: pray.

16.

Deferred Love

T wo months after the transplant in the summer of 2007, David's new kidney was functioning perfectly. But he was just as le-thargic as he had been before the operation. Kim told him to exercise more, but even walking just a few blocks was exhausting. He returned to his endocrinologist for tests.

Weeks later, the doctor called with some deeply disturbing results. David had a rare form of thyroid cancer that had metastasized to his lungs. By leaving part of his thyroid intact during the first surgery, doctors had missed some aggressive cells. Now David would have to undergo another operation to remove the rest of it, and be treated with radioactive iodine to destroy the cancer elsewhere in his body. His treatment options were limited because of the immunosuppressant drugs he had to take for the kidney transplant. The news was shat-tering.

He tried to put on a bright face. One day when I was visiting him at home not long after the diagnosis, he asked aloud, to no one in particu-lar: "Why does God make this happen?" He answered his own question: "Because I'm used to this. My kids are used to seeing me being in bed; they're used to me going to the hospital. My poor wife's used to me kvetching."

And then, quietly, he added: "The hardest part is not knowing."

For the next several years, his only vocation was trying to get himself well. He and Kim traveled frequently to Houston for cancer treatment at MD Anderson. The prognosis was grim. Together the family decided that they, and not a nurse, would tend to David as he grew frailer, as the cancer spread from his lungs to his bones. Kim had become a financial planner in order to support the family, but cared for David at night. Noah and Sam helped support him as he walked, but David continued to focus on their hockey—and had extra advice for Noah, who had become a talented goalie himself. Estee, who was home the most, helped him bathe and dress. The boys had spent so much time with their dad as they drove to and from hockey, across town in Portland, and on trips to Canada

Now Estee, entering middle school, had her time with her father too. But they were marooned in their Portland living room. Afternoon after afternoon, Estee came home from school, made a snack, and brought David his pills and his Diet Coke. They played with his little caramel-colored dog, Gordie, named for the legendary Canadian hockey player Gordie Howe, and hung out.

People looked up to David and came to him with their troubles. In Portland, for many, he'd become an authority of kindness, someone who listened intently and offered sage advice. But now David was sick and needed tending. Other kids went to the mall or soccer practice after school; Estee came home to take care of her dad. She sat next to him on the couch as she did her homework, and he'd tell her the stories of Ephraim and Esther that he'd shared with the boys on their hockey trips.

They also watched TV and listened to music. Sometimes he'd try to sing along, with a voice fighting for its old strength. But it would crack, and then he would be silent, smiling as his daughter projected her clear alto. One time, while listening to Estee's playlist, they heard Billy Joel's song "Vienna." Estee was anxious, and together they listened to the melancholy lyrics urging listeners to slow down and savor their lives. But now, the song's lines about the rush of time seemed freighted with extra meaning.

Where's the fire, what's the hurry about?
You'd better cool it off before you burn it out

David had once heard Billy Joel, the son of a Jewish refugee from Nazi Europe, explain the inspiration for the song. Joel's parents had divorced while he was young, and his father, Helmut, had returned to live in Europe. When Billy was in his early twenties, he visited Helmut in Vienna and noticed an old woman sweeping the streets with a broom. He was horrified. Why did an elderly woman have such a task? he asked. Helmut had an immediate reply. The state paid the woman to do her job, he told Billy, and she relished her work. Unlike life in the United States, where older people are pushed aside, senior citizens in Austria could still find purpose.

Perhaps the story had resonated. David was facing the possibility that he might not experience old age, but as he listened to Estee sing the lyrics, he tried to banish the thought. He had the best doctors, he told himself, he told his friends, again and again. He was trying experimental treatments; he had hope. He had no intention of leaving his sons and daughter fatherless, his wife a widow.

But the cancer was worsening. When Sam graduated from high school in 2013, David marshaled his strength for days so he could attend. For his birthday, Kim, who had consistently urged David to seek his birth family, bought him a kit from the DNA testing company 23andMe. They had only rarely spoken about his adoption, and didn't mention it now. Because she didn't want him to feel he was betraying Esther and Ephraim, she suggested that he might discover Sephardic roots. He spat into a vial and sent his saliva off, along with a consent form. On it, he checked a box that allowed him to receive mail from relatives.

By the early 2010s, great numbers of adoptees were using consumer DNA tests as new tools for finding relatives, especially those in states in which original birth certificates remained closed. Adoptee-rights activists had succeeded in opening birth certificates in Oregon in 2000, followed by a handful of others, including Maine, Hawaii, and Alabama. Before then, the only option for adoptees and birth mothers who sought to reunite with their lost family was hiring private investigators. In the 1980s and 1990s, some companies emerged that specialized in locating lost family members, and through them, reunions between birth mothers and their adult children continued to surface in the news. Many also turned to people within the adoption community who had advanced research skills. Called "search angels," they used a combination of DNA matching with searches of public records to locate birth parents and adoptees.

But David never said out loud that he was hoping to find birth relatives. Perhaps he didn't want to risk hurting the family he had created; he didn't want them to think his tight-knit clan of five hadn't provided enough love. He just wanted to find out if his origins were Sephardic. If they were, it would ease the strict dietary rules of the eight days of Passover—a possibility he welcomed. (Sephardic Jews, who trace their origins to Spain, are allowed to eat rice; until recent changes, Eastern European Jews had to endure a far more limited diet, food that David despised.)

Several weeks later, he began receiving messages from the California company. The test determined that his roots were almost entirely Eastern European. But soon he heard from a woman named Sandy Baumwald. 23andMe had identified her as a distant cousin. When Sandy, who was riveted by the intricacies of ancestry, asked if they could discuss their shared family tree, David told her he could be of no help. He was adopted, he said, and aside from his three children, she was the first blood relative he'd ever spoken to.

"Do you want me to find your birth mother for you?" she asked.

He had never been terribly curious, he responded. He'd been comforted to know that his birth parents were Jewish, he told her, and that

he'd been lucky to be adopted by loving parents. He described his severe health problems, adding that he had long outlived the predictions
of his doctors in Houston. Each day, he told her, was a blessing. He
continued: "With how my health has been these last few years I feel like
it would be nice to connect with relatives from my birth parents, but
mainly to see if I can help anyone with similar health issues." Perhaps
he was protecting himself; perhaps he was struggling with loyalty. He
was not pinning hopes on finding help for his medical troubles. But it
did occur to him that by sharing his medical history, he might be able
to help someone else who suffered from the same afflictions. And perhaps his sense of limited time had prompted him to create a narrative
about why he was taking the test, one that didn't put his allegiance to
the Rosenbergs in question.

As the daughter of Holocaust survivors, Sandy was deeply committed to reuniting separated families, no matter how distant. An attorney
in Athens, Georgia, she had investigative skills that had allowed her to
help hundreds of adoptees locate family members as a search angel
herself. Sandy sensed David's ambivalence about searching for his birth
family. He remained careful, decades after Esther's and Ephraim's
deaths, to tell Sandy how much he loved them, asserting again that he'd
only been looking for clues to his heritage. This was something she had
seen with many adoptees before him. It would not diminish his love for
his adoptive parents if he found his first ones, she assured him.

Her directness did not waver. "Do you want to find her?" she asked
again. He hesitated. What if his birth mother didn't want the intrusion?
he asked. If she didn't, Sandy told him, he'd soon learn.

"OK," David told her. "OK."

Because she'd had two previous clients who'd been adopted through
Louise Wise, Sandy was familiar with the procedures required to search
for original birth names in New York. As she well knew, the original
birth certificate remained under seal. But, as Margaret had learned decades earlier, Sandy knew that there were four digits assigned by New

York City officials on the amended birth certificate, which David provided to her. And the magic number would also be on the original notation of his birth, along with his original name.

The New York City birth indexes were now available online, so she could search the endless list of names at home, just as Margaret had done with the brown ledgers at the city library decades earlier. The records were just scans, however. The city had created no search function that would allow her to retrieve the entry that matched the four numbers on David's birth certificate. There was no alternative for finding David's birth name. She would have to go line by line, number by number.

David, exhausted by illness, offered to help. Sandy said that if after several letters of the alphabet she had not found the record, she'd share the task with him. She bought herself an ample supply of her favorite coffee, settled in with her computer, and told David she hoped his birth name wasn't Zuckerberg. And one afternoon, after three weeks of searching, she found a baby boy born on Staten Island that matched. She leapt from her computer in tears. She immediately emailed David.

"I FOUND IT!!!!!!" read the subject line. In the email, she told him his birth name.

He called her instantly. "Stephen Erle," he said, over and over. "Stephen Erle."

"What do we do now?" he asked quietly.

SANDY'S INSTRUCTIONS WERE EXPLICIT: "Write this all down," she advised, so he wouldn't forget. He was to call Spence-Chapin—the agency that inherited Louise Wise's records after it finally shuttered in 2004—and ask for any "non-identifying information" about his adoption. And even though he now knew his birth name, she was adamant. Do not, under any circumstances, reveal what he now knew to officials at Spence-Chapin; it might make them less willing to help. Since New York State's original birth certificates were all still sealed, there was a legal barrier that blocked David, a dying fifty-two-year-old man, from the truth about his own past.

David requested his file from Spence-Chapin. A few weeks later, he received a four-page document of "non-identifying" information about his birth family, newly written by the agency social worker with whom David had spoken. The social worker had compiled a report from information she had gleaned from records written by Louise Wise social workers beginning from the moment Margaret and Gertrude walked into the agency in the summer of 1961; it continued with the observations of the social worker who visited David while he was in foster care, and ended abruptly with his meeting Esther and Ephraim for the first time in late 1962. It was the only record of his first two years. He had ample photographs and stories from his arrival at the Rosenberg home, but until he received that document, he had had no facts about his early life.

When the record arrived in early March, David forwarded it to Sandy. She fastened on the notation that David's birth mother was a talented student who'd been accepted to a "prestigious science high school" in New York. There were only a few public schools that fit that description. Sandy had a New York cousin, a successful surgeon who had attended the Bronx High School of Science, and her scholarly family had been proud of his distinction there. The school's cachet had made a lasting impression on her, so she began to search graduating classes from the early 1960s. Within no time, she found a graduate named Allen Erle. She felt she was getting closer.

Next, she Googled "Erle." One of her first hits was an American-born winemaker in Israel named Ari Erle. Sandy, an outgoing southerner, decided to call him directly, pretending she needed advice about wine for Passover, which was just a few weeks away. She chatted with Ari for a few moments, and ordered two cases of his wine, which he would send from his California distributor. Then she casually dropped into the conversation that she had some Erle relatives too. Was Ari any relation to Allen? "He's my dad," he told her. She didn't miss a beat. "Doesn't he have an older sister?" she asked. "Yes," Ari told her—he had an aunt in New Jersey. In a cosmically improbable irony, the lie Louise Wise officials had concocted about Margaret's proficiency as a science student had, decades later, helped David's cousin search in precisely the right place.

Sandy logged on to Facebook. Minutes later, she had found a profile of a New Jersey grandmother named Margaret Erle Katz.

THE FULL NAME WAS NO COINCIDENCE. Like many birth mothers who hoped their lost sons and daughters would someday locate them, Margaret had intentionally included her maiden name in her profile even though she was Margaret Katz to everyone who knew her. She had written her most recent post on the anniversary of George's death.

"My Love and best friend since we were 15&16. Cannot believe you are gone today 14 years." Sandy had no doubt that not only was Margaret David's birth mother, it was plausible that her high school sweetheart, now dead, was David's father. The timing of their teenage romance fit the chronology of David's birth. She located Margaret's phone number and address in public records and forwarded them along with George's online obituary and a link to Margaret's Facebook page with the line "I think I found your birth mother."

David clicked on the link and stared at the profile. The resemblance between him and the attractive Jewish grandmother embracing a granddaughter was incontrovertible. She even had a cleft chin like his. Was George Katz his father? Had they had other children? A tall, striking woman with long black hair and olive skin also appeared in Margaret's feed. Was that his sister? Half sister?

Still, he was nervous. "I don't want to interfere," he told Sandy again. "Go for it," she told him. "What have you got to lose?"

On the first night of Passover that year in Portland, the Rosenbergs read from two documents: the Haggadah describing the Jews' exodus from Egypt, and the four-page description of his birth family the social worker had written. David loved the holiday—its songs, and its story. But on this night, he beamed from ear to ear as the family read aloud from both narratives. Noah watched in wonder as his father's face bloomed with an array of new emotions—pride, contentment, and above all, a peace he had never seen before. Kim felt as if she were witnessing a miracle. One line from the adoption agency document mentioned that his parents "had great feelings for him." Another was one Sandy had pointed out to him, a sentence mentioning that his birth mother had approached the agency in the hope of making contact in 1981. (There was no reference to its sending her away.)

"David," she told him, "if she did this, you were not a secret." It was as revelatory as it was liberating.

A FEW DAYS AFTER the end of Passover, David dialed the landline number in Roosevelt, New Jersey, that Sandy had passed along. Margaret didn't recognize the Oregon number. Thinking it was a telemarketer, she let the call go to voice mail. The next morning, May 1, she was setting out to meet Mark for lunch and to visit George's grave; it would have been his seventy-first birthday. But just before she left, she remembered to check the message.

"Hello, Margaret Erle Katz? My name is David Rosenberg, and I'm calling you from Portland, Oregon. I hope you're sitting down, because I think you might be my birth mother. I don't want to disrupt your life, but if you'd like to make contact, here's my number."

Tears sprang to her eyes, and her heart pounded so forcefully in her chest, it felt like there was a baby kicking there. She played the message again and again, listening to the faint voice she had been waiting to hear for a half century.

But she did not just pick up the phone. She went out to meet Mark. They spoke of the usual things—work, Judy, Rachel—and kissed goodbye. Then she set out for the cemetery, her mind racing so fast she didn't remember how she got there. She hurried to George's grave, marked by a handsome granite headstone inscribed in Hebrew and English. She brushed off the pine needles that had covered it, and as is Jewish custom, put some stones on top.

"Georgie," she said, choking back sobs. "He found us. Our son found us."

Back at home, Margaret waited to phone David until the hour he had called her, 8:00 p.m. eastern time. He answered on the first ring, and mother and son spoke for the first time in their lives. Margaret had slipped under the down comforter on her New Jersey bed; David lay sprawled on his bed in Portland. Even in this first talk, he did not shy away from telling her the truth of his condition, and of his dwindling hopes for a cure. But first, he had several questions. Was she upset that he had called?

"David," she told him, "I looked for you for years. I left messages for you at the agency. When you were twenty, I came by to leave my contact number."

He paused, thinking of the line in the records about her 1981 visit.

"I just had no idea," he said.

Over the next hour, David listened, stunned, as Margaret told him about all the efforts she had made to get him back, and then about the calls she'd carefully made about the illnesses in the family tree that had robbed George of old age.

Margaret felt rage rise from her belly to her throat. How could they not have told him? How could he not have known? She told him that she'd married George at nineteen in a desperate attempt to prevent the adoption. Fact by fact, she dismantled the story he had always believed about how she'd voluntarily given him up to further her career.

"Wait," he said. "What about the science?" he asked, referring to the fallacious claim that she had been accepted to a science high school.

"Science?" she asked, incredulous. Her only experience with science was taking care of her three children and of dying relatives: her parents, her husband, even her bitter father-in-law. She'd been a mother, a wife. There'd been no future career in science, and he had never been in the way. He had been loved and wanted. She'd sung German lullabies to him in the maternity home. She had desperately wanted to keep him, and resisted every effort to separate from him until the end.

David was silent on the other end, pausing to let the information sink in.

Margaret also told David that through George, he was a kohen—a member of the priestly class of Jews descended from Aaron, as are most Jews named Cohen, Katz, Cohn, and Kahane. The status passes from father to son, and imparts special duties and responsibilities.

He had so many questions. "Did anyone like sports?" David asked. Yes, Margaret said—George had won, and relinquished, a baseball scholarship the year he was born in order to get married. And he'd been such a dedicated Rangers fan, he wore the team's blue jersey when he came home from work, and often bought season tickets. In fact, she told David, in the early days of her pregnancy, she and George went to the top of the bleachers at Madison Square Garden to watch the games.

"You're kidding," David said. He told her he'd been recruited by the team. With each disclosure, Margaret felt another wave of goose bumps. That led to another question: Was there musical talent in the family?

Margaret laughed. "Your youngest sister is an opera singer in Berlin."

"I have a sister who's an opera singer?" he said, astounded—and immediately checked Cheri Rose Katz's website. The woman on Margaret's Facebook page not only looked like him; they had similar talent, and both had had successful careers in a field in which very few can make a living. David clicked through her YouTube videos of performances in Germany and Italy. He noticed her powerful mezzo-soprano, her wavy hair, expressive dark eyes, and disciplined posture. It was like looking at, and hearing, a female version of himself.

Fearful of wearing him out, Margaret suggested they speak again after he had some rest. Margaret waited for several hours to Skype Cheri in Berlin. It was 2:00 a.m. eastern time, so Cheri was perplexed by the early call. She knew Margaret had visited George's grave that day, and expected to hear a heaviness in Margaret's voice. Instead, her tone seemed strangely light—even happy. Had something happened? Cheri asked.

Margaret replied with a question of her own: "You know how I always say every family has skeletons in their closets?"

Cheri paused. "Ye-ahh?" She cocked her head toward the microphone.

"Well, I've got a big one," Margaret told her daughter, and took a deep breath. "You have another brother. I got pregnant at seventeen and your dad and I had to give him up. He grew up in New York and Toronto and became a wonderful cantor. He's got a beautiful wife, three beautiful kids—and he just found me. We talked this evening," she said, and paused.

At that moment, a blurry peculiarity in Cheri's life snapped into focus. Margaret had always been obsessively curious about her and Lisa's boyfriends—their birthdays, their parents, their origins. Suddenly, her questioning made sense. From the moment her daughters were teenagers, Margaret had been fearful that one day her son might meet her daughters and start dating. She'd read about that sort of coincidental meeting in magazines.

"Are you angry with me?" Margaret asked.

"Angry?" Cheri responded. "I'm thrilled!"

Over the next few weeks, Cheri and Margaret spoke with David, his wife, Kim, and Sam, Noah, and Estee. With some renewed vigor, David propelled himself to attend Noah's high school graduation, expending energy, Noah would say, that he didn't have. David could feel, and see, himself physically melting away. He confessed to a friend in Israel that it was difficult for him to keep a smile going. But in calls and emails with Margaret, he asked if she and her children could come visit them in Portland. They'd all been talking and writing, but it was clear that David and Cheri, the two singers, had developed an instant bond. Cheri canceled her concerts in Germany, flew home to Newark to meet her mother, and in July the two traveled to Portland for a two-week visit.

Margaret was heading to a blind date with her own son. During the long flight to Portland, she was so nervous she took a Xanax. Her back was bothering her so much—and her anxiety was so high, despite the pill—that they ordered a wheelchair for the Jetway. Kim, nervous and excited, welcomed them in the waiting area. A half hour later, they pulled up to the Rosenberg home, amid lush hills and tall fir trees.

David, thin and pale, stood outside. Margaret clambered out of the car, and the two embraced.

It was only the third time she had ever touched him, and she could hardly let go.

David turned to Cheri. "My sister," he said, his arms opened wide. "My sister."

David and Kim had insisted that they stay at the house. Noah had moved to the living room so that Cheri could have his room; Kim installed Margaret in the guest room. As she recited the Shema she'd said every night since girlhood, she was aware of a fundamental difference: for the first time since the hospital on Staten Island, she and her son were under the same roof. The next morning, she awakened from a dream in which she saw Esther Rosenberg smiling down from heaven.

In addition to singing opera, Cheri practiced the Japanese healing art Reiki. She performed sessions on David, and whipped up wheatgrass shakes. (David stuck to his Diet Cokes.) Kim, understanding the decades of deferred love, stepped aside. Margaret rose early to eat breakfast with David and to run errands with him. "Let me do this," she begged Kim. "Please." Her first instinct was to add weight to his thin frame. She made chocolate-chip cake and Gertrude's stuffing to go along with roast chicken. She accompanied David to every medical appointment.

When during their visit his oncologist suggested that it was time for David to consider hospice, Margaret insisted that the doctor was wrong.

She was so elated to learn that her son had had a good life, and was surrounded by family and friends, she couldn't acknowledge what was obvious to everyone, including her son: David was dying. Just as she had batted away thoughts, at seventeen, of his pending adoption, now she dismissed the evidence that she might lose him again. He would recover, she told herself, told him. After every checkup, they went out for Thai food.

And everywhere mother and son went, he introduced her: "This is my birth mom."

At night, the family sat on David and Kim's bed and watched DVDs of the family that Margaret had brought along. She showed the family the pictures of the original Polaroids she and George had snapped on their visits while he was in foster care—the only images he had ever seen of himself as an infant. She poured out the Erle and Katz family histories. Sometimes they spoke of her stay at Lakeview, and of her efforts to try to keep him. He had seen the movie *Philomena*, and asked Margaret if she had endured the same harsh conditions the pregnant Irish girls experienced. The family went on day trips to the Oregon coast and took in Portland's natural beauty.

One Saturday afternoon, Marshal came with his wife, Shari, for a Shabbat lunch they'd arranged to be FedExed from a kosher deli in New York. With wide-eyed wonder, David surveyed the commotion of what he called his "new-old family," gathered in his large, open dining room. Margaret was talking to Marshal and Shari. His sons were playing with Gordie and Cheri's tiny Maltese, who had come along on the trip. Estee, who bears an unmistakable resemblance to Cheri, was next to her newfound aunt on the couch. Kim prepared plates, making sure everyone was comfortable. Everybody was talking; everybody was interrupting one another.

With the platters on the table, David summoned his family to the meal. Everyone did the ritual handwashing, and David chanted blessings over the wine, food, and his family. His voice rang with a clarity it had lacked for months as he gazed upon a scene he could never have dreamed of. The children, who had never known any of David's parents, suddenly had a grandmother and an aunt fussing over them, an aunt and uncle they'd never met, first cousins in Florida and Pennsylvania. All his life, David had known one reality. Now he was learning another. Margaret had only a few weeks to transmit nearly fifty-three years of deferred love, and David basked in it. For the first time, he wasn't thinking of how finding his birth family might be disloyal to his adoptive one. He was a grown man, a husband and father, a spiritual caretaker in his community. But at this moment, he was also a little boy who was, at long last, learning from his mother where he came from.

There is no blueprint for such a meeting, and it was at once both intimate and challenging. For much of their lives, the children had anxiously watched every downturn of their father's health. Now, as they anticipated the grief of his passing, they made room. As Margaret and Cheri's planned two weeks drew to a close, the family called a meeting to discuss how everyone felt about extending their stay. The ayes won. Sam was in college, playing hockey at the University of Oregon; Noah, who had also made the team, was about to enroll. Estee was midway through high school. The children had conflicting feelings. On one hand, they were delighted to see their father's newfound serenity. But they also felt unsettled as their long-lost family assumed the caretaking duties they had all shouldered for so long.

There were also moments of levity, and astonished recognition over shared traits and characteristics. At one point, Kim was driving with Cheri, and gasped as Cheri reached to move her purse. "Oh my God," she said aloud. "You have David's exact hands." During one visit to a seaside arcade, Cheri and David were stunned to learn that they shared a skill at the game Fascination. It had been George Katz's favorite. And they both discovered that they had developed their raw vocal talents early on. Unlike many professional singers, they learned music by ear—not from the typical formal methods of sight-reading.

In mid-August, Margaret and Cheri packed to go home. Cheri had concerts scheduled for the autumn and needed to return to Germany. David, pale and in pain, drove his mother and sister to the airport. On the way, he spoke of taking the family to Miami to see Cheri's next US concert—maybe they could all go on a cruise afterward. He stopped his gray SUV at the departure curb, and everyone got out of the car in slow motion. He hugged Margaret, then Cheri, then Margaret again. Tears spilled down his face.

"I don't want you guys to go," he said.

He would get better, Margaret told him. He would recover. Have faith. They had just experienced a miracle. More, surely, were in store.

THE JEWISH NEW YEAR CAME. David ordinarily felt energized by the High Holidays, but having just absorbed so much, he was drained. A few weeks later, David grew so ill he was hospitalized once more. When he was released, Sam figured out how they could watch Cheri's concert in a live stream, and David saw his sister perform from his bed in Portland. It hurt to talk, and Kim ordered a hospital bed for the living room. David resisted, but he also lacked the strength to make it up the stairs. Kim slept on the couch next to him.

Shortly after returning home, Margaret had decided to go and stay with Cheri in Berlin for a while; it was too overwhelming to return to her empty house in New Jersey.

On November 24, 2014, nearly seven months after their first phone call, they spoke again. David still dreamed, he said, of going on the cruise.

"Save your strength," Margaret told him. "You'll get better, and we'll go. It's something to look forward to."

David paused. "I love you," he whispered to his mother. "Thank you so much for trying so hard to find me."

"I love you too," Margaret said. "I always have, and I always will."

The next day, David Rosenberg died at home.

⁓

FRIENDS AND ADMIRERS CROWDED into Shaarie Torah for the funeral.
David was remembered, eulogized, beloved; his friends spoke of the joy
he'd experienced by meeting Margaret and Cheri. One after another,
people at the shiva spoke of how much David had helped them, changed
their lives, brought out their best. They described his generosity, his appetite for fun, his temper, his passions, his loves. It was difficult to absorb it all. As Sam listened, sometimes he thought the stories revealed
more about the storytellers than his father. Noah remembered how he
felt one time as a little boy, hearing David lead a Passover service. He
had felt a warmth spread through his belly and to each of his digits. His
dad, he understood, was special. People confirmed it, over and over.
Estee, just fifteen, mourned the robust version of her father that people
invoked. She had known only the sick one. Kim tried to maintain composure for her children; inside, she felt numb.

Half a world away, Margaret and Cheri grieved too. Margaret's sorrow, for so long so repressed, for so long so secret, flooded her. Whenever
she thought of the loss, of the unfairness, of the rupture, she told herself
she was lucky. She had met her son; he had had what the social workers
promised: a better life. Was it one she and George could have delivered,
as teenage parents? She didn't allow herself to make that calculation.
She directed her thoughts toward the column of benefits, the ledger she
kept in her head. David had had wonderful parents and a large family
who had loved him deeply. He was embraced everywhere he'd lived—
New York, Toronto, Jerusalem. He'd had a gorgeous, intelligent, spiritual
wife, a loving marriage. He had three beautiful children—grandchildren
she already loved, grandchildren she could get to know.

Shortly after David died, Margaret went to a Berlin synagogue to
pray for him. She stepped up into the crowded women's balcony, un-
zipped her jacket, and placed it on the seat next to her. Moments later,
a young woman came in. Margaret picked up her coat and motioned for

her to sit. The two women began chatting. Margaret explained that she had come to say kaddish, the prayer for the dead, for her son, who had recently died in Portland. "That's strange," said the woman. "I'm here with my dad, who's saying kaddish for my grandmother. She was also in Portland!"

Margaret replied: "I had to give up my son for adoption when I was seventeen, and I only recently met him. He was a cantor there."

The young woman's eyes grew wide. "My grandfather was a rabbi there for forty-five years. His name was Yonah Geller."

"Rabbi Geller?" Margaret asked, her jaw growing slack. "My son was David Rosenberg."

"David Rosenberg, the cantor for my grandfather?" asked the woman, who introduced herself as Rebecca Geller. "I've known your son my whole life."

For so long, Margaret had consoled herself with the thought that she'd put an angel on earth. She'd understood from her brief time in Portland that her son had made a difference. In Judaism, to heal one life is to heal the whole world. He had healed so many. He had repaired the wounds of the living, over and over. She had seen it, felt it, witnessed it. And now she took this chance encounter in the country of their ancestors as a message from a realm she could only hope existed: David was letting her know that he was all right.

IN 2016 Cheri moved back to the United States, and gave birth to a baby girl she named for her father and brother, Georgiana Della. Kim, Sam, and Noah came for the baby's naming ceremony in New Jersey, and met David's brother, Mark, for the first time. Sam and Noah took turns leading the service in Margaret's house in Roosevelt; those gathered spoke of the baby's namesakes.

When it was Margaret's turn to speak, she tilted her head back, and directed her voice to the sky. "George and David," she said, "I hope you are together in heaven."

THE STORY OF MARGARET Erle Katz and David Rosenberg does not have a tidy ending; it was never a tidy story. Their two families, linked once more, tread cautiously around each other. There is love; there is respect; there is compassion. They live on opposite sides of the country; they have different lives. They share biology, but not history, and a half century of lost time is irretrievable. It is almost as if they are relatives, removed, who met at a wedding or a bar mitzvah: the people gathered are there to celebrate the person they have in common. But now, the person they have in common is gone.

Margaret, at home in the house where she raised her children, where she dreamed of David in the backyard, helps care for little Georgie, who is already showing signs of carrying on the family musical tradition. She is not exactly at peace. But she feels reassured, at long last, to have found at least some answers to the questions that had tormented her for fifty-two years.

Now she surrounds herself with images of the things that matter to her the most, and the only thing she ever desired: her complete family. Her refrigerator door is plastered with school photos and holiday cards. In the center is an image of David, Sam, Noah, Estee, Margaret, and Cheri on the Oregon coast. Everyone is smiling, the gentle mist of the ocean air softening the frame. She is never far from her iPhone, and frequently talks and texts her children and grandchildren from Portland to Pennsylvania, from New York to Florida.

Sometimes at night when Margaret is alone, she listens to CDs that David had given her. On them, she can hear her son sing the ancient melodies of their ancestors, full of bittersweet longing for peace. She closes her eyes as she listens, envisioning him as the strong young man he once was, comforted by their brief, shared memories, and her ability, however short, to immerse him in her love.

She listens as the singing mounts and descends, summoning the divine. It is the voice of her son—so very long lost. And so, very fleetingly, found.

David Rosenberg and Margaret Katz, Portland, July 2014

17.

No More Secrets

This book chronicles two journeys, a lifelong separation, and a bittersweet reunion. The experiences of Margaret and David were part of a hidden chapter of US history, a reproductive- and civil rights story that remains unresolved for millions of Americans. If there is a basic human right to know your parents or the fates of your sons and daughters, then a significant number of our fellow citizens have been deprived of something as fundamental as life, liberty, and the pursuit of happiness.

The United States had little understanding of the possible long-term consequences when it launched a social experiment in which millions of babies were raised by families with whom they shared no genetic bond and who knew little or nothing of their inheritance. Closed adoptions of babies born to single women were universally seen as a societal gain, a win-win-win for the mothers, adoptees, and adoptive couples. Most often, they were anything but that.

Children love to hear their origin stories, from where Mommy and Daddy met to the address of the hospital in which they were born. For many adopted people in the United States, that story begins with a lie: their selfless birth mothers gave them to strangers to be raised because they loved them so much. Many adult adoptees told me this well-meaning fable had the opposite of its intended effect, leaving them with pervasive, sometimes crippling anxieties. If the person who is most supposed to love you surrenders you, they would ask, how can you ever trust any relationship to last?

Today we have a more nuanced understanding of the needs of children than did the pseudoscientific clinicians of the mid-twentieth century (although bizarrely, some pediatric researchers continue to cite Karelitz's work). A succession of studies conducted using modern, evidence-based techniques show that many adoptees often feel grief, anxiety, and fear at the loss of their birth parents, even when they were raised in loving homes with parents who cherished them. These feelings often intensify during emotionally charged milestones such as marriage or the birth of a child. Similarly, researchers have found that birth mothers' enduring guilt, shame, and sorrow are not assuaged by the belief that their sons and daughters might be living a "better" life. When outcomes were compared, children involved in open adoptions in which they remain in contact with their birth mothers reported feeling far more satisfied, at ease, and positive than adoptees in closed processes. Separately, birth mothers in open adoptions reported experiencing far less unresolved grief than comparable women in closed adoptions. In the United Kingdom, where authorities unsealed adoption records in 1975, a longitudinal study of birth mothers and adoptees who reunited found that the reconnection had been overwhelmingly positive, helping to dissolve the adoptees' feelings of rejection and the mothers' anxiety. The report also found that reunions had not changed the adoptees' thoughts and emotions toward their adoptive parents.

The scientific findings are consistent with the inherent human interest to know where we come from. Genealogy is one of America's favorite pastimes, both in real life (as a hobby, it's second to gardening) and online (only porn sites are more popular). They're also in line with my observations from hundreds of interviews with adopted people. Sooner or later, nearly every conversation with them circled back to the foundational fact of closed adoption: it begins with an erased past, and facts replaced with myths. Birth mothers I interviewed expressed similar skepticism about the "it was all for the best" argument they heard as young women. I never met anyone who relinquished a newborn because she loved him or her so much. They did so out of shame, a lack of support from their families, or both. Their pain at having done so persisted, often for a lifetime.

In many quarters, today's adoption practices are different. (But for adoptive parents willing to pay large sums, it is still possible to arrange exactly the sort of closed domestic adoption that separated Margaret from David.) The number of babies placed for domestic adoption began to fall in the early 1970s and adoption social workers came up with the idea of open adoptions, in which birth parents have varying degrees of contact with their child and the adoptive family. They quickly became common. The crushing pressures that made surrendering a newborn seem like the only rational choice have largely vanished. The deal Margaret was forced to accept—surrender your child forever or we'll throw you in juvie—is far from the only possibility for a young woman pregnant outside marriage. To be an unmarried mother, even as a teenager, is no longer aberrant; nearly a quarter of all children now live with single mothers. Society's expectations of women have seen a comparable shift. While the notion of teen mothers raising babies is sometimes viewed as less than ideal, it is no longer inconceivable, or evidence of an unimaginable moral failing. Almost everyone has sex before marriage and most teenagers have easy access to birth control. Women have had the right to abortion since 1973, although it is increasingly restricted in many states.

The millions of sealed birth records that made the twentieth-century system possible remain a deeply contentious political issue, one of the few that transcend the red/blue divide. Ten states, including cobalt Oregon and vermilion Alabama, allow adoptees unrestricted access to their original birth certificates. Records remain closed in some of the nation's biggest states, including California, Texas, and Florida. It took adoptee-rights advocates in deeply liberal New York four decades to persuade the state legislature to pass a law allowing access to original birth certificates, signed into law in 2019. The legislation made available an estimated 650,000 previously sealed records.

The debate has been, and remains, intense and emotional, pitting the value of personal privacy against people's right to know their original identity. In many states, it has also become entangled with the struggle over abortion. In New York and elsewhere, Catholic officials and others opposed to abortion have lobbied against granting adoptees access to their original birth certificates, contending it would lead to more abortions. They argue that many more women would reject adoption if it meant giving birth to a child who could someday find them. Although frequently cited, there is no evidence for this proposition. States that have opened their original birth certificates have not seen a jump in abortion rates.

Another argument against opening the records is that to do so would renege on a long-ago promise of secrecy made to birth parents. The truth is that while some birth parents may have felt an implicit guarantee of privacy, no surrender documents could have ever legally guaranteed that their identities would be permanently concealed. A detailed analysis of documents signed by women in twenty-six states found no language promising lifelong anonymity.

Certainly, many of the mothers who relinquished children assumed their identities would remain secret, even if that promise was not written down. But few birth mothers oppose opening the records. In states that have passed what are called "partial access laws," birth mothers have been allowed to redact their names before any files are released. Hardly any have done so. A study found that an average of one out of every two thousand birth mothers in those states removed their names from the documents—one-half of 1 percent. That's consistent with my reporting. The vast majority of the more than one hundred birth mothers I met had been coerced into surrendering their children. (Admittedly, it was a group composed of those who had either reunited or hoped to reunite with their sons and daughters.) Nearly all of them told me they were not able to forget their missing child, not for a single day.

Their longing, their worry, and their loss influenced their lives in immeasurable ways.

Adoptee-rights advocates say the states' secrecy laws are an anachronism from a time when single women were viewed as inherently unable to govern themselves. Shawna Hodgson, an adoptee-rights activist reformer and mediator who was born and adopted in Texas, offers an even more compelling argument against the laws that keep the records closed: they infantilize adoptees. At this point in the twenty-first century, why, she asks, should people who were adopted have fewer rights than those who were not? Why should adoptees have to live their lives with so many unknowns? People, she says, are not secrets. To Hodgson and other adoptees searching for their genetic backgrounds and families, it seems astonishing that in an era in which privacy has been obliterated, in which apps track our whereabouts, in which targeted ads stalk our computer screens, and in which surveillance cameras record our every gesture, they remain barred from finding their kin or seeing records of their birth.

For the half million international adoptees from China, Korea, Guatemala, Ethiopia, and elsewhere, the issues are even more complex. Reared predominantly by white families, they often struggle to establish their racial identities as people of color as they contend with the loss of language and cultural traditions. As Stephanie Drenka, a Texas-based writer who was adopted from Korea in 1986, told me, "We were raised with white privilege in white worlds, and yet we are perpetual foreigners within it." Many transracial adoptees, she says, grapple with internalized racism that is reinforced by casual bigotry: compliments, for example, on how well they speak English and thoughtless commentary on hair type or skin color.

Their path to finding their birth families is even more daunting. In Korea, some adoption registries exist. Drenka, for example, reunited with her birth family in 2013, and learned that the story her agency had told her adoptive parents—that her mother was a disgraced single mother with little choice but to surrender her child—was utterly false. Her parents had been married, and her late birth father had insisted that her mother relinquish her, a third daughter, in a culture that favored sons. Their reunion has been both joyful and fraught: Stephanie speaks little Korean, and her birth mother has difficulty surmounting her guilt. And while she loves and appreciates her adoptive parents, who'd suffered through several miscarriages but who had a biological son within a year of her adoption, Stephanie has struggled with the feeling of being a "second-choice backup plan." She is outspoken about the need for transracial, international adoptees to reshape the narrative of their lives, moving beyond the simplified tales of abandonment and dramatic rescue. It is true, she says, that many grew up with advantages and have flourished in American society. But she and many others are deeply aware of what was lost and left behind.

ADOPTIVE PARENTS, who provide nurture and love with the very best of intentions, must also understand that adoption always equates to loss for the adoptee. People who are adopted are often told that they are "lucky," like Drenka, like David, like so many others. There is no disputing that their families love them, and in that sense, of course, they are lucky. But love and devotion can only go so far in annulling loss, even if—especially if—it is not verbalized. So often in adoption, each party carries grief. One set of parents mourns the loss of the child they had to surrender. Adoptive parents relish the chance to make that child their own. But infertility also carries stigma and shame. No matter how much a child is wanted, there often remains the ambiguous loss of the child they were unable to create. Adoptees, meanwhile, are torn between loyalty to the family that raised them—often with love and opportunities—and longing for their absent kin.

Perhaps bridging that complex reality is why efforts to unseal the records have been painstakingly slow.

Opening these vital documents can be a life-changing experience for adoptees. One advocate I know likens the effects of government secrecy in adoption, at any time, to being sequestered in, say, the East Wing of a museum of one's own life. Tim Monti-Wohlpart, who was born and adopted in New York State in 1971, describes the experience this way: "Imagine that one day you look across the rotunda and finally grasp that there was always a West Wing too." Naturally, he says, you understand that it's yours. You also know that if you explore it, you might find some unpleasant things. That, he argues, is the choice every adoptee deserves—whether or not to see and assimilate the reality of the other wing. "But then, as you approach, a guard enters. He blocks your path and says, 'You can't go there.' And you say, 'But it's my right to understand the truth of where I came from. To know my own self.' And the guard steps closer and says, 'Sorry, pal—not for you.'"

For David, the mystery of his identity was more than an issue of wondering why his mother had "given him up." Every time he filled out a medical form asking for his family history, he had to say he didn't know. The medical records that Margaret so valiantly—obsessively—tried to pass on, and which Louise Wise refused to share, might have altered his life's path. Had he known he was at risk for diabetes, he might have made choices that would have forestalled the cascade of illnesses to which he eventually succumbed. Likewise, Margaret Katz lived most of her life keeping her identity as the mother of her firstborn son a secret. Her sexuality, her fertility, and her pregnancy were viewed, in the mid-century United States, as an existential threat, a social menace.

When you think about the march toward rights, it is important to remember that every abstract girl "in trouble" was a real woman like Margaret Erle. One Friday afternoon in Israel, I sat with David's aunt Yafa at a bustling café. She was smiling as she described how thrilled her late sister Esther was to become a mother. Yafa was eighty-eight at the time and speaking in her third language. We had just paid, and I was about to put my notebook back in my purse. But just as I did, she reached across the table and touched my hand. She motioned for me to write down what she was about to say. It was a message for Margaret.

"Please tell David's mother that I am so happy that she had him," she said. "And that I am happy for my sister that Esther had her boy."

Then her expression shifted, and her blue eyes got sad. "But I am also sorry for David's mother that she has this tragedy." She drummed her pink fingernails on the table. "You know when someone is very sick, and waiting for a new heart or kidney? The family of the sick person prays for a miracle. Then the miracle comes—you get the call that a new heart or kidney is waiting in the hospital. But you realize what is responsible for this miracle: the death of someone else. The tragedy in someone else's family becomes the joy, the life, for another."

IT IS POSSIBLE THAT the arguments about concealing the identities and histories of biological parents are made with an eye not just to the past, but also to the present and the future. In 1978 in England, Louise Brown, the first baby conceived by in vitro fertilization, was born just as the number of infants available for adoption was dropping. With that announcement, the miracle of human existence hurtled forward into a new world of assisted reproductive technology. Artificial insemination—the process by which doctors impregnated women by injecting sperm directly into the cervix—had been around since the late nineteenth century. But now people who'd had no hope of conceiving could turn to an additional array of helpers, including egg donors and gestational surrogates, to create babies in a laboratory.

Those breakthroughs, while bringing joy to couples unable to conceive, have opened up a new set of issues. The tens of thousands of people created each year from anonymously donated eggs and/or sperm face the same questions that have confounded adoptees. Many conceived with these new methods are already asking, What rights do they have to know about their genetic origins? What right do the donors have to lifelong confidentiality? The donors in these cases are entirely willing. Does that mean they have a stronger claim to permanent privacy? Each year, an estimated thirty thousand to sixty thousand babies are conceived with sperm from US sperm banks, yet the $6 billion reproductive medicine industry is as unregulated as adoption was in the mid-twentieth century. Sperm banks and fertility clinics typically market their sperm and egg donors as tall, attractive, athletic, and intellectually gifted. Already, some of those claims have proved as fanciful as Margaret the scientist. In one instance, DNA tests revealed that more than thirty half siblings purportedly fathered by an assortment of sperm donors were actually the offspring of a single fertility doctor who used his own sperm to impregnate their mothers. In another, the tests have discovered that at least a dozen children of a single donor have autism, in addition to ADHD, dyslexia, and mood disorders.

As for the future of adoption, it's likely to remain part of society as long as there are unwanted pregnancies and people unable to raise their own children in a safe environment. In the United States, the chief alternative to adoption is a foster care system whose flaws have been repeatedly exposed by investigative journalists. Modern adoption, with its openness and efforts to recognize the cultural needs of adoptees, is preferable to the poorly funded and regulated foster parent arrangements common in many states. It is tragically unfair to criminalize parents for poverty. But there are instances in which people who feel ill equipped to parent, sometimes willingly, or under legal sanction, give up their parental rights. In those cases, adoption can place a child in a secure, loving environment that offers a permanency that is in the child's best interest. This is also true for children born to single mothers in countries that treat sex outside marriage as a crime. While international adoption has come under increased scrutiny for its abuses, a significant number of intercountry adoptions can and do offer such children a nurturing, enriching life. But it is almost never guaranteed that adoption will provide a child with a better life. Most often, it is a different life.

෴

THE RIGHTS OF ADOPTEES have emerged as a global political issue. Closed, secretive adoption practices like those in the United States were widespread. In post–World War II Canada, Australia, the United Kingdom, and Ireland, authorities also orchestrated the coerced adoptions of babies born to hundreds of thousands of single mothers. As in the United States, officials in Canada and Australia also forcibly took children from indigenous communities and gave them to white families.

Authoritarian regimes in Spain, Greece, and Argentina stole the babies of women who were political opponents and gave them to their allies to raise. In Argentina, the mothers were tortured while pregnant and murdered after they gave birth. And in the 1950s, Israeli officials took as many as 4,500 babies from Yemeni parents living in migrant camps, told their parents they had died, and gave them to light-skinned European Israelis.

The methodologies may have differed, but the outcome was the same as officials sought to raise new generations by separating them from parents they deemed undesirable. Most countries in the European Union have opened adoption records, and some national lawmakers, including Justin Trudeau of Canada and Leo Varadkar in Ireland, have publicly recognized the pain and inequities of a system that gave women and their children no choice.

No political figure has spoken more eloquently and forthrightly on this issue than Australian prime minister Julia Gillard. In 2013, she addressed the Australian Parliament and directly acknowledged the government's complicity in the estimated 150,000 forced adoptions in the decades after World War II. To a crowd of eight hundred, many in tears, Gillard recognized the losses suffered by everyone involved in the system, including fathers, grandparents, siblings, and extended family. But her most moving remarks were directed toward the mothers and their lost children, now adults.

We deplore the shameful practices that denied you, the mothers, your fundamental rights and responsibilities to love and care for your children. You were not legally or socially acknowledged as their mothers. And you were yourselves deprived of care and support.

To you, the mothers who were betrayed by a system that gave you no choice and subjected you to manipulation, mistreatment and malpractice, we apologise. . . . For the loss, the grief, the disempowerment, the stigmatisation and the guilt, we say sorry.

To each of you who were adopted or removed, who were led to believe your mother had rejected you and who were denied the opportunity to grow up with your family and community of origin and to connect with your culture, we say sorry.

With profound sadness and remorse, we offer you all our unreserved apology.

SUCH WORDS WOULD OFFER great comfort to Margaret and millions of other mothers, adoptees, fathers, sisters, and brothers trapped in the closed American system.

They are still waiting.

ACKNOWLEDGMENTS

T his book took me on a journey in telling many stories: two deeply personal ones, and that of a little-explored period in the United States. It began in 2007, when I first met David Rosenberg. His memory served as both a blessing and a beacon as I set out to learn what had happened to him, to his birth mother, Margaret Erle Katz, and to the millions of other Americans who were caught in this country's system of closed adoptions. I am grateful to have known him, and for his encouraging me to tell this story.

Thank you to Margaret Katz, who shared her life's most intimate, painful, and joyous moments, unraveling the secret she contained for fifty-two years. She is the most generous of Jewish mothers, and I'm humbled by her faith, love, and resilience. My gratitude to Kim Danish Rosenberg, and to her and David's children, Sam, Noah, and Estee, is immense. It was difficult to have me explore their memories of David as they mourn his loss, yet they welcomed me with warmth, love, humor, grace, and breathtaking introspection. Cheri Rose Katz also shared her experiences of the brother she only briefly met. Her daughter, Georgie, is still tiny, but it's clear she possesses the same talents as her family. It's impossible to thank everyone adequately for the time we spent together—so much of it wrenching—and for all of my questions. They are mensches, all.

David touched people everywhere, and his friends mobilized to connect me with people who remembered him. Ron Goldner and Marshal Spector responded to the most minute of questions, and when they couldn't answer them, directed me to those who could. Ron and Caryn Gersh Ben-Simchon welcomed me to their table in Tel Aviv; Ron's daughters, Romi and Shelly, joined in offering stories and correspondence. Marshal and his wife, Shari Levinson, spoiled me in Portland. Thanks also to Marden Paul, Larry Zeifman, David Klein, Suzanne Wintrob, Rabbi David Berk, and Debbie Cherniak for Toronto details; to Udi Barzily, Riki Barzily, Motti Ohana, Rachel Ohana, and Adam Emanuel for Jerusalem recollections; to Barry Benson, Karla Benson, and Rabbi Ariel Stone for Portland ones. In Netanya, Yafa Kuperman, David's late aunt, shared memories of her late nephew, sister, and brother-in-law. In New York, thanks to David's cousins: Chen Serok, Mitch Herstic, and Bryan Herstic. In Athens, Georgia, Sandy Baumwald was as enthusiastic a host and source to me as she was in linking David to Margaret through their chance meeting on 23andMe.

I was lucky to work at the *Oregonian* in the 2000s; it laid the foundation for this book. Michael Rollins encouraged me to explore adoption and reproductive medicine as a beat (I'll never stop thinking about the story that got away). Joany Carlin gave me time and space to write about David's kidney transplant. Sandy Rowe was a tireless supporter of the work we all did there. Jack Hart read my proposal and gave suggestions for how to execute this project. I miss you all.

I had great help from many scholars. I owe enormous thanks to two professors who have examined the history of adoption in the United States: E. Wayne Carp at Pacific Lutheran University and, over the years, Ellen Herman at the University of Oregon. University of Minnesota historian Elaine Tyler May offered keen insights on society's expectations of women during the Cold War. Evergreen State College historian Stephanie Coontz offered wisdom on the way we never were. New York University historian Zvi Ben-Dor Benite produced forgotten documents that were instrumental in my research. NYU psychiatrists Glenn Saxe and Joanna Bures helped explain the neurobiology of trauma, loss, and the importance of the work of John Bowlby; Robert Marvin at the University of Virginia and Heidi Bailey from the University of Guelph did too. University of Baltimore law professor Elizabeth Samuels read portions of this book and answered many questions. At New York's American Museum of Natural History, paleoanthropologist Ian Tattersall helped shed light on proceedings at the museum many decades ago.

Thanks to archivists Steve Novak and Cameron Mitchell at the Augustus C. Long Health Sciences Library at Columbia University; Trevor Sandgarhe at Oregon State University; and the staff at the Missouri Valley Special Collections at the Kansas City Public Library, particularly Dr. John Horner. In Memphis, Steve McFarland gave me access to the files of Abe Waldauer and the Tennessee Children's Home Society. In Portland, Aya Fujii shared her extraordinary personal documents. Thanks, too, to Lori Shenseki for sharing documents, and to Jill Benson for allowing access to the former Lakeview home on Staten Island.

At the *New York Times*, Amy Virshup and Todd Heisler worked sensitively with me to help capture Margaret's story in 2015. Thanks also—so much—to Kathleen O'Brien and Beth Flynn.

So many in the adoption-reform community were patient with an adoption outsider. Enormous thanks are owed to Pam Hasegawa, who responded immediately to every phone call, text, and email; to Florence Fisher, adoptee-rights pioneer, wonderful cook, and storyteller; to Cathi Swett, so generous with her time and knowledge of the law. Thank you to Erica Babino, Peter Franklin, Rudy Owens, April Dinwoodie, Suzanne Bachman, Gregory Luce, Annette O'Connell, Stephanie Drenka, Valerie Duckett Charles, Lisa Munro, Christopher Philippo, Marty Juman, and Adrian Jones (especially) for their graciousness. Kris Probasco and Marilyn Mendenhall Waugh welcomed me to Kansas City. They guided me through the new world of assisted reproductive technology, as well as the city's and Marilyn's history. Ronny Diamond, Gretchen Viederman, Jim Gritter, and Maxine Chalker described their evolving years as adoption social workers. Bert Hirsch, a New York attorney who drafted numerous pieces of adoption-reform legislation, spent hours reviewing several sections of this manuscript. Marty and Phyllis Juman spoke of their lives with Michael, and of battling Louise Wise.

I'm deeply grateful for the candor and bravery of many women who offered insight on the shame of their pregnancies and the anguish of losing their sons and daughters. In New Jersey, Lori Posner Zapin depicted her time at the Lakeview home for unwed Jewish mothers and the sexual expectations of young women in the *Mad Men* era. Her memory, style, and wit are unmatched. Lorraine Dusky offered her experiences of having lost, found, and then lost her daughter once more. Her books, blog, emails, memory (and hospitality in Sag Harbor) were extremely helpful. I also had help from Jane Edwards and Delores Sullivan in Portland; from Sarah Burns in Los Angeles; from Amy Seek, Carol Schaefer, Lynn Franklin, Claudia Corrigan D'Arcy, and Dr. Judy Kelly (who bequeathed me her adoption library) in New York; and from Leslie Pate Mackinnon in Atlanta. In Santa Cruz, Maya Lama shared her encyclopedic knowledge of the shocking manner in which girls and their babies were treated; her research helped strengthen this book. There is so much more to say about what they all experienced; I hope I have done justice to the larger story.

Many of my writer friends helped me when I was stuck. Tracy Quan offered gimlet-eyed advice on matters editorial and otherwise. Lettie Teague studded the calendar with glamorous dates. Barbara Bisantz Raymond read portions for clarity, and introduced me to sources in Memphis. Dale Russakoff was a human thesaurus.

At services in Portland I took solace from J. D. Kleinke's clear tenor on the bimah. I'm so honored by the time he took to help sharpen my own voice in telling this story. His sensitivity and active-verb vocabulary elevated this project. I lack the ones I need to articulate my thanks.

Thanks to Netaya Anbar, always, for her dazzling sixth sense, and to

Flip Brophy for her generosity—with everything. Thank you to Mitch and Wendi Glaser, Amy Putman, Nina Rosenstein, Leslie Mitchel Bond, Melissa Deutsch, Ray Bonner, Robin Long, Robin and Cliff Kulwin, Nomi Kehati, Naomi Rand, Shimon Dotan, and Dave Austin for their enthusiasm; Rabbi Elliott Tepperman for his knowledge and for Wednesday meditations. Thanks to Carlos Alvare for his well of compassion. And to Victoria Britt for her vision and kindness, so much of it.

Members of my clan in Oregon helped support me during my visits there. Many thanks to Stephanie Hagerty, Lyn Jenks, and Ann Olsen.

I am lucky to be in the gifted orbit of so many in the publishing world. At WME, my brilliant, bold agent, Dorian Karchmar, envisioned a big story from the outset—and pushed me to improve it. She has brains and empathy in equal measure. Thanks also to Jamie Carr and Alex Kane. At Viking, my magnificent editor, Wendy Wolf, helped frame this story by reminding me that it was the biography of not only an adoption but also an era; she and Terezia Cicel helped streamline this work in profoundly elegant ways. Thanks also to Lindsay Prevette, Kate Stark, Mary Stone, Andrea Schulz, Carolyn Coleburn, Sara Leonard, Jeanette Gingold, and so many other resourceful thinkers at Viking.

I'm indebted to adoptee-rights activists Tim Monti-Wohlpart in New York and Shawna Hodgson in Houston. I am honored by their trust, friendship, and partnership. They deepened the scope of this book immensely by conveying essential facts, by suggesting editorial changes, and especially by alerting me to the chilling studies conducted on vulnerable newborns at the hands of society's most powerful. I hope this work makes a difference.

My biggest debts are to my family, who help repair the world—and me. To my gentle, wise, and clever daughters, Ilana, Moriah, and Dalia— I am thankful to be your mother every day. Finally, to Steve, editor and seer: so generous with his prodigious talents, and so patient with this process, again and again. His optimism and foresight sustained me when my own escaped—also again and again. I am deeply grateful.

AUTHOR'S NOTE

American Baby is a work of nonfiction, based on four years of reporting on David Rosenberg's adoption in New York City in 1963, research on the forces that coerced his birth mother, Margaret Erle, to surrender him, and on the historical context in which it and millions of other US adoptions took place. I use the term "birth mother" throughout, understanding that many women who were forced to relinquish their sons and daughters in secret adoptions often prefer the terms "natural mother" or "first mother." Many of those women also use the terms interchangeably, and I recognize that the language of adoption is evolving.

In order to recreate dialogue and scenes in Margaret Erle Katz's story, I conducted hundreds of interviews with her and her daughter Cheri Katz; consulted the many personal documents and photographs in her possession; and went with her to visit many of the locations where events took place, from the apartment buildings of her childhood and early adulthood to the Staten Island maternity home where she was sequestered in 1961. While no one's memory is infallible, Margaret's is enviably detailed and complete. This is not entirely coincidental: most of what we experience leaves no trace in our memory, but the trauma of losing a child is impossible to forget.

The scenes from David's life are based on many interviews I had with his widow, Kim Danish Rosenberg, as well as their children, Sam, Noah, and Estee, and his wide circle of friends. I visited his former neighborhood and synagogue in Toronto, and met with childhood and high school friends; I traveled to Israel to meet his indomitable aunt Yafa in Netanya; his close friend Ron Goldner in Tel Aviv; and many friends from his student days at Hebrew University in Jerusalem. In places where I quote David directly, his words come from the recollections of his friends and family; our own conversations, which began in 2007; an in-depth interview conducted with him by the Oregon Jewish Museum in 2009; correspondence with friends and family; and an autobiography he wrote in or around 1980.

To tell the larger history of adoption in the United States, I relied on extensive archival documents and photographs; historical and scientific research; and interviews with a wide range of birth mothers, adoptee-rights activists, adoptive parents, social workers, genealogists, and others whose work or lives connect with adoption. Occasionally people wished to remain anonymous. My historical reporting took me to many places: to the private Memphis archives of Georgia Tann's Tennessee Children's Home Society, a baby-stealing and baby-selling operation for America's elite that helped spawn secret adoptions; to archives in Kansas City, Missouri, which because of the city's centrality on the nation's rail lines operated a disproportionate number of maternity homes to which anxious parents could send their shamed daughters; and to archives at Oregon State University, which operated a "practice home" using babies surrendered for adoption as human dolls in its home economics department. I also spent many weeks exploring the Columbia University archives of Viola Bernard, a psychiatrist at Louise Wise Services in New York City, the adoption agency that handled Jewish adoptions, including David's.

The story of David and Margaret and the millions of others involved in secret adoptions raises crucial questions about ethics, the law, gender, and human and civil rights. I have done my best to try to present these issues fairly and lucidly. As in every examination of post–World War II history in America, race plays a role. The world of closed adoptions into which Margaret and David were thrust was overwhelmingly white. White middle-class parents were the primary customers of the adoption industry. The experiences of black women with unplanned pregnancies unfolded in an entirely separate realm, typical of our segregated nation.

Notes

Author's Note

Prologue

8 **The adoption agencies:** Elizabeth J. Samuels, "Surrender and Subordination: Birth Mothers and Adoption Law Reform," *Michigan Journal of Gender and Law*, vol. 20, issue 1, 2013, pp. 33–81. https://repository.law.umich.edu/cgi/viewcontent.cgi?article=1030&context=mjgl. Accessed May 20, 2018.

1. Secrets

13 **Gertrude had grown up:** From both Margaret's recollections and Fulda's official website. https://www.tourismus-fulda.de/fileadmin/user_upload/tourismus-fulda.de/bilder/souvenirs-prospekte/Willkommen_engl.pdf. Accessed Oct. 28, 2019.

When describing Margaret's life and history throughout this book, I rely on Margaret's memories and our many interviews. Her recollections are bolstered by newspaper articles, Margaret's personal documents, the memories of other women whose children were adopted through Louise Wise Services, as well as social workers who worked in the adoption field in the postwar period.

14 **Divorce was shameful:** Brandon Ambrosino, "Recent US Divorce Rate Trend Has 'Faint Echo' of Depression-Era Pattern," Johns Hopkins University HUB, Jan. 29, 2014. https://hub.jhu.edu/2014/01/29/divorce-in-time-of-recession/. Accessed Nov. 14, 2017.

14 **After a few years:** The German-Jewish Club was founded in the nineteenth century for German-speaking Jews around the world. It was later

renamed the New World Club, and published its own newspaper, called the *Aufbau*. *Aufbau*, Leo Baeck Institute. https://www.lbi.org/collections/library /highlights-of-lbi-library-collection/periodicals/aufbau-york-ny-periodical/. Accessed Jan. 4, 2018.

15 **By the late 1940s:** Supermarkets first appeared during the Depression. One chain called King Kullen launched in Queens in 1930. https://www .kingkullen.com/about-us/. Accessed Nov. 8, 2017. D'Agostino was founded in Manhattan a few years later. http://www.fundinguniverse.com/company -histories/d-agostino-supermarkets-inc-history/. Accessed Nov. 8, 2017.

2. *Teenagers in Love*

19 **Born to a wealthy:** Cheri Katz, Margaret Erle Katz's daughter, has visited the addresses of her grandparents. She showed me photographs of the buildings on Nov. 6, 2017.

19 **Fritz and his father, Isidor:** Interview with Margaret, Nov. 6, 2017. For more about the deportations of Viennese Jews, see Martin Gilbert, *The Holocaust: A History of the Jews of Europe during the Second World War* (New York: Henry Holt, 1987), pp. 58–61.

20 **At Dachau . . . them:** Read more about the forced labor of Jews in Dachau at the US Holocaust Memorial Museum website. https://www.ushmm.org /wlc/en/article.php?ModuleId=10005214. Accessed Nov. 7, 2017.

20 **Jews were assigned:** Gilbert, *The Holocaust*, p. 58.

20 **They were often:** Interview with Margaret, Nov. 8, 2017. For more on the treatment of prisoners before the start of the war, see Christian Goeschel and Nikolaus Wachsmann, eds., *The Nazi Concentration Camps, 1933–1939: A Documentary History* (Lincoln: University of Nebraska Press, 2012), p. 225.

20 **A few months later:** Read more about wartime rationing in Britain here: Stephen Wilson, "Rationing in World War II," Historic UK. https://www .historic-uk.com/CultureUK/Rationing-in-World-War-Two/. Accessed Oct. 28, 2019.

20 **The camp had been converted:** "The Kitchener Camp for Refugees," Weiner Holocaust Library, https://www.wienerlibrary.co.uk/The-Kitchener -Camp-for-Refugees. Accessed Oct. 31, 2017. Photo seen Nov. 5, 2017.

20 **Fritz spoke little about his year as a laborer:** Interview with Margaret, Nov. 6, 2017.

20 **George's mother, Lizzie:** Interview with Margaret, Nov. 6, 2017.

21 **German officials claimed:** While this scene comes from Margaret's memory of her conversation with Lizzie, I also consulted the US Holocaust Memorial Museum's website. https://www.ushmm.org/wlc/en/article.php?ModuleId= 10005201. Accessed Nov. 1, 2017. My late father-in-law, Professor Edward Engelberg, grew up in Munich and often recalled those terrifying days in chilling detail. Also see Gilbert, *The Holocaust*, pp. 68–70.

22 **Not knowing the fates:** Lizzie and George married before the war's end, but swift pairing would soon become a pattern. After the war, the marriage and birth rates among Jews in displaced persons camps were among the highest in the postwar world. Michal Shapira, "'Hitler Married Us': The Chaotic Life of Jews in Post–WWII German Displaced Persons Camps," *Haaretz*, April 18, 2017. https://www.haaretz.com/world-news/europe/.premium-1.783291. Accessed Dec. 17, 2017.

22 **Fritz, meanwhile, never stopped:** Interview with Margaret, Jan. 17, 2017, but see more here: Eleanor Sontag, *Second Generation: Memoir of a Child of Holocaust Survivors* (Bloomington: Xlibris, 2011), p. 26.

3. *"We're Going to Have to Take Care of This"*

34 **He said goodbye:** This is Margaret's memory, as well as that of Lori Posner Zapin, who was also remanded to Lakeview. (She gave birth to a daughter just days after her seventeenth birthday.) I also found several fundraising pamphlets, including one that made reference to it. "Louise Wise Services: Affiliated with Jewish Philanthropies of New York, Member of Child Welfare League of America, 1958," p. 4.

34 **From the back corridor . . . plant:** Louise Wise Services, fundraising pamphlet, 1958, p. 1.

4. *Girls in Trouble*

39 **The number of babies born:** Stephanie J. Ventura, "Recent Trends and Differentials in Illegitimacy," *Journal of Marriage and Family*, vol. 31, no. 3, Aug. 1969, pp. 446–450. https://www.jstor.org/stable/349764?seq=1. Accessed March 23, 2018.

39–40 **was a stark contrast . . . "dynamite":** Elaine Tyler May, *Homeward Bound: American Families in the Cold War Era* (New York: Basic Books, 2008), pp. 106–108. Also see her chapter on sexuality at home: "Brinkmanship: Sexual Containment on the Home Front," pp. 109–128.

40 **novels and films:** Caitlin Healy, "Banned Books That Shaped American Literature," *Miami Herald*, Feb. 8, 2018. https://www.miamiherald.com /news/nation-world/national/article179666311.html. Accessed Oct. 28, 2019.

The National Coalition Against Censorship's website has a list dating to the late nineteenth century. http://ncac.org/resource/a-brief-history-of-film-cen sorship. Accessed Jan. 15, 2018. Note that the National Legion of Decency, founded in 1933 by American Catholics, assigned films an A, B, or C (for "Con-demned) based on their moral suitability. A film boycott by American Catholics could be devastating for filmmakers.

40–41 **Consider this 1957 . . . line:** High school students throughout North America watched McGraw-Hill's Marriage and Family Living series. https:// www.worldcat.org/title/how-much-affection/oclc/61513261. This comes from "How Much Affection?" https://bit.tube/play?hash=QmT4XN8U193x4C 44gA4zJRPcX2om5TCuuiy7nRCd5Jcp22&channel=183445. This link pre-view says 1958, but the date stamped on the film is 1957. Accessed Oct. 31, 2019.

There are more, including one called "How to Say No," in which high school boys and girls discuss petting. "Nora" tells her friend "Lucy": "Naturally, Lucy, we're partly to blame. We invite a little attention. It goes on—and then it's hard to stop."

Also see: Beth Bailey, *From Front Porch to Back Seat: Courtship in Twentieth-Century America* (Baltimore: Johns Hopkins University Press, 1988) in a chapter called "Sex Control," particularly pp. 80–83.

41 **In one popular . . . bowling:** Harriet Cynthia London, *How Every Girl Can Choose, Win, Hold and Enjoy a Man* (Brooklyn, NY: Daycliffe Company, 1948), pp. 72–73.

41 **Access to the birth control pill:** The landmark 7–2 Supreme Court decision in 1965 found that two appellants, Estelle Griswold, a feminist activist, and Dr. C. Lee Buxton, a gynecologist, birth-control rights activist, and professor of medicine at Yale University, were charged with violating an 1873 statute pre-venting advising married couples about contraception. They claimed the stat-ute violated the Fourteenth Amendment to the US Constitution, the right to privacy, and won. Read more here: *Griswold v. Connecticut*, Case Briefs, https:// www.casebriefs.com/blog/law/family-law/family-law-keyed-to-weisberg/pri vate-family-choices-constitutional-protection-for-the-family-and-its-members /griswold-v-connecticut-2/. Accessed Jan. 12, 2018.

42 **At the time . . . states:** You can see the laws in "The Prosecution of American Sex Laws," *'48 Magazine* 2, no. 2, Feb. 1948. Alfred Kinsey's books are a tough slog, and he has since come under (understandably) heavy criticism for his repeated interviews with many subjects, including those who sexually abused children. Alfred Kinsey, *The Sexual Behavior of the Human Male* (Bloomington: Indiana University Press, 1948) and Alfred Kinsey, *The Sexual Behavior of the Human Female* (Bloomington: Indiana University Press, 1953). Also see Rebecca Clay, "Sex Research at the Kinsey Institute," *Monitor on Psychology*, The American Psychological Association, vol. 46, no. 9, Oct. 2015. Accessed Jan. 15, 2018. See more from David Halberstam in part 4 of the History Channel documentary based on his book *The Fifties* (New York: Fawcett Books, 1993). https://www.youtube.com/watch?v=x_OkKiV92I8. Accessed Jan. 13, 2018.

43 **On one side of popular culture . . . baby:** Halberstam, *The Fifties*, pp. 197–201. *I Love Lucy* fans can read more here: Phil Dyess-Nugent, et al., "More than 60 Years Ago, a Pregnant Lucille Ball Couldn't Call Herself 'Pregnant,'" A.V. Club. https://tv.avclub.com/more-than-60-years-ago-a-pregnant -lucille-ball-couldn-1798239435. Accessed Jan. 8, 2018.

43–44 **Meanwhile, a new upstart . . . "truths":** Steven Watts, *Mr. Playboy: Hugh Hefner and the American Dream* (Hoboken: Wiley, 2008). Also, Laura Mansnerus, "Hugh Hefner, Who Built the Playboy Empire and Embodied It, Dies at 91," *New York Times*, Sept. 27, 2017. https://www.nytimes.com/2017/09 /27/obituaries/hugh-hefner-dead.html?_r=0. Accessed Jan. 14, 2018.

44 **He integrated his staff:** Amber Batura, "How Hugh Hefner Invented the Modern Man," *New York Times*, Sept. 28, 2017. http://nyti.ms/2DxwVFr. Accessed Jan. 15, 2018.

45 **Newspaper society pages:** Ads for girdles, nightgowns, and mink coats on the wedding pages of the *New York Times*'s TimesMachine tell a story of their own. Read the *Times*'s account of the first African American couple featured in its pages, Jewelle and James Gibbs Jr. https://timesmachine .nytimes.com/timesmachine/1956/08/26/91647619.html?pageNumber=96. Accessed Jan. 13, 2018.

45 **Elizabeth Taylor's serial:** "Conrad Hilton Was the First of Elizabeth Taylor's Seven Spouses," cbsnews.com, March 24, 2011. https://www .cb snews.com/news/conrad-hilton-was-first-of-elizabeth-taylors-seven-spouses/. Accessed Jan. 9, 2018.

45 **paparazzi besieged Marilyn:** "Marilyn Monroe Marries Joe DiMaggio,"
This Day in History, History.com, Jan. 14, 1954. http://www.history.com/this
-day-in-history/marilyn-monroe-marries-joe-dimaggio. Accessed Jan. 9, 2018.

45 **and millions watched:** "Grace Kelly Shadows Royal Wedding of Her Son in
Monaco," July 1, 2011. https://www.cbsnews.com/news/grace-kelly-shadows
-royal-wedding-of-her-son-in-monaco-pictures/. Accessed Jan. 9, 2018. The
Oscar-winning Kelly agreed to retire permanently from acting in order to take
on her responsibilities as Prince Rainier's wife. He promptly banned her many
films from being shown in Monaco. See more: http://www.telegraph.co.uk
/news/obituaries/royalty-obituaries/1487262/Prince-Rainier-III-of-Monaco
.html. Accessed Jan. 9, 2018.

45 **The marriage rate:** Ana Swanson, "144 Years of Marriage and Divorce in the
United States, One Chart," *Washington Post*, June 23, 2015. https://www.wash
ingtonpost.com/news/wonk/wp/2015/06/23/144-years-of-marriage-and
-divorce-in-the-united-states-in-one-chart/?utm_term=.e240f0b417b8.
Accessed Jan. 15, 2018.

45 **and in 1950, the marriage age:** May, *Homeward Bound*, p. 3.

45 **One guide to marriage:** London, *How Every Girl Can Choose, Win, Hold
and Enjoy a Man*. Demographic tips appear on p. 28; personality types are
listed on pp. 65–69; dressing hints show up on pp. 79–88.

46 **By Margaret's sixteenth:** Bill Osgerby, *Youth Media* (New York: Routledge, 2004), p. 22.

46 **Parents now had:** Miriam Forman Brunell, *Babysitter: An American History* (New York: New York University Press, 2009), pp. 49–50.

46 **Elvis represented a kind of:** We now know about his private predilec-
tions; today, justifiably, he'd be in the Polanski/Weinstein camp. See more:
Elizabeth King: "Elvis Was the King of Treating Women Like Shit and Luring
14-Year-Olds into Bed," *Vice*, Oct. 7, 2016. https://broadly.vice.com/en_us
/article/3k8z39/elvis-was-the-king-of-treating-women-like-shit-and
-luring-14-year-olds-into-bed. Accessed Jan. 31, 2018.

5. *"Children of Your Own One Day"*

50 **It didn't take Margaret long:** Margaret, her daughter Cheri Katz, and I visited the former Lakeview home in August of 2015. The home, now called Geller
House, is a residential youth home, and its director, Jill Benson, gave us a tour
of the facility. The visit helped solidify Margaret's memories of the place.

52 **Before the war . . . babies:** Sara B. Edlin, *The Unmarried Mother in Our Society* (New York: Farrar, Straus & Young, 1954), pp. 26–29. Edlin was Lakeview's director for forty years before her 1952 retirement.

53 **A few minutes:** Roger Horowitz, *Kosher USA: How Coke Became Kosher and Other Tales of Modern Food* (New York: Columbia University Press, 2016), "The Great Jell-O Controversy," pp. 47–74.

53 **On one hand:** Minutes from the Louise Wise Services board meeting, Nov. 2, 1960, Viola W. Bernard Papers, Box 155, Folder 3, Archives and Special Collections, Augustus C. Long Library, Columbia University.

54 **One girl said . . . "born":** Edlin, *The Unmarried Mother*, p. 47

54 **That was deliberate . . . mail:** Edlin, *The Unmarried Mother*, p. 49.

54 **as well as some journal entries . . . "disturbed":** Edlin, *The Unmarried Mother*, pp. 67–68.

54 **The scene at Lakeview:** Tables 1–17, "Number and Percent of Births to Unmarried Women, by Race and Hispanic Origin: United States, 1940–2000." Centers for Disease Control and Prevention. https://www.cdc.gov /nchs/data/statab/t001x17.pdf. Accessed May 15, 2015.

55 **By 1965, there:** Rickie Solinger, *Wake Up, Little Susie: Single Pregnancy and Race before* Roe v. Wade (New York: Routledge, 2000), p. 103.

55 **It began to:** Jewish Women's Archive, Encyclopedia. "Louise Waterman Wise, 1874–1947," https://jwa.org/encyclopedia/article/wise-louise-waterman. Accessed Dec. 12, 2018.

55 **But there was:** Minutes from the Louise Wise Services board meeting, June 2, 1971, Viola W. Bernard Papers, Box 155, Folder 5, Archives and Special Collections, Augustus C. Long Library, Columbia University.

55 **One couple adopting in the 1940s:** Elaine Tyler May, *Barren in the Promised Land: Childless Americans and the Pursuit of Happiness* (New York: Basic Books, 1995), p. 145.

55 **By the early 1950s:** Louise Wise Services, "A Half-Century of Service," p. 17.

55 **It was a situation that:** Samuel Karelitz, moderator, "Adoptions: A Panel Discussion," *Pediatrics*, vol. 20, no. 366, Aug. 1957, p. 368. Katherine Bain, MD, and Martha M. Eliot, MD, from the Children's Bureau at the Department of Health, Education, and Welfare, use "seller's market" in the portion called "Adoption as a National Problem."

56 **In 1955, Louise:** Minutes, Annual and Special Meeting of Board of Directors, Louise Wise Services, June 2, 1971, Viola W. Bernard Papers, Box 155,

Folder 5, Archives and Special Collections, Augustus C. Long Library, Columbia University.

56 **One estimate found:** Solinger, *Wake Up, Little Susie,* p. 104.

56 **The price to hide:** Solinger, *Wake Up, Little Susie,* pp. 114–115.

56–57 **At a Salvation Army . . . table:** Phone interview with Delores (Swigert) Sullivan, Feb. 16, 2019.

57 **at the Florence Crittenton . . . girl:** Email, Marilyn Mendenhall Waugh, Feb. 17, 2019.

57 **In 1965, at Seton House . . . church:** Carol Schaefer, *The Other Mother: A Woman's Love for the Son She Gave Up for Adoption* (New York: Soho Press, 1991). Carol discusses this in her book, but told me about her "jobs" over lunch in New York on Jan. 21, 2015.

57 **Many homes were like:** Solinger, *Wake Up, Little Susie,* p. 119.

57 **some girls slept on:** Solinger, *Wake Up, Little Susie,* p. 114.

57 **When women dared:** Interview with Marilyn Mendenhall Waugh, Kansas City, MO, June 9, 2017.

57–58 **At Portland's Salvation Army . . . parents:** Phone interview with Delores (Swigert) Sullivan, Feb. 16, 2019.

59 **Perched at the top:** Willows pamphlet (Kansas City, MO: E. P. Haworth, 1925), p. 2, Missouri Valley Special Collections, Kansas City Public Library.

59 **Indeed, it cost:** Associated Press, "Adopted People Fighting to Learn Real Life History," *Daily Capital News,* Jefferson City, MO, July 2, 1975.

59 **Its fee for:** Jennifer Howe, "Where Women Went to Hide," *Kansas City Star,* Dec. 29, 1991.

59 **Most important, patients . . . "experience":** *By-Paths and Cross-Roads: Accidents of Fair Travelers on the Highways of Life,* The Willows Maternity Sanitarium, A Primer for Physicians (Kansas City, MO: E. P. Haworth, 1918). Missouri Valley Special Collections, Kansas City Public Library.

59 **and the state had earned:** Interview with E. Wayne Carp, Tacoma, WA, June 14, 2017. One of his books, *Family Matters: Secrecy and Disclosure in the History of Adoption* (Cambridge: Harvard University Press, 2000), gives an immensely detailed history of adoption in this country.

60 **Couples could arrive:** Interview with Kris Probasco and Marilyn Mendenhall Waugh, Kansas City, MO, June 7, 2017.

60 **Home studies were:** Laws regulating interstate adoptions were not passed until 1960, and even then it took many years for states to ratify them. The Interstate Compact on the Placement of Children and Interjurisdictional

Placements was established in 1960. US Department of Health and Human Services, Child Welfare Information Gateway. https://www.childwelfare.gov /topics/permanency/interjurisdictional/icpc/. Accessed Sept. 26, 2018.

60 **Kansas City's geography:** *A Ten Years' Survey of Seclusion Maternity Service*, The Willows Sanitarium: 1937, p. 26. Missouri Valley Special Collections, Kansas City Public Library.

60 **Not everyone was:** Edlin, *The Unmarried Mother,* p. 23.

63 **In most homes . . . "preserve the figure":** Debbie Miller, "Pregnancy Weight Gain Guidelines in the US—a Historical Overview," DoctorsLounge, Oct. 12, 2010, https://www.doctorslounge.com/index.php/articles/page/14732. Accessed Jan. 31, 2019.

63 **In the 1967 memoir . . . wrote:** Jean Thompson (pseudonym), *The House of Tomorrow* (New York: Harper & Row, 1967), p. 45.

63 **The book had many admirers:** Thompson, *The House of Tomorrow,* back jacket copy.

64 **William Tarnasky was assigned . . . "way it was":** Phone interviews with Dr. William Tarnasky, June 19–20, 2019.

64–65 **Delores Swigert, a patient . . . taken away:** Phone interview with Delores (Swigert) Sullivan, June 20, 2019.

65 **In 1936, Herbert Lehman:** The law sealing the original birth certificates of adopted people was signed by Gov. Lehman on June 4, 1936. Laws of New York, chapter 854, vols. 1–2, pp. 1779–1784.

66 **The agency recognized . . . "them":** In an unsigned document in the papers of Viola Bernard, Louise Wise Services' consulting psychiatrist, a memo describing the need for a film extolling the virtues of agency adoptions described the process in particularly frank and wrenching terms. It was clearly at odds with the reassurances social workers gave to birth mothers and adoptive parents. "Presentation for a Film on Adoption." Undated, unsigned, in a folder of correspondence from the years 1950–1953, Viola W. Bernard Papers, Box 162, Folder 1, Archives and Special Collections, Augustus C. Long Library, Columbia University.

67 **Her job was to find:** "Louise Wise Services 1916–1966," pp. 7–8.

70 **A few days later:** Hanukkah began on the night of Dec. 3, 1961. Timeand date.com. https://www.timeanddate.com/calendar/?year=1961&country=34. Accessed Feb. 21, 2018. Read more about its commercialization here: Daniel Luzer, "Why Is Hanukkah So Closely Associated with Christmas? It's All About the Benjamins," *Pacific Standard*, Dec. 10, 2013. https://psmag.com/so

cial-justice/jewish-arbor-day-christmas-holiday-shopping-hanukkah-71203.
Accessed Feb. 21, 2018.

6. *"You Don't Get to Hold Your Baby"*

71 **As often as possible . . . fares:** Minutes from the Louise Wise Services board
meeting, Dec. 4, 1964, Viola W. Bernard Papers, Box 158, Folder 1, Archives
and Special Collections, Augustus C. Long Library, Columbia University.

73 **a combination of:** William Camann and Kathryn Alexander, *Easy Labor:
Every Woman's Guide to Choosing Less Pain and More Joy in Childbirth* (New
York: Ballantine, 2006), p. 223.

76 **When Margaret stepped out:** Breast-binding has been found to be incon-
clusive at best. Kathy Swift and Jill Janke, "Breast Binding . . . Is It All That
It's Wrapped Up to Be?" *Journal of Obstetric, Gynecologic, and Neonatal Nurs-
ing*, vol. 32, no. 3, May 2003, pp. 332–339. https://10.1177/0884217503253531.
Accessed March 5, 2018.

76 **"Lactation suppressants and":** One of the lactation suppressants most commonly administered in the early 1960s was the drug DES, which has been
shown to have had a multitude of dangerous health effects for women decades
later, including breast cancer. See more at Helmuth Vorherr, *The Breast: Mor-
phology, Physiology, and Lactation* (New York: Academic Press, 1974), p. 201.

76 **In a 1954 book:** Sara B. Edlin, *The Unmarried Mother in Our Society* (New
York: Farrar, Straus & Young, 1954), pp. 39–40.

77 **Fog, snow, and rain:** Weather Underground, Weather History for New York,
NY, Dec. 17–23, 1961. https://www.wunderground.com/history/airport/KJFK
/1961/12/20/WeeklyHistory.html?req_city=&req_state=&req_statename=&
reqdb.zip=&reqdb.magic=&reqdb.wmo=. Accessed March 6, 2018.

79 **This wasn't common . . . daughters:** Interview with retired adoption social worker Ronny Diamond, New York, NY, May 30, 2019.

79 **(Gertrude was more correct):** Louise Wise Services came under fire from
the New York Board of Rabbis for its practice of promising mothers that
mohels would perform their sons' circumcisions. In fact, that happened only
rarely, despite the agency's vociferous protestations to the contrary. Doctors
were far more likely to perform the procedure in the hospital. The rabbis
claimed the agency was "undermining American Jewry" with its practices.
Correspondence from shortly after this period also suggests that the
agency may have circumcised non-Jewish boys in an attempt to pass them off
as Jewish ones. Letters to rabbis from Justine Wise Polier, March 11, 1965;

letter from Viola Bernard to Justine Wise Polier and LWS executive director Florence Brown, March 22, 1965; and letter from Brown to Bernard, March 25, 1965, Viola W. Bernard Papers, Box 158, Folder 1, Archives and Special Collections, Augustus C. Long Library, Columbia University.

7. *"This Never Happened"*

81 **Eleven days after:** Information about David Rosenberg's life as a foster child comes from David Rosenberg's personal files, which he forwarded to me in May of 2014. The file, transferred to Spence-Chapin Services to Families and Children after Louise Wise ceased operations in 2004, is called simply "Biological Background Narrative for David Rosenberg, 3/31/14." See pp. 3–6. Easily half the details, including the date at which Margaret signed the adoption papers (March 5, 1961; she had not yet even lost her virginity, and did not sign the papers until she was threatened with juvenile detention more than fourteen months later) are completely fictionalized.

81 **A brochure for Louise Wise's:** "Louise Wise Services 1916–1966," p. 9.

81 **Louise Wise Services:** "Louise Wise Services," p. 14.

81 **The prolonged process:** Interview with Cathi Swett, attorney and adoption-rights reformer, May 14, 2016.

81 **Between 1950 and 1966:** Louise Wise Services, "A Half-Century of Service," pp. 9–10.

83 **foster mothers had . . . visits:** Interview with Cathi Swett, May 14, 2016.

88 **Her job at the Cort . . . Night:** Here's the Playbill from the revival: http://www.playbill.com/production/long-days-journey-into-night-cort-theatre-vault-0000003530. Accessed March 13, 2018.

90 **The threat was not idle:** Though the definition of the offenses—and prosecution of them—varied from state to state, juvenile jurisprudence fell into its own category until the 1967 Supreme Court decision *In re Gault*. It declared that juveniles accused of crimes in delinquency proceedings must be afforded the same rights as adults. Until then, however, there was little if no oversight of the treatment of minors who committed offenses, regardless of whether they were making prank calls or could simply be described as "delinquent." United States Courts, Facts and Case Summary—*In re Gault*. http://www.uscourts.gov/educational-resources/educational-activities/facts-and-case-summary-re-gault. Accessed Sept. 13, 2018.

The nineteenth-century wayward minor law remained on the books in New York until 1971. Read more here: Karen M. Staller, *Runaways: How the*

Sixties Counterculture Shaped Today's Practices and Policies (New York: Columbia University Press, 2006), p. 128.

90 **The long list of vague, punishable offenses:** Saidiya Hartman, "Revolution in a Minor Key," *Jezebel*, Feb. 20, 2019. Excerpted from *Wayward Lives, Beautiful Experiments* (New York: W. W. Norton, 2019). https://pictorial .jezebel.com/revolution-in-a-minor-key-1832623264. Accessed June 20, 2019.

91–92 **millions of other babies:** Only Alaska and Kansas allowed adoptees access to their original birth certificates.

92 **When she left**: It was, and is, a federal crime to knowingly alter an original birth certificate, a government document. Clearly, Dr. Grunstein was trying to protect Margaret in the event she married another man and wished to keep her first pregnancy a secret, and his aims seemed kind to Margaret despite their illegality. The birth certificate of Margaret's second child, signed by Dr. Grunstein after her birth in 1964, listed her as a first-time mother. Interview with New York and New Jersey attorney Cathi Swett, an adoptee-rights activist, Feb. 8, 2018. Read more here: June Gibbs Brown, "Birth Certificate Fraud," Department of Health and Human Services, Office of the Inspector General, Sept. 2000, p. 2. https://oig.hhs.gov/oei/reports/oei-07-99-00570.pdf. Accessed Feb. 8, 2018.

8. *Blue-Ribbon Babies*

95 **The agency also claimed:** "Biological Background Narrative for David Rosenberg," pp. 1–3.

96 **The professed idea:** Ellen Herman, a professor of history at the University of Oregon, has developed a comprehensive website called the Adoption History Project that allows visitors to understand, as she puts it, the "personal, political, legal, social, scientific, and human dimensions of this particular form of kinship." It is an indispensable resource for anyone interested in adoption. She writes about the history of "matching" here: http://pages.uore gon.edu/adoption/topics/matching.html. Accessed March 28, 2018.

96 **(Redheads, who make up):** Interview with Ronny Diamond, New York, NY, Feb. 20, 2017.

96 **Premium parents deserved:** Matching gone awry was in the news. While adoption agencies were mostly worried about pleasing adoptive parents, there was also occasional concern for children. Mr. and Mrs. Richard Combs, a New Jersey foster family trying to adopt Alice Marie, a four-year-old they had grown to love, became engaged in a custody battle with the

state. The New Jersey State Board of Child Welfare claimed that the child was "too bright" for the Combses to adopt. Emma Harrison, "Adoption Experts Disclaim I.Q. Use," *New York Times*, March 9, 1960.

97 **The goal was to . . . "automobile":** Brian Paul Gill cites this example in "Adoption Agencies and the Search for the Ideal Family, 1918–1965," Wayne Carp, ed., *Adoption in America* (Ann Arbor: University of Michigan Press, 2004), p. 169. It is a quote from St. Louis adoption worker Abraham Simon in Michael Schapiro, *A Study of Adoption Practice* (New York: Children's Welfare League of America, 1956), pp. 160–163.

97 **One woman said:** Interview with retired social worker G., who requested that her name not be used, New York, NY, Jan. 13, 2017.

97–98 **If the files can . . . "husband":** Minutes from the Louise Wise Services Adoption Committee Meeting, Jan. 17, 1961, Viola W. Bernard Papers, Box 161, Folder 11, Archives and Special Collections, Augustus C. Long Library, Columbia University.

98–99 **In one assessment . . . "frigid":** Molly Harrower, PhD, "Psychological Report on Mrs. Sylvia (redacted)," undated, Viola W. Bernard Papers, Box 160, Folder 4, Archives and Special Collections, Augustus C. Long Library, Columbia University.

99 **Another psychologist . . . "arms":** Miriam G. Siegel, PhD, "Psychological Examination, 7/2/58," Viola W. Bernard Papers, Box 160, Folder 4, Archives and Special Collections, Augustus C. Long Library, Columbia University.

99 **A national authority on:** See Samuel Karelitz in this PDF about the group of hospitals to which Long Island Jewish Medical Center now belongs: Jeffrey L. Rodengen, "Northwell Health: Shaping the Future of Healthcare," p. 49. https://www.northwell.edu/sites/northwell.edu/files/d7/ShapingTheFutureOfHealthcare.pdf. Accessed Dec. 20, 2018.

99 **haughty, clipped voice:** "A Doctor Who Deals with Affection and Infection," Oct. 22, 1968, WNYC archives, NYPR Archive Collections. https://www.wnyc.org/story/a-doctor-who-deals-with-affection-and-infection/. Accessed Dec. 20, 2018.

99 **Board members at Louise Wise:** Letter from Florence Kreech to Judge Justine Wise Polier, Dec. 9, 1966; Letter from Samuel Karelitz to Judge Justine Wise Polier, Dec. 8, 1966, Viola W. Bernard Papers, Box 158, Folder 2, Archives and Special Collections, Augustus C. Long Library, Columbia University.

99 **He had a strange idea:** Karelitz interview, WNYC, Oct. 22, 1968.

100 **Karelitz and Vincent Fisichelli:** You can read more about this sickening experiment, which the NIH began funding in 1957. This one describes the rubber-band gun: Samuel Karelitz and Vincent Fisichelli, "The Cry Thresholds of Normal Infants and Those with Brain Damage: An Aid in the Early Diagnosis of Severe Brain Damage," *Journal of Pediatrics,* vol. 61, no. 5, Nov. 1962, pp. 679–685. This one describes the induced cries of babies who were ten minutes old: V. R. Fisichelli, S. Karelitz, and A. Haber, "The Course of Induced Crying Activity in the Neonate," *Journal of Psychology,* vol. 73, no. 2, Dec. 1969, pp. 183–191. There are at least nine more, which you can find listed on Research-Gate, Samuel Karelitz's research while affiliated with CUNY Graduate Center and other places. https://www.researchgate.net/scientific-contributions/673591 93_Samuel_Karelitz. Accessed Aug. 4, 2018.

101 **In 1962, Karelitz:** Karelitz and Fisichelli, "The Cry Thresholds of Normal Infants and Those with Brain Damage," pp. 679–685.

101 **The federal government . . . 1975:** A generous source at the National Archives who prefers to remain anonymous helped locate figures for National Institutes of Health grant M2875 and National Institutes of Health grant HD00332. They come from tallying the grants listed in the Public Health Service Grants from the National Institutes of Health at Hathi Trust. The NIH destroys documents and grant materials after twenty years if studies do not yield major scientific discoveries or cures. Karelitz's studies were scientifically ludicrous, and a FOIA request seeking the grant proposal and other materials turned up nothing in the archives. I was able to tally figures that totaled $150,000 from grants listed in Hathi Trust. Here is a link to one: https://babel .hathitrust.org/cgi/pt?id=uiug.30112106694299;view=1up;seq=221. Accessed Oct. 15, 2018. The grants are numerous. For the total of what my source was able to provide, please see my website: www.gabrielleglaser.com.

While the National Institutes of Health and the National Institute of Mental Health dispensed repeated grants to the New York researchers between the late 1950s and early 1970s, the paperwork had been destroyed, since NIH grant files are considered temporary unless they are of historical importance, yielding cures or scientific breakthroughs. In this case, there was no such medical advance, just a horrifying record, published in respected peer-reviewed journals, of sinister experimentation on infants. I located a co-author of many of these studies, a psychologist in Florida. She is in her eighties now, and while she is still working at a research facility, she claimed she did not remember the aim of them.

101 **Karelitz, who was president of a New York:** Zoom Info, Zoom People Information, Aug. 2018. https://www.nexis.com/results/enhdocview.do?doc LinkInd=true&ersKey=23_T28048201493&format=GNBFI&start DocNo=0&resultsUrlKey=0_T28048201495&backKey=20_T28048 201496&csi=345234&docNo=1. Accessed Aug. 27, 2018.

101 **In subsequent studies:** Samuel Karelitz, Vincent R. Fisichelli, et al., "Relation of Crying Activity in Early Infancy to Speech and Intellectual Development at Age Three Years," *Child Development*, vol. 35, no. 3, Sept. 1964, pp. 769–777.

101–102 **Dr. Joyce Brothers . . . "IQ":** Dr. Joyce Brothers, "Worried Mother Fears Baby Cries Too Much," *Terre Haute Star*, Terre Haute, IN, March 30, 1966, p. 7.

102 **Dr. Walter Alvarez . . . "damage":** Dr. Walter Alvarez, "Dr. Alvarez Reports: A Crying Baby," *Simpson's Leader Times*, Kittanning, PA, Feb. 20, 1967, p. 17. Alvarez was an emeritus consultant in medicine to the Mayo Clinic, and an emeritus professor of medicine at the Mayo Foundation in Rochester, MN.

103 **Trained at Harvard:** Eric Pace, "Harry L. Shapiro, Anthropologist, Dies at 87," *New York Times*, Jan. 9, 1990. https://www.nytimes.com/1990/01/09 /obituaries/dr-harry-l-shapiro-anthropologist-dies-at-87.html. Accessed Oct. 23, 2018. Information about Shapiro's joining Louise Wise comes from Viola W. Bernard Papers, Box 158, Folder 1, Archives and Special Collections, Augustus C. Long Library, Columbia University.

103 **Over the course . . . family:** Anna Quindlen, "About New York: The Art of Drawing Meaning from Mute Bones," *New York Times*, Nov. 20, 1982.

103 **Shapiro even offered:** Minutes from the Louise Wise Services board meeting, March 7, 1956, Viola W. Bernard Papers, Box 155, Folder 2, Archives and Special Collections, Augustus C. Long Library, Columbia University.

104 **in the early 1960s . . . forty-two for men:** Louise Wise Services, fund-raising pamphlet, 1958, p. 8.

104 **No one really knows:** Interview with University of Baltimore professor of law Elizabeth Samuels, June 28, 2019.

104 **Some news reports . . . "forgotten":** William Rice, "'Unadoptable' Babies Want Homes with Loving Hearts," *New York Newsday*, July 21, 1963.

104 **"Where then can we draw":** Minutes from the Louise Wise Services board meeting, Oct. 8, 1958, Viola W. Bernard Papers, Box 155, Folder 3, Archives and Special Collections, Augustus C. Long Library, Columbia University.

105 **Social workers lined up . . . Jews:** This comes from two sources. One is Ian Tattersall, an anthropologist at the American Museum of Natural History, who arrived at the museum as a young scientist from England in the early 1970s. He worked down the hall from Shapiro, and recalled the practice. "It made me very uncomfortable," he said, as he pointed out Shapiro's former office on Oct. 12, 2018. The practice was first described to me by Ronny Diamond, a retired adoption social worker on Dec. 11, 2015.

105 **this precaution might:** Minutes from the Louise Wise Services board meeting, Oct. 8, 1958, Viola W. Bernard Papers, Box 155, Folder 3, Archives and Special Collections, Augustus C. Long Library, Columbia University.

106 **Like Karelitz and Shapiro:** Wolfgang Saxon, "Viola Bernard, 91, Psychiatrist Who Helped Ease Young Fears," *New York Times*, April 6, 1998. https://www.nytimes.com/1998/04/06/nyregion/viola-bernard-91-psychiatrist-who-helped-ease-young-fears.html. Accessed Aug. 25, 2019.

106 **This amused Neubauer:** Elyse Schein and Paula Bernstein, *Identical Strangers: A Memoir of Twins Separated and United* (New York: Random House, 2007), pp. 221–226.

107 **The birth mothers:** This study is infamous and the source of at least two documentaries. One was 2018's *Three Identical Strangers*, by Tim Wardle. Another is Lori Shinseki's 2018 *The Twinning Reaction*, which you can see here: https://www.thetwinningreaction.com/. Accessed June 23, 2019.

107 **Bernard seemed unperturbed . . . "twins":** Letter from Florence Brown to Viola Bernard, Nov. 14, 1961, Viola W. Bernard Papers, Box 156, Folder 8, Archives and Special Collections, Augustus C. Long Library, Columbia University.

108 **"natural laboratory situation":** Letter from Viola Bernard to Dr. John A. P. Millett, Jan. 29, 1963, Viola W. Bernard Papers, Box 36, Folder 2, Archives and Special Collections, Augustus C. Long Library, Columbia University.

108 **That guideline was:** The film makes clear that the brothers were separated at roughly six months, having been housed together at first. Newspaper articles routinely and erroneously say that the brothers were "separated at birth," but they were not. The headline of this story repeats the error, but the story's timeline is correct. Sara Stewart, "Separated-at-birth Triplets Met Tragic End after Shocking Psych Experiment," *New York Post*, June 23, 2018. https://nypost.com/2018/01/23/these-triplets-were-separated-at-birth-for-a-sick-scientific-experiment/. Accessed Oct. 15, 2019.

108 **Each was concerned:** Rokhl Kafrissen, "Why Did 'Three Identical Strangers' Ignore Just How Jewish This Story Was?" *Cleveland Jewish News,* Jan. 16, 2019. https://www.clevelandjewishnews.com/jta/why-did-three-identical-strangers-ignore-just-how-jewish-this/article_78a7a757-1442-5273-8d03-cabf28e12210.html. Accessed Oct. 15, 2019.

108 **Other twins from . . . killed themselves:** Shinseki, *The Twinning Reaction.*

108 **It has long been understood:** David J. Sharrow and James J. Anderson, "A Twin Protection Effect? Explaining Twin Survival Advantages with a Two-Process Mortality Mode," *PLOS One,* May 18, 2016. http://journals.plos.org/plosone/article?id=10.1371/journal.pone.0154774. Accessed April 6, 2018.

109 **One adoptive father:** Shinseki, *The Twinning Reaction.*

109 **these "practice homes" . . . old:** "What Were Practice Apartments?" Cornell University Library, Rare and Manuscript Collections. http://rmc.library.cornell.edu/homeEc/cases/apartments.html. Accessed April 2, 2018. Author Lisa Grunwald also explores the history of "practice houses" in her novel *The Irresistible Henry House* (New York: Random House, 2010).

110 **At Oregon State University:** Kate Taylor, "Scars of 'practice baby' run deep, long," *Oregonian,* Jan. 1, 1999. The piece has a small error in the dates during which the homes ran. They were operational beginning in 1926, but ran until 1950, not 1947, as the piece notes.

110 **At Withycombe House:** The dates of the program and description of Withycombe House are noted in an undated file at the Oregon State University Special Collections and Archives Research Center.

110 **Aya Fujii was . . . "just cuddled it":** Interview with Aya Fujii, Sept. 29, 2017, Portland, OR. We spoke about her experiences as an interned Japanese American, and a practice mother. You can see a photograph of her holding the little girl in OSU's 1949 yearbook. Oregon State University digital archives, *The Beaver,* 1949. https://oregondigital.org/sets/osu-yearbooks/oregondigital:xd07gt12w#page/178/mode/2up. Accessed April 1, 2018.

111 **In the book:** John Bowlby, *Maternal Care and Mental Health: A report prepared on behalf of the World Health Organization as a contribution to the United Nations programme for the welfare of homeless children* (Geneva: World Health Organization, 1952), p. 11.

111–112 **He was raised . . . dog:** Barbara Tizard, "Looking Back: The Making and Breaking of Attachment Theory," *The Psychologist,* British Psychological Society, vol. 22, Oct. 2009, https://thepsychologist.bps.org.uk/volume-22

/edition-10/looking-back-making-and-breaking-attachment-theory. Accessed May 21, 2019.

112 **"This deprivation will":** Bowlby, *Maternal Care and Mental Health*, p. 12.

112 **"In both these . . . "dangers":** Bowlby, *Maternal Care and Mental Health*, p. 47.

112 **The book was:** Inge Bretherton, "The Origins of Attachment Theory: John Bowlby and Mary Ainsworth," *Developmental Psychology*, vol. 28, no. 5, Sept. 1992, pp. 759–775. http://www.psychology.sunysb.edu/attachment/online /i_origins.pdf. Accessed May 19, 2019.

112 **It was influential:** F. C. van der Horst and R. van der Veer, "Changing Attitudes towards the Care of Children in Hospital: A New Assessment of the Influence of the Work of Bowlby and Robertson in the UK, 1940–1970," *Attachment and Human Development*, vol. 11, no. 2, March 2009, pp. 119–142. https://www.ncbi.nlm.nih.gov/pubmed/19266362. Accessed June 24, 2019.

112 **During the same . . . months:** "Louise Wise Services 1916–1966," p. 9.

112 **This was an understatement:** There was a great deal of discussion about testing during the waiting period. At one agency meeting, Carl Schoenberg, Louise Wise's assistant director, said that psychological "testing" on two-month-olds was routine in adoption practice. He mentions that some Wise officials had questioned the validity of the tests, and how well they could "predict" where a child should go. Bernard and Dorothy Krugman, the agency's staff psychologist, also favored the use of the testing. Minutes from the Louise Wise Adoption Committee, Oct. 11, 1960, Viola W. Bernard Papers, Box 155, Folder 3, Archives and Special Collections, Augustus C. Long Library, Columbia University.

112–113 **One doctor who had . . . "body":** Helen Fradkin and Dorothy Krugman, PhD, "A Program of Adoptive Placement for Infants under Three Months," *American Journal of Orthopsychiatry*, vol. 26, issue 3, July 1956, pp. 577–593. This comes from the "Discussion" section by Ner Littner, MD, p. 590.

113–114 **Stephen's early months . . . his boarding mother:** "Biological Background Narrative for David Rosenberg," pp. 3–4. Other information in this chapter about Stephen's time in foster care also comes from the document.

115 **Ephraim Fishel Rosenberg:** David Rosenberg described his father's remarkable résumé in an interview with the Oregon Jewish Museum. David Rosenberg, interview with David Fuks, March 23, 2009, p. 3. Other background information on Ephraim and Esther in this and other chapters comes from this comprehensive document.

115–116 **No doctor anywhere . . . crushed:** Interview with Yafa Kuperman, Esther Rosenberg's sister, Netanya, Israel, Dec. 1, 2017.

116 **To be considered . . . forty-two:** Louise Wise Services, fundraising pamphlet, 1958, p. 8. Like David's biological background, some of the material in this brochure was also untrue. Note: This undated pamphlet was in a catch-all file at Columbia that said "1957" on the front. But in reading the fine print, I realized it had to have been published in 1958, since it alludes to the adoption agency having been in operation for forty-two years. It was founded in 1916.

9. *"Better" Families*

117 **This is why:** Karen Wilson-Buterbaugh is among those who have examined the history of the period in depth. She is a birth mother, researcher, and author of the book *The Baby Scoop Era: Unwed Mothers, Infant Adoption, and Forced Surrender* (Kindle edition, 2017).

117 **Federal statistics show:** Not all states and territories fully participated in the count every year, but between 1951 and 1975, they did report that courts recorded the adoptions of 2.7 million children. P. Maza, "Adoption Trends: 1944–1975," Child Welfare Research no. 9 (Administration for Children, Youth, and Families, Washington, DC, 1984). Not all of those adoptions were to strangers; the figures include adoptions of a stepparent or other family members. The number of non-stranger adoptions began rising when the divorce rate increased in the late 1960s. See more at University of Oregon history professor Ellen Herman's excellent website on adoption history: http://pages.uoregon.edu/adoption/archive/MazaAT.htm. Accessed March 21, 2018.

117 **One researcher estimate:** Rickie Solinger explores these complex transactions. She not only examined the harsh treatment of women but also explored the differences between how black and white Americans responded to the increase of babies born to single mothers. In *Wake Up, Little Susie* (New York: Routledge, 2000), she looks at market forces on pp. 29–34. On p. 32, Solinger cites an estimate that as many as 39 percent of unwed mothers in the 1950s and '60s were involved in independent, or more clearly, black market, adoptions.

119 **In the colonial era:** US Census Bureau, United States Population 1790 to 1990, Urban and Rural. https://www.census.gov/population/censusdata/ta ble-4.pdf. Accessed April 25, 2018.

120 **It's now estimated:** Charles Loring Brace, *The Dangerous Classes of New
York, and Twenty Years' Work among Them* (New York: Wynkoop and Hallen-
beck, 1872), pp. 317–319, Internet Archive. https://archive.org/details/danger
ousclasses00bracuoft. Accessed April 25, 2018.

There's a wealth of information about this forced resettlement of children. Christina Baker Kline depicts the story of an Irish immigrant girl
transplanted to Minnesota by the Children's Aid Society in her 2013 novel
Orphan Train (New York: William Morrow, 2013). And here are some press
accounts: Staff report, "'Orphan Train' Riders Share Common Bond," *Pioneer Press,* Sept. 18, 2007. Recollection of Sophia Kral. https://www.twin
cities.com/2007/09/18/orphan-train-riders-share-common-bond/. Accessed April
25, 2018. One more: Joe Duggan, "Orphan Train Rider Finds It in Her Heart
to Forgive, Heal," *Lincoln Journal Star,* March 5, 2010. http://journalstar.com
/news/local/orphan-train-rider-finds-it-in-her-heart-to-forgive/article
_6fe526f8-2805-11df-8417-001cc4c002e0.html. Accessed April 25, 2018.

121 **The contracts varied:** The Children's Aid Society, National Orphan Train
Complex. https://orphantraindepot.org/history/the-childrens-aid-society/. Accessed June 23, 2019.

122 **Walker wrote that:** George Walker, *The Traffic in Babies: An Analysis of the
Conditions Discovered during an Investigation Conducted in the Year 1914* (Baltimore: The Norman, Remington Co., 1918), p. 134. I found my copy on eBay.

000 **The vast majority:** Walker, *The Traffic in Babies,* p. 152.

122 **"He put it":** Walker, *The Traffic in Babies,* pp. 3–4.

122 **At least one:** Ellen Herman, *Kinship by Design* (Chicago: University of Chicago Press, 2008), p. 34.

124 **The declining birth rate:** Minnesota Public Radio, *The Fertility Race, Part
Four: Race Suicide.* http://news.minnesota.publicradio.org/features/199711
/20_smiths_fertility/part1/f4.shtml. Accessed Nov. 26, 2018. The Theodore
Roosevelt Center at Dickinson State University Digital Archive has a 1903
cartoon featuring an "idle stork" standing back smoking in a wealthy neighborhood, and several "strenuous storks" flying around in a frenzy in a dirty,
overcrowded one in the next frame. https://www.theodorerooseveltcenter
.org/Research/Digital-Library/Record/ImageViewer?libID=o277250. Accessed
Nov. 26, 2018.

124 **in Minnesota marked . . . parents:** E. Wayne Carp, ed., "Introduction: A
Historical Overview of American Adoption," *Adoption in America: Historical
Perspectives* (Ann Arbor: University of Michigan Press, 2004), p. 8. The Min-

nesota law also provided for the confidentiality of adoption records. It allowed the adopted person, the birth parents, and the adoptive parents access to the records, but sealed them to the public.

124 **In the years:** Interview with Ellen Herman, March 7, 2019.

125 **The approach came:** Herman, *Kinship by Design*, p. 45.

125 **Chapin, who was childless:** "Mrs. Henry D. Chapin, 84, Dead; Founder of the Adoption Service," *New York Times*, Feb. 21, 1964. https://www .nytimes.com/1964/02/21/archives/mrs-henry-d-chapin-84-dead-foun der-of-the-adoption-service.html. Accessed Jan. 8, 2019.

125 **Spence, along with:** Elizabeth Titus, "Clara B. Spence: Ahead of Her Time," *Ms.* magazine blog, March 6, 2015. http://msmagazine.com/blog /2015/03/06/clara-b-spence-ahead-of-her-time/. Titus says that Spence and her partner, Charlotte Baker, were likely among the country's first same-sex couples to adopt. Accessed Jan. 8, 2019.

125 **New York codified:** Justine Wise Polier, "A Memorandum Concerning Adoption across Religious Lines," 1955, Adoption History Project. https:// pages.uoregon.edu/adoption/archive/PoliermemoNCRAC.htm. Accessed Jan. 8, 2018.

125 **religious-matching law:** Laura J. Schwartz, "Religious Matching in Adoption Law: Unraveling the Interests Behind the 'Best Interests' Standard," *Family Law Quarterly*, vol. 25, no. 2, Summer 1991, pp. 171–192.

126 **Many Americans still:** "Timeline of Adoption History," Adoption History Project. https://pages.uoregon.edu/adoption/timeline.html. Accessed Jan. 8, 2019.

126 **The Cradle, the Illinois:** "History of The Cradle." https://www.cradle.org /about-us/history-cradle. Accessed Jan. 8, 2019.

127 **To avoid the disgrace:** Rachel Gordan, "A Single Adoptive Mother—in 1937," *New York Times, Motherlode: Adventures in Parenting*, April 25, 2014. https://parenting.blogs.nytimes.com/2014/04/25/a-single-adoptive-mot her-in-1937/. Accessed Dec. 19, 2018.

127 **And then there was . . . alike:** These details come from Christina Crawford, *Mommie Dearest: A True Story* (New York: William Morrow, 1978). If you haven't read it, you should.

127 **Notably, she obtained:** Shirley Downing, "Quest Led Crawford Twins, Others to Tenn," *Memphis Commercial Appeal*, Sept. 11, 1995.

128 **Tann realized that:** Information about Georgia Tann comes from many sources. Most important is the fastidiously documented book by Barbara

Bisantz Raymond, *The Baby Thief: The Untold Story of Georgia Tann, the Baby Thief Who Corrupted Adoption* (New York: Union Square Press, 2007). Read about Tann's methodology in "Georgia's Methods," pp. 89–125.

128 **Eleanor Roosevelt:** Raymond, *The Baby Thief,* pp. 90–91.

129 **The stories, timed:** Raymond, *The Baby Thief,* p. 110, pp. 112–115.

129 **She became a millionaire . . . Tennessee:** Ray Hill, "Judge Camille Kelley & Miss Georgia Tann," *Knoxville Focus,* Sept. 29, 2013. http://knoxfocus .com/2013/09/judge-camille-kelley-miss-georgia-tann/. Accessed Jan. 3, 2019.

129 **Abe Fortas, a future:** Letter from Abe Fortas to Abe Waldauer, March 1, 1948. This letter is from the files of Abe Waldauer, at the home of Steve Mc-Farland, Millington, TN. I combed through them on Dec. 12, 13, and 14, 2016.

130 **To one customer:** Letter from Abe Waldauer to a potential client in Indiana, Aug. 4, 1941. Waldauer's files, Millington, TN.

130 **Following state laws:** Interview with Marymor "Boo" Cravens, at her home in Sewanee, TN, Dec. 15, 2016. Boo, ninety-four when I met her, was a young social worker in Memphis when Tann's activities were being investigated, and she was tasked with managing many out-of-state cases that had fallen under scrutiny. Boo told me that it had come to the attention of New York family courts that a boy Tann provided to a Jewish family had in fact been born to a Protestant woman. A judge ordered the boy, then a teenager, to go to a Protestant foster home. Panicked Jewish adoptive parents called the Tennessee Children's Home Society, fearful about the fates of their children, and Cravens clambered to reassure them. "Sometimes I'd just tell them, oh, it says right here, her mother's name was Cohen, or his mother's name was Levine. Don't you worry." I asked her how she had felt about lying. She didn't flinch. "I was knee-deep in files of that woman's deceit! But I didn't want more harm to come to those innocent children as the result of this woman's crimes." Cravens died on May 9, 2018.

130 **It's not as if:** Raymond, *The Baby Thief,* p. 108.

130 **The new system . . . father:** Carp, *Adoption in America,* p. 8.

130–131 **Tann didn't have to:** Kenneth Neill, "Adoption for Profit: Conspiracy and Cover-Up," part 1, *Memphis* magazine, vol. 3, no. 7, Oct. 1978, p. 39.

131 **(It is possible that):** Letterhead, American Friends of the Hebrew University, letter to Albert Sabin from Michael Nisselson, Oct. 31, 1963. The two men's names are on the second page. https://drc.libraries.uc.edu/bitstream/handle/23 74.UC/695051/1959-63_006.pdf?sequence=1. Accessed June 3, 2017.

131 **In 1936, Lehman:** Laws of the State of New York, 1936, chapter 864, pp. 1779–1784.

131 **At the time . . . pass:** Janet Golden, *Babies Made Us Modern: How Infants Brought America into the Twentieth Century* (New York: Cambridge University Press, 2018), pp. 201–202.

131–132 **A Louise Wise brochure . . . "adoptive parents":** Louise Wise Services, 1957, p. 17.

132 **In this sappy . . . "future":** *Close to My Heart*, Warner Bros., 1951. Unbelievably sentimental, with no mention of the child's birth mother.

10. *The Right Future*

134 **Although they had access . . . children:** Elaine Tyler May, *Homeward Bound: American Families in the Cold War Era* (New York: Basic Books, 2008), pp. 130–131.

134 **As Betty Friedan:** Betty Friedan, *The Feminine Mystique* (New York: Norton, reprint 2001), p. 115.

134 **For the growing:** Elaine Tyler May, *Barren in the Promised Land: Childless Americans and the Pursuit of Happiness* (New York: Basic Books, 1995), p. 145. p. 18.

135 **It is important to note:** May, *Homeward Bound*, p. 10. See more here: Bruce Lambert, "At 50, Levittown Contends with Its Legacy of Bias," *New York Times*, Dec. 28, 1997. http://www.nytimes.com/1997/12/28/nyregion/at -50-levittown-contends-with-its-legacy-of-bias.html. Accessed Jan. 15, 2018.

135 **A 1963 article . . . "sterility.":** May cites this in *Barren in the Promised Land*, p. 141.

135 **In 1953, doctors:** W. Ombelet and J. Van Robays, "Artificial Insemination History: Hurdles and Milestones," *Facts, Views & Vision: Issues in Obstetrics, Gynaecology and Reproductive Health*, vol. 7, no. 2, 2015, pp. 137–143.

135 **in 1967, when:** Eli Y. Adashi, "Clomiphene Citrate at 50: The Dawning of Assisted Reproduction," *Fertility and Sterility*, vol. 108, no. 4, Oct. 2017.

135 **Between 1947 and 1967:** The Statistics Portal, "Percentage of the U.S. population who have completed four years of college or more from 1940 to 2018, by gender." https://www.statista.com/statistics/184272/educational -attainment-of-college-diploma-or-higher-by-gender/. Accessed April 1, 2018.

136 **Not only did:** Louise Wise Services, "A Half-Century of Service," p. 10.

136 **Their story is:** Rickie Solinger examines this history throughout *Wake Up, Little Susie: Single Pregnancy and Race before* Roe v. Wade (New York: Routledge, 2000).

136 **In 1965, the . . . crisis:** Daniel Patrick Moynihan, "The Negro Family: The Case for National Action," Office of Policy Planning and Research, US Department of Labor, March 1965. In his explosive report on the problems in black families, Assistant Labor Department Secretary Moynihan predicted that children raised in homes with unwed mothers would grow up with serious disadvantages. https://web.stanford.edu/~mrosenfe/Moynihan's%20The%20 Negro%20Family.pdf. Accessed April 10, 2018.

136 **"Let's not mince words":** Interview with Carol Schaefer, New York, Jan. 15, 2015. Her book *The Other Mother: A Woman's Love for the Child She Gave Up for Adoption* (New York: Soho Press, 1991) was made into an NBC movie of the same name in 1995.

137 **In his 1957 . . . "father":** Edmund Pollock, "An Investigation into Certain Personality Characteristics of Unwed Mothers," 1957, New York University PhD dissertation, pp. 4–7.

137 **It would have been hard:** Pollock, "An Investigation into Certain Personality Characteristics of Unwed Mothers," p. 2.

137 **One psychiatrist said:** Solinger quotes Harry Gianakon's article "Ego Factors in the Separation of Mother and Child" in *Wake Up, Little Susie,* p. 88. Solinger explored the scientific literature of unwed mothers deeply in her chapter "The Girl Nobody Loved: Psychological Explanations for White Single Pregnancy," pp. 86–102.

137 **Two Harvard psychiatrists:** Solinger also discovered this gem. *Wake Up, Little Susie,* p. 87.

137 **Another NYU scholar . . . women:** Wyatt C. Jones, "Correlates of Social Deviance: A Study of Unmarried Mothers," 1965. New York University PhD dissertation, p. 76.

137 **Not surprisingly, he declared them:** Jones, "Correlates of Social Deviance," p. 149.

137–138 **A journal article . . . "desires":** Sally Finger, "Concurrent Group Therapy with Adolescent Unmarried Mothers and Their Parents," *Confinia Psychiatrica,* vol. 8, 1965, pp. 21–26.

138 **One found they:** Norman Reider, "The Unmarried Father," *American Journal of Orthopsychiatry,* vol. 18, no. 2, April 1948, pp. 230–237. https://onlinelibrary .wiley.com/doi/pdf/10.1111/j.1939-0025.1948.tb05081.x. Accessed April 10, 2018.

138 **"Every time we place":** Emma Harrison, "Adoption Experts Disclaim I.Q. Use," *New York Times,* March 9, 1960.

138 **During the 1950s . . . belief:** Josephine Johnston, "The Ghost of the Schizophrenogenic Mother," *AMA Journal of Ethics,* Virtual Mentor, vol. 15,

no. 9, Sept. 2013, pp. 801–805. http://journalofethics.ama-assn.org/2013/09
/oped1-1309.html. Accessed April 7, 2018.

I met with New York University bioethicist Arthur Caplan on February
28, 2017, to discuss some of the studies on children in the adoption system.
He was unaware of them, but listened intently as I unfolded the history, and
agreed that they were egregious. But he also pointed out that perhaps some
of the Jewish refugees, in particular NYU's Austrian-born Peter Neubauer,
were motivated in part by the wish to disprove Nazi theories about biology.
He did not, by any means, excuse Neubauer and Bernard's approach to the
twins study.

138–139 **But how much to reveal . . . "misgivings":** In a staff meeting on Jan. 20,
1964, Bernard discussed the "conflicts" about telling adoptive parents
about "the likelihood of Puerto Rican or Negro admixture when the child's
appearance is ambiguous" and continued "misgivings about mental illness,
retardation, socially inadequate mothers." Minutes from the Louise Wise Services staff meeting, Jan. 1, 1964, Viola W. Bernard Papers, Box 158, Folder
1, Archives and Special Collections, Augustus C. Long Library, Columbia
University.

139 **As late as the 1960s:** There have been several instances of such treachery.
Dozens of women in St. Louis were told their babies had died at birth in the
mid-1960s, only to reunite later. You can read more here: Abby Phillip, "They
Were Told Their Babies Had Died. Now, These Black Women Wonder: Was
It a Lie?" *Washington Post*, May 6, 2015. https://www.washingtonpost
.com/news/morning-mix/wp/2015/05/06/they-were-told-their-babies-had
-died-now-dozens-of-black-women-wonder-if-it-was-all-a-lie/?utm_term
=.286c2d20ba57. Accessed Feb. 13, 2019. And at the end of 2018, a Florida
woman who'd been told her daughter had died in 1949 was reunited with her
when a DNA test linked them. Rima Abdelkader and Dennis Romero,
"Woman Reunites with Daughter She Thought Had Died at Birth Nearly 70
Years Ago," NBC News, Dec. 5, 2018. https://www.nbcnews.com/news/us
-news/woman-reunites-daughter-she-thought-had-died-birth
-nearly-70-n944556. Accessed Feb. 13, 2019.

139–140 **When sixteen-year-old . . . abused him:** Phone interview and email exchanges with Delores (Swigert) Sullivan, Feb. 16–17, 2019. Information regarding Swigert's oldest son and their reunion originally appeared in *Rolling
Stone*. Randall Sullivan, "The Bastard Chronicles, Part Two: The Birth
Mother's Story," *Rolling Stone*, vol. 861, March 1, 2001, pp. 41–48. At the
time, Swigert's surname was Teller. Now she is Delores Sullivan.

140–141 **Jane Edwards, who . . . double blow:** Phone interviews and email exchanges with Jane Edwards, Feb. 13–15, 2019.

141–143 **Another woman, from . . . Child Welfare:** Phone interviews and email exchanges with a private source, Feb. 13–17, 2019, and again on May 20–28, 2019.

143 **Sara Edlin acknowledged . . . "human pain of it":** Sara B. Edlin, *The Unmarried Mother in our Society* (New York: Farrar, Straus & Young, 1954), p. 188.

11. *Childless Mother*

154 **The sacrifice of David's birth mother:** Interview with Yafa Kuperman, Netanya, Israel, Dec. 1, 2017.

158 **They had been abducted:** *Murder in Mississippi.* PBS, *American Experience.* http://www.pbs.org/wgbh/americanexperience/features/freedomsummer -murder/. Accessed May 30, 2018.

159 **By 1960, nearly all:** Neal Devitt, "The Transition from Home to Hospital Birth in the United States, 1930–1960," *Birth, Issues in Perinatal Care,* vol. 4, no. 2, June 1977, pp. 47–58. The article lists the number of hospital deliveries at 96 percent. https://onlinelibrary.wiley.com/doi/pdf/10.1111/j.1523-536X .1977.tb01207.x. Accessed May 17, 2018.

159–160 **Women were shaved . . . tightness:** Faith Gibson, a midwife and natural childbirth advocate who began her career in the segregated South as a labor and delivery nurse, describes this in a YouTube video: https://www.youtube .com/watch?v=GV3UFv-5AqU. She discusses racial disparities between black and white wards in a Florida hospital in a second video: https://www .youtube.com/watch?v=qlvjDRje__M. She also writes about the history of medicalized childbirth on her website. Read about how normal childbirth became a surgical procedure here: https://faithgibson.org/this-months-new -read/chapter1_nctwhx_15-apr-08-b/. Videos accessed May 17, 2018.

163 **She could not know:** Phone interview with David Rosenberg, May 13, 2014.

12. *Breathing Exercises*

171 **David Rosenberg lived . . . borough:** In this section about David's early life, I rely on the observations and recollections of several sources: Yafa Kuperman, whom I met in Netanya, Israel, on Dec. 1, 2017, and May 30, 2018,

and who spoke with great authority about her late sister and brother-in-law as well as David's childhood and adolescence; David's cousins Mitch and Bryan Herstic, whom I met in Riverdale, NY, on Oct. 30, 2017; and Marden Paul, whom I met in Toronto on Jan. 20, 2017. I also had phone interviews with several of David's friends from Toronto: Larry Zeifman on Nov. 26, 2018; David Klein on Nov. 19, 2018; and Suzanne Wintrob on Nov. 26, 2018. In addition, I consulted David Fuks's interview of David on March 23, 2009. I also referred to an autobiography David had written as a young man and had given to his friend David Berk, now a rabbi in Brooklyn, for safekeeping, before he went to Israel. It appears to have been written in or around 1980. I also interviewed Rabbi Berk in Brooklyn on Feb. 28, 2019.

174 **New York was . . . spooked:** Albin Krebs, "Assailant Wounds Passer-by and Sprays 138th Street with Bullets before Vanishing into Tenement," *New York Times*, July 12, 1968. And Tom Buckley, "Man Shot in Park by Angelof Dies," *New York Times*, July 12, 1968.

177 **Still, she felt fulfilled:** In a large report that aggregated the small amount of research on birth parents, the Donaldson Adoption Institute found: "These include feeling more detached than they would have liked, particularly with the child born directly after the one who was placed; overprotectiveness; setting impossibly high standards for themselves as parents; and smothering their children with an overabundance of affection and material goods (Howe et al., 1992). Many birth mothers also reported extreme fears of losing additional children, separation anxiety, and difficulty allowing children to become independent." *Safeguarding the Rights and Well-Being of Birthparents in the Adoption Process*, Evan B. Donaldson Adoption Institute, Jan. 2007, p. 61. http://www.adoptioninstitute.org/old/publications/2006_11 _Birthparent_Study_All.pdf. Accessed July 28, 2018.

178 **To those who had lost:** Lucette Lagnado, "Stern Summer Camp Is Happy Memory, and to Some It's an Obsession," *Wall Street Journal*, Aug. 1, 2003. https://www.wsj.com/articles/SB105969072538318000. Accessed Sept. 21, 2018.

179 **One of George's colleagues:** You can read more about the history of Roosevelt, NJ, here: "History of Roosevelt, New Jersey," Rutgers University Libraries. https://www.libraries.rutgers.edu/scua/roosevelt-history. Accessed May 22, 2018.

185 **He revered Ephraim . . . "whose son I am":** Interview with Mitch and Bryan Herstic, Riverdale, NY, Oct. 30, 2017.

185 **David's fleeting curiosity . . . loneliness:** David M. Brodzinsky, "A Stress and Coping Model of Adoption Adjustment." In *The Psychology of Adoption,* David M. Brodzinsky and Marshal D. Schechter, eds. (New York: Oxford University Press, 1990), p. 6.

186 **The psychologist Erik Erikson . . . self-esteem:** Arthur D. Sorosky, Annette Baran, and Reuben Pannor, *The Adoption Triangle* (New York: Anchor Press, 1978), p. 110.

187 **And another teacher:** Paul Lungen, "Former Teacher Charged with Sexual Assault," *Canadian Jewish News,* Sept. 12, 2012. http://www.cjnews.com /news/canada/former-teacher-charged-sexual-assault. Accessed Aug. 1, 2018.

188 **Adoptees often show . . . yours:** Sorosky, Baran, and Pannor, *The Adoption Triangle,* pp. 105–106. There is a great deal of literature about this cycle, but this book was revolutionary in describing it. Sorosky was a child psychiatrist, and Baran and Pannor were social workers. They had had years of experience with treating and researching adoptive families when they wrote *The Adoption Triangle.*

189 **What was so wrong with me:** This isn't an actual citation. Adoptees in hundreds of interviews—from Carlsbad, CA, to New York, NY; from Portland, OR, to Atlanta, GA; from Morristown, NJ, to Houston, TX—have told me that they asked some version of this question. But you can also find it highlighted in Sorosky et al., *The Adoption Triangle,* especially chapters 8 and 9, "The Adoptee: Adolescence" and "The Adoptee: Adulthood," pp. 105–142. Also, Brodzinsky, "A Stress and Coping Model of Adoption Adjustment," pp. 6–10.

189 **he said very little:** Interview with Yafa Kuperman, Netanya, Israel, Dec. 1, 2017.

189 **This is common:** Sorosky, Baran, and Pannor: *The Adoption Triangle,* p. 108.

13. *Agency*

191 **Founded in New York:** I met Florence Fisher with Pam Hasegawa at her Brooklyn apartment on Jan. 29, 2016. Where not noted, the information in these paragraphs comes from both her book and our interview that day. Please note that Jean Paton, an adoptee, author, and adoptee-rights reformer, first pioneered the idea of a registry in the early 1950s. E. Wayne Carp, *Jean Paton and the Struggle to Reform American Adoption* (Ann Arbor: University of Michigan Press, 2014), p. 1.

193 **At first, he . . . "deal":** Florence Fisher, *The Search for Anna Fisher* (New York: Arthur Fields Books, 1973), p. 68.

195 **While everyone has . . . life:** Interview with Florence Fisher, Jan. 29, 2016.

195 **The lawsuit was dismissed:** Interview with attorney Bert Hirsch, Great Neck, NY, Sept. 12, 2018. Here's the lawsuit: *ALMA Society Inc. v. Mellon*, Justia.com, https://law.justia.com/cases/federal/district-courts/FSupp/459/912/1389292/. Accessed Aug. 25, 2019.

195–196 **One organization called . . . "maladjusted":** Enid Nemy, "Adopted Children Who Wonder, 'What Was Mother Like?'" *New York Times*, July 25, 1972. Fisher told me many of the same things.

196 **Betty Jean Lifton:** Betty Jean Lifton, *Twice Born: Memoirs of an Adopted Daughter* (New York: McGraw-Hill, 1975); *Lost and Found: The Adoption Experience* (New York: Dial, 1979).

196 **Together, adoption-rights:** American Adoption Congress, https://www.americanadoptioncongress.org/aac_history_and_awards.php. Accessed June 15, 2019.

196 **At its first:** Carp, *Jean Paton and the Struggle to Reform American Adoption*, pp. 236–237.

196 **In 1976 she founded:** Concerned United Birthparents, "Past." https://www.cubirthparents.org/past.php. Accessed July 18, 2018.

197 **In 1979 journalist . . . one told her:** I have both of Lorraine Dusky's books about adoption: *Birthmark* (New York: M. Evans, 1979) and *hole in my heart* (Sag Harbor: Leto Media, 2015). She told me this at an interview in Sag Harbor, NY, on Dec. 3, 2018.

197–198 **She saw the headline . . . "desperate to be found":** Sally Moore, "An Adopted Woman Who Finally Found Her Real Parents Helps Others Search for Theirs," *People*, Aug. 18, 1975.

199–200 **And then she'd think . . . icily:** Interview with Margaret's neighbor, who preferred to keep her identity private, and Margaret Katz, March 6, 2019.

201 **a headline that read . . . certificates:** "Parents Want Proposal Defeated," *Asbury Park Press*, Dec. 19, 1976.

203 **Her mission, and:** Pam Hasegawa was and remains an adoption reformer and advocate. We have spent many days together in her home in Morristown, NJ. She was instrumental in drafting the legislation that eventually opened original birth certificates in New Jersey in 2014.

204 **Hasegawa, citing figures:** Pam was citing figures from the US Census, but the figures are also in Moore, "An Adopted Woman Who Finally Found Her Real Parents."

204 **By adding birth:** Phone call with Pam Hasegawa, June 10, 2018.

208 **It was cold:** Weather Underground for Dec. 18, 1981. https://www.wunder ground.com/history/daily/us/ny/new-york-jfk/KJFK/date/1981-12-18. Accessed July 19, 2018.

14. *"You Are a Man"*

215 **"You Are a Man":** The reconstruction of David's late adolescence and early adulthood comes from the sources mentioned above, and was verified, as best as possible, by Kim Danish Rosenberg and Ron Goldner. From Toronto, the information comes from extensive interviews and emails with his friends Larry Zeifman, David Klein, David Berk, and Suzanne Wintrob. I also consulted his own long interview, his autobiography, and a letter he wrote to Suzanne on Sept. 7, 1984. I also exchanged many emails with Debbie Cherniak on Nov. 28, 2018.

I conducted comprehensive interviews in Israel. For this chapter, I owe an enormous debt to Ron Goldner and Caryn Ben-Simchon in Ramat Gan, who hosted me on Dec. 4, 2017, and again on June 1, 2018. I also spoke to Ron's daughters, Romi Goldner and Shelly Goldner, and over the course of my reporting for this book we spoke and corresponded extensively. I drew on my conversations with Yafa Kuperman, who passed away in Oct. 2018, and with David's friends from Hebrew University. I spoke to Adam Emanuel in Washington, DC, on Nov. 15, 2016. In Tel Aviv, I met with Udi Barzily on May 30, 2018, and Riki Barzily on May 31, 2018; in Jerusalem, I interviewed Motti and Rachel Ohana on June 2, 2018. I also consulted the memory book Kim made of David's life in 2014. Friends and family worldwide contributed to the book.

219 **Some believe that:** Aron Moss, "Why the Rush for the Jewish Funeral?" Jewish Practice, Chabad.org. https://www.chabad.org/library/article_cdo/aid /1488006/jewish/Why-the-Rush-for-the-Jewish-Funeral.htm. Accessed Jan. 23, 2019.

224 **Many adoptees are drawn:** Observation of Peter Franklin, a British-born adopted man. He is an Iraq War veteran, a pharmacist, an adoptee-rights activist, and the founder of a group called Adoptees Without Liberty. Interview, Fairfield, NJ, Nov. 20, 2017. For more, visit AWOL's Facebook page: https://www .facebook.com/awolobc/?eid=ARBHdhYiv4dVh5nA-mJW5K3bw8VkgTM wU0U3hvu VezDL6bfcxtYtXH1zFq8HuPTnmhFQlEWKbBE5FJO3&timeline _context_item_type=intro_card_work&timeline_context_item_source= 1274223383&fref=tag. Accessed Jan. 29, 2019.

227 **"God forbid they starve":** Recollection of Ron Goldner. Interview with Ron Goldner, Ramat Gan, Israel, Dec. 4, 2017.

230 **Sometimes:** Recollection of Riki Barzily. Interview with Riki Barzily, Tel Aviv, Israel, May 31, 2018.

15. *Going West*

231 **Going West:** For this chapter of David's life, I relied on extensive interviews with David's friends and family in Portland, my own work from 2007, and David's interview with David Fuks of the Oregon Jewish Museum. My material is drawn from interviews from 2016 to 2019 with Kim Danish Rosenberg, Sam Rosenberg, Noah Rosenberg, and Estee Daveed, as well as Marshal Spector. I also drew on the recollections and observations of my friend J. D. Kleinke, who knew David as a fellow musician in Portland's small Jewish circle, as well as my Portland rabbi, Ariel Stone, who also knew David. Information also came from Mitch and Bryan Herstic, David's memory book, and an interview and emails with Barry Benson on March 11, 2018, as well as emails exchanged with him and Karla Benson on July 12, 2019.

231 **The other was from:** Congregation Shaarie Torah, History. http://shaari etorah.org/history/. Accessed March 5, 2019.

232 **Rabbi Stephen Wise . . . stay:** Joe Rooks-Rapport, "Louise Waterman Wise 1874–1947," Jewish Women's Archive Encyclopedia. https://jwa.org/encyclo pedia/article/wise-louise-waterman. Accessed March 5, 2019.

232 **In the sanctuary of . . . heaven:** A version of this paragraph appeared first in my story about David's kidney donation. Gabrielle Glaser, "Timeless Faith, Renewed Life: Portland Man Donates Kidney to Best Friend," *Oregonian*, Sept. 16, 2007.

234 **He informed David . . . daunting:** Email, Mitch Herstic, March 12, 2019. You can read more about the infantilizing registry here: Associated Press, "Data on Adoptions Given Out by New York State Registry," *New York Times*, Dec. 11, 1983. https://www.nytimes.com/1983/12/11/nyregion/data-on-adoptions-given -out-by-new-york-state-registry.html. Accessed March 12, 2019.

238 **But then he:** Glaser, "Timeless Faith, Renewed Life."

239 **The number of . . . 1975:** Penelope L. Maza, "Adoption Trends: 1944– 1975," Child Welfare Research Notes #9, US Children's Bureau, Aug. 1984, pp. 1–4. You can see them online at https://pages.uoregon.edu/adoption/ar chive/MazaAT.htm. Accessed June 11, 2019.

239 **the federal government . . . incomplete:** Ellen Herman, "Adoption Statistics," Adoption History Project. https://pages.uoregon.edu/adoption/topics /adoption statistics.htm. Accessed July 1, 2019.

239 **Louise Wise Services . . . 1971:** Minutes from the Louise Wise Services board meeting, June 2, 1971, Viola W. Bernard Papers, Box 155, Folder 5, Archives and Special Collections, Augustus C. Long Library, Columbia University.

239 **To make up for . . . heritage:** For more on the adoption of roughly 12,000 African American children by white families between 1960 and 1976, see Arnold R. Silverman, "Outcomes of Transracial Adoption," *Future of Children*, vol. 3, no. 1, Spring 1993. https://pdfs.semanticscholar.org/5ff9/38abf6346f26e42e 07a63b11c796265420d7.pdf. Accessed July 2, 2019. In 1972, the National Association of Black Social Workers issued a statement of vehement opposition to the practice of white families raising black children. The group argued that such adoptions were a form of cultural genocide and extended the chattel status of black people in the United States.

For more on the roughly 12,500 Native American children adopted in the 1960s and 1970s in the federally supported Indian Adoption Project, see Claire Palmiste, "From the Indian Adoption Project to the Indian Child Welfare Act: the resistance of Native American communities [*sic*, capitalization]," *Indigenous Policy Journal*, vol. 22, no. 1, Summer 2011, p. 5. Native activists argued that the program extended the century-old forced removal of Native children from traditional lands, and worked with attorneys for the 1978 passage of the Indian Child Welfare Act (ICWA). The federal law oversees Native American children in state foster care. In order to reinforce a child's Native cultural identity, it gives tribes priority to adopt them.

240 **pioneered the idea of . . . Korea:** Herman, "Bertha and Harry Holt," Adoption History Project. https://pages.uoregon.edu/adoption/people/holt.htm. Accessed June 16, 2019.

240 **The Holt Agency continued . . . families:** "Adoption History," *First Person Plural*, Point of View Films, PBS.org, http://archive.pov.org/firstperson plural/history/4/. Accessed July 6, 2019.

241 **In the 1990s:** Kathryn Joyce, "The Truth about China's Missing Daughters," *New Republic*, June 1, 2016. https://newrepublic.com/article/133845 /truth-chinas-missing-daughters. Accessed July 5, 2019.

241 **Meanwhile, many agencies:** "Agency Questionnaire on Sharing Information from Adoption Records," Child Welfare League of America, New York, NY, April, 1976, p. 15. Viola W. Bernard Papers, Box 158, Folder 4,

Archives and Special Collections, Augustus C. Long Library, Columbia University.

241 **Among those deeply . . . "strangers":** Interview with Jim Gritter, Nov. 22, 2016.

242 **In city after city . . . families:** Private correspondence and email, Jan. 15, 2015.

242 **Some of the new . . . "else":** Interview with Maxine Chalker, July 10, 2019.

243 **Researchers have documented . . . adoptions:** "Working with Birth and Adoptive Families to Support Open Adoption," Bulletin for Professionals, Child Welfare Information Gateway, Jan. 2013. https://www.childwelfare .gov/pubPDFs/f_openadoptbulletin.pdf. Accessed April 15, 2019. This bulletin provides a summary of findings on closed versus open adoptions that have been ongoing since the 1990s. Incidentally, while open adoptions do provide more satisfaction among the participants, in most states there is no legally binding contract to make sure they remain open.

243–244 **In one widely . . . heart attack:** You can read more about the case here: *Juman v. Louise Wise Services*, FindLaw.com. https://caselaw.findlaw.com/ny -supreme-court/1223757.html. Accessed July 6, 2019.

245 **"They told us" . . . "perfect mother."** Interview with Marty Juman, July 8, 2019.

245 **As Barbara Miller:** Lisa Belkin, "What the Jumans Didn't Know about Michael," *New York Times Magazine,* March 4, 1999. https://www.nytimes .com/1999/03/14/magazine/what-the-jumans-didn-t-know-about-michael .html. Accessed May 31, 2019.

245 **The Jumans refused:** Interview with Marty Juman, July 8, 2019.

246 **It was, she wrote . . . "relationship":** *Ross v. Louise Wise Servs*, Supreme Court, New York County, May 12, 2004. https://law.justia.com/cases/new -york/other-courts/2004/2004-24159.html. Accessed July 6, 2019.

16. *Deferred Love*

249 **Deferred Love:** The information from this chapter comes from David's family: Kim Danish Rosenberg, Sam Rosenberg, Noah Rosenberg, and Estee Daveed, who recently changed her name to honor her father's memory. Of course, I also relied heavily on the recollections of Margaret and Cheri Katz. I also had extensive interviews, in person and on the phone, with Sandy Baumwald, who shared her correspondence and phone messages with David;

with Ron Goldner; and with Caryn Gersh Ben-Simchon, who also shared the messages she and David exchanged. I also frequently relied on the memories of Marshal Spector and Barry and Karla Benson. (Everyone was so patient; I know I asked the same questions twice.)

In addition, I refer to my own reporting from 2007. And Tim Monti-Wohlpart helped impart the concerns of many adoptees, who feel torn between allegiance to their adoptive family and a thirst to know about their biology, as we discussed the thoughts of many adoptees when they search.

249 **Weeks later, the . . . "not knowing":** Gabrielle Glaser, "Timeless Faith, Renewed Life," *Oregonian*, Sept. 16, 2007.

250–251 **Now Estee, entering . . . still find purpose:** You can hear Billy Joel explain the lyrics in this interview: https://www.youtube.com/watch?v=sWRii H2MJ2U. Accessed March 11, 2019.

252 **Perhaps he didn't:** Interview with Estee Daveed, David's daughter, Bronxville, NY, Nov. 2, 2018.

254 **the agency that:** Elizabeth Cady Brown, "Wise Demise: Foster Care Group Closes under Fire," CityLimits.org, March 1, 2004. https://citylimits.org /2004/03/01/wise-demise-foster-care-group-closes-under-fire/.

267 **They share . . . gone:** Interview with Sam Rosenberg, Portland, OR, March 27, 2019.

17. *No More Secrets*

270 **(although bizarrely, some):** Finley R. Lewis, ed., *Focus on Nonverbal Communication Research* (New York: Nova Science Publishers, 2007), pp. 33, 34, 49, 58, 60. Also: Stephen J. Sheinkopf, Jana M. Iverson, Melissa L. Rinaldi, and Barry M. Lester, "Atypical Cry Acoustics in 6-Month-Old Infants at Risk for Autism Spectrum Disorder," *Autism Research*, vol. 5, no. 5, Oct. 2012, pp. 331–339. https://www.ncbi.nlm.nih.gov/pmc/articles/PMC3517274/. Accessed Sept. 10, 2019. There are many more sources.

270 **A succession of studies:** There is a large body of literature cataloging the loss adoptees feel. Here is a government summary of recent literature: "Impact of Adoption on Adopted Persons," Factsheet for Families, Child Welfare Information Gateway, Aug. 2013. https://www.childwelfare.gov/pubpdfs/f _adimpact.pdf. Accessed June 27, 2019.

270 **Similarly, researchers have:** Numerous studies have detailed the loss birth mothers experience. Here is a government summary of many of them:

"Impact of Adoption on Birth Parents," Factsheet for Families, Child Welfare Information Gateway, Aug. 2013. https://www.childwelfare.gov/pubpdfs/f _impact.pdf. Accessed April 18, 2019.

270 **Separately, birth mothers:** "Impact of Adoption on Birth Parents, Factsheet for Families."

270 **In the United Kingdom . . . parents:** John Triseliotis, Julia Feast, and Fiona Kyle, "The Adoption Triangle Revisited: Summary, A Study of Adoption, Search, and Reunion Experiences," British Association for Adoption and Fostering, Jan. 2005. http://citeseerx.ist.psu.edu/viewdoc/download?doi=10.1.1.475.915& rep=rep1&type=pdf. Accessed July 27, 2019. Or: https://www.researchgate.net /publication/265047307_The_Adoption_Triangle_Revisited.

270 **Geneaology is one:** Gregory Rodriguez, "Roots of Genealogy Craze," *USA Today*, May 12, 2014. https://www.usatoday.com/story/opinion/2014/05/12 /genealogy-americans-technology-roots-porn-websites-column/9019409/. Accessed Aug. 28, 2019.

271 **The number of babies . . . norm:** "Working with Birth and Adoptive Families to Support Open Adoption," Child Welfare Information Gateway. https://www.childwelfare.gov/pubPDFs/f_openadoptbulletin.pdf. Accessed July 2, 2019.

271 **nearly a quarter:** US Census Bureau Newsroom: "The Majority of Children Live with Two Parents, Census Bureau Reports," Nov. 17, 2016. https://www .census.gov/newsroom/press-releases/2016/cb16-192.html. Accessed July 9, 2019.

271 **It took adoption-rights . . . records:** This is the estimate of Tim Monti-Wohlpart, a New York adoptee, an adoptee-rights advocate, and the American Adoption Congress's national legislative chair. He is also the New York State representative of the American Adoption Congress.

272 **Although frequently cited:** Lawrence B. Finer, Lori F. Frohwirth, Lindsay A. Dauphinee, Susheela Singh, and Ann M. Moore, "Reasons US Women Have Abortions: Quantitative and Qualitative Perspectives," *Perspectives on Sexual and Reproductive Health*, vol. 37, no. 3, Sept. 2005, pp. 110–118. https:// www.guttmacher.org/sites/default/files/pdfs/journals/3711005.pdf. Accessed April 14, 2019.

272 **States that have:** American Adoption Congress, "Reform Adoption Data: Abortion and Adoption Access from States Who [sic] Have Enacted Access." Compiled April 2010. https://www.americanadoptioncongress.org/reform_adop tion_data.php. Accessed April 22, 2019.

272 **Another argument against:** The Women's Bar Association of the State of New York has repeatedly argued that opening the records would be a breach of birth mother confidentiality. Read here: "Position Statement, Adoption Registry/Adoption Rights." https://www.wbasny.org/leg islation/34184/. Accessed April 12, 2019.

272 **The truth is:** Interview with Bert Hirsch, Sept. 3, 2019.

272 **A detailed analysis:** Elizabeth J. Samuels, "Surrender and Subordination: Birth Mothers and Adoption Law Reform," *Michigan Journal of Gender and Law*, vol. 20, no. 33, March 2013. https://papers.ssrn.com/sol3/papers.cfm ?abstract_id=2233400. Accessed April 12, 2019. I also had two detailed conversations with Professor Samuels on June 13 and June 15, 2018.

272 **In states that . . . percent:** "Statistics for States Implementing Access to Original Birth Certificate (OBC) Laws since 2000." American Adoption Congress, Feb. 2016. https://www.americanadoptioncongress.org/docs/Stats _for_States_with_access_Feb_-_2016.pdf. Accessed April 22, 2019.

273 **Shawna Hodgson, an . . . secrets:** Interview with Shawna Hodgson, April 3, 2019.

273 **For the half million . . . traditions:** There is so much excellent work on this topic, including Nicole Chung's recent memoir, *All You Can Ever Know: A Memoir* (New York: Catapult, 2018). Also see this report: Holly McGinnis, Susan Smith, Scott Ryan, and Jeanne Howard, "Beyond Culture Camp: Promoting Healthy Identity Formation in Adoption," Evan B. Donaldson Adoption Institute, Nov. 2009. https://www.adoptioninstitute.org/wp-content/uploads /2013/12/2009_11_BeyondCultureCamp.pdf. Accessed April 17, 2019.

273 **"We were raised . . . skin color":** Interview with Stephanie Drenka, July 5, 2019.

274–275 **One advocate I know . . . "not for you":** Phone interviews with Tim Monti-Wohlpart, April 14–16, 2019.

276–277 **The tens of thousands . . . century:** In the US in 2007, 16,488 babies conceived with donor eggs were born; by 2016, that number had risen to 19,102, according to the CDC. "Assisted Reproductive Technology, National Summary Report 2016," Centers for Disease Control and Prevention. https:// www.cdc.gov/art/pdf/2016-report/ART-2016-National-Summary-Report .pdf#page=56, p. 52. This report does not include the number of babies conceived by sperm donors, which is estimated to be between 30,000 and 60,000 per year. Sperm donations are not regulated, and neither the fertility industry nor any other governing body is required to report on these figures.

Read more here: Karen Clark and Elizabeth Marquardt, "The Sperm-Donor Kids Are Not Really All Right," *Slate*, June 14, 2010. https://slate.com /human-interest/2010/06/new-study-shows-sperm-donor-kids-suffer.html. Accessed April 16, 2019.

277 **In one instance, DNA tests:** Sarah Zhang, "The Fertility Doctor's Secret," *Atlantic*, April 2019. https://www.theatlantic.com/magazine/archive/2019/04 /fertility-doctor-donald-cline-secret-children/583249/. Accessed April 12, 2019.

277 **In another, the tests:** Ariana Eunjung Cha, "The Children of Donor 989," *Washington Post*, Sept. 14, 2019. https://www.washingtonpost.com/health/the -children-of-donor-h898/2019/09/14/dcc191d8-86da-11e9-a491-25df61c78dc4 _story.html. Accessed Dec. 13, 2019

278 **Most countries in:** European Union Agency for Fundamental Rights, "Accessing Adoption Files and Information on the Biological Family, Year 2017." https://fra.europa.eu/en/publication/2017/mapping-minimum-age -requirements/accessing-adoption-files. Accessed Sept. 7, 2019.

278–279 **No political figure . . . "unreserved apology":** Australian Government Attorney-General's Department, "National Apology for Forced Adoptions." Read more and also watch the powerful video here: https://www.ag.gov.au /About/ForcedAdoptionsApology/Pages/default.aspx. Accessed July 13, 2019.

INDEX

Note: Page numbers in *italics* refer to illustrations.

Resource List

I f you are an adopted person, a birth parent, or a relative seeking to reunite with family lost to adoption (or simply wish to know more about adoption), these groups, websites, and people may be of help. Laws governing access to original birth certificates vary by state.

Adoptee Rights Law Center

The Adoptee Rights Law Center is an adoptee-focused legal practice founded by adoptee Gregory Luce, a Minnesota lawyer.
https://adopteerightslaw.com/

Adoptees' Liberty Movement Association

ALMA, founded in 1971, offers a birth registry that helps family members connect.
http://almasociety.org/

Adoption History Project

The Adoption History Project, created by University of Oregon historian Ellen Herman, is a comprehensive site devoted to the history of adoption in the United States and elsewhere.
https://pages.uoregon.edu/adoption/index.html

American Adoption Congress

The American Adoption Congress was created in the late 1970s as an umbrella organization by the search-and-support adoption reform groups sprouting up across the United States, Canada, and around the world.
https://www.americanadoptioncongress.org/

Ann Fessler

Artist Ann Fessler is the author of the 2006 book *The Girls Who Went Away*. Fessler, an adoptee, interviewed one hundred women who had lost sons and daughters to adoption in the decades after World War II. Her 2011 film, *A Girl Like Her*, combines the women's voices with footage from the era.
http://www.annfessler.com/

Bastard Nation

Bastard Nation, founded in 1996, advocates for the civil and human rights of adult citizens adopted as children.
http://bastards.org/

CeCe Moore

CeCe Moore is a genetic genealogist who appeared on the PBS series *Finding Your Roots*. She has extensive experience in helping solve cold cases with DNA, and in helping adoptees identify their birth family.
https://thednadetectives.com/
https://www.facebook.com/groups/DNADetectives/

Child Welfare League of America

Founded in 1921, the CWLA is the oldest child-welfare organization in the United States. It works with public and private agencies.
https://www.cwla.org/

Concerned United Birthparents

Concerned United Birthparents was founded in the mid-1970s as an organization for parents who had lost children to adoption. Today it serves all those affected by adoption and all who are concerned about adoption issues. https://cubirthparents.org/

Donaldson Adoption Institute

DAI, a national adoption research, education, and advocacy organization, closed in 2018. Its website, which features extensive publications, remains live. https://www.adoptioninstitute.org/

Joyce Maguire Pavao

Dr. Joyce Maguire Pavao is an adoptee and a therapist with more than forty-five years of experience in the fields of adoption and complex families, child welfare, family therapy, and family systems. She is also the author of *The Family of Adoption*. http://www.pavaoconsulting.com/

Rudy Owens

Rudy Owens, a Michigan-born adoptee and journalist, is the author of the 2018 memoir *You Don't Know How Lucky You Are*, which explores US adoption, adoptee rights, and the public health impacts of adoption on adoptees. https://www.howluckyuare.com/